DEEPENING DEMOCRACY
IN LATIN AMERICA

PITT LATIN AMERICAN SERIES

Billie R. DeWalt

General Editor

Reid Andrews

Associate Editor

Carmen Diana Deere

Associate Editor

Jorge I. Domínguez

Associate Editor

DEEPENING DEMOCRACY

IN LATIN AMERICA

Edited by

Kurt von Mettenheim

and

James Malloy

UNIVERSITY OF PITTSBURGH PRESS

Published by the University of Pittsburgh Press, Pittsburgh, Pa. 15261
Copyright © 1998, University of Pittsburgh Press
Manufactured in the United States of America
Printed on acid-free paper

10 9 8 7 6 5 4 3 2 1

Library of Congress Cataloging-in-Publication Data
Mettenheim, Kurt von, 1957–
    Deepening democracy in Latin America / Kurt von Mettenheim and
James Malloy
       p. cm.—(Pitt Latin American series)
    Includes bibliographical references and index.
    ISBN 0-8229-4060-4 (alk. paper). — ISBN 0-8229-5664-0 (pbk. : alk. paper)
    1. Latin America—Politics and government—20th century.
    2. Democracy—Latin America.   3. Political parties—Latin America.
    4. Elite (Social sciences)—Latin America.   I. Malloy, James M.
    II. Title.   III. Series.
    JL 960.M48   1998
    320.98—dc21   97-45396

A CIP catalog record for this book is available from the British Library.

CONTENTS

ACKNOWLEDGMENTS

This volume is based on a research conference held under the auspices of the University of Pittsburgh Center for Latin American Studies. Professor Burkhart Holzner, director of the University of Pittsburgh University Center for International Studies, and B. Guy Peters, chair of the Department of Political Science, provided additional financial support and intellectual encouragement that made the conference and subsequent editorial process possible. Special thanks are in order to Reid Andrews, John Booth, Ernest Cabrera, Robert Chisholm, Annabelle Conroy, Ricardo Cordoba, Jamie Jacobs, Brooke Larson, Peggy Lovell, John Markoff, John Martz, Carmelo Mesa-Lago, Carlos Parodi, Orlando Perez, Ben Schneider, Mitchell Seligson, and Andrew Stein, who generously participated in the conference or commented on papers. The editors also wish to acknowledge the extensive editorial and academic efforts of the University of Pittsburgh Press, especially the interest of Director Cynthia Miller, the persistence of Pitt Latin American Studies General Editor Billie R. DeWalt, and the profound insights of several anonymous reviewers who improved the organization and content of this volume.

DEEPENING DEMOCRACY
IN LATIN AMERICA

INTRODUCTION

KURT VON METTENHEIM and
JAMES MALLOY

This book seeks to shift scholarly debate from matters of regime transition and democratic consolidation to the prospects for deepening democratic politics in Latin America. Both the false realism of competitive democratic theory that focuses exclusively on elections and elites, and the easy appeals for greater participation that define participatory democratic theory, fail to capture the new developments of post-transition in Latin America.[1] By focusing both on new patterns of party and electoral politics in Latin America and on how political elites are forging new patterns of governance that reconcile party politics, interest groups, economic policy teams, and political economic constraints, the analyses presented in this volume seek to identify new problems of democratic theory and practice as the region prepares to enter the twenty-first century.

The dizzy pace of political change and the protracted character of economic problems bring an urgency to this reassessment of events and scholarly assumptions. An unprecedented number of Latin American countries from the Southern Cone to Central America did indeed experience transitions from military to civilian government in the last decades. But political realities in the 1990s counsel against inferring easy or inexorable trends of democratization. While countries that provided traditional models of democratic stability such as Venezuela and Colombia struggled to maintain democratic government amid civil strife and military coups, Peru succumbed to emergency rule and dictatorship to confront economic crisis and revolutionary insurgency. In Mexico, economic crises, revolutionary movements, an entrenched monolithic government party, and movements for political reform continue to defy standard political concepts.

On the economic front, the difficulties are also imposing. After decades of rapid industrialization and modernization throughout Latin America, the 1980s and 1990s will be remembered as a decade of lost economic opportunities; of successive packages attempting to reduce inflation, foreign debt, and fiscal deficits. With some notable exceptions, renewed growth during the 1990s through privatization and liberalization came only at the expense of further income concentration. Despite this troubled record, for neoliberal ideologues Latin America prefigured transitions in Eastern Europe and the new republics of the former Soviet Union because Latin American leaders often attempted to stabilize economies through austerity and encourage new investment through liberalization and privatization.[2]

But far from confirming a necessary relation between democracy and markets, even neoliberal scholars agree that austere economic policies are notoriously unpopular in Latin America.[3] These policies impose further social costs on the very same groups that bore the brunt of economic policies under military rule, such as labor, peasants, and the informal sector. While many of these social groups opposed authoritarianism and supported democratic openings, few are now disposed to accept another round of austerity, no matter how democratic the government that seeks to implement them. And simple appeals to political will are insufficient for the tasks of building democratic institutions and surpassing economic crisis. As the studies in this volume show, such calls tend to reinforce the inclinations of post-transition economic teams and governments to adopt decidedly authoritarian styles of policy making.

The problems of generating governmental capacity, extending democracy, and producing economic growth in Latin America are more complex than both prevailing notions in neoliberal economics and the stale debate between elite and participatory democratic theory. Recent democratic theories fail to account for events in the region because they either restrict the meaning of democracy to competitive elections or emphasize ideal standards of citizen participation without providing means of achieving these standards amid the realities of mass politics. Not that there are easy answers about post-transition change. This volume emphasizes the complexities and contradictions encountered in specific Latin American experiences of democratization. The editors and contributors do not seek to measure national experiences or bend the processes of the region into accord with some one or another theory of democracy. Nor have we sought to develop models capable of generating nomothetic propositions of explanation, conceptual maps for liberal but top-down reforms, or guidelines for "constitutional engineering." We also do not view the region as passing through structurally determined sequences or phases, such as "transition" followed by "consolidation," which can be rendered in some set of synchronic propositions or theory above and beyond complex national contexts. In sum, this volume breaks with existing social science theories and approaches to democracy in Latin America.

Instead, contributors seek to communicate the substance of political creativity in Latin America by focusing on new patterns of party electoral politics and new experiences of liberal democratic governance throughout the region. Recent Latin American experiences reveal a broad range of creative attempts that simultaneously grapple with the political problems of building democratic institutions while recasting national economies around the common themes of adjustment, economic opening, and the retreat of the state. New and creative patterns of competitive politics, coalition building, political negotiation, and economic policy making—in sum, statecraft—have emerged throughout the region. While both scholarly divisions of labor and Latin American realities inform this distinction between electoral representation and governance, the studies contained herein highlight interesting and contradictory amalgams; of new types of direct popular appeals mixed with traditional electoral systems, of competitive mass politics mixed with traditional notions of pluralist representation through organized groups, and of tensions between technocratic policy processes and the traffic of political demands.

Deepening democracy means not only that competitive elections select those who will govern, but that this process produces governments with initiative and capacity. Unfortunately, elections in Latin American history have served largely to circulate elites rather than provide a forum for airing and debating national issues, forming governments, and endowing those governments with the capacity to act. The complex problem of linking elections to both more open policy-making styles and the capacity of governments is a fundamental theme that runs throughout the analyses of national experiences presented herein. Indeed, a central methodological principle that shapes this collection of essays is that national experiences can be interpreted as a series of variations around common problems or themes that confront the region.

The concept of deepening democracy taps an analogy with a classic contribution to economic theory by Latin Americans to surpass lacunae in the comparative analysis of democracy. The tasks of post-transition politics today in Latin America can be clarified by a comparison to the need to deepen industrialization at the end of the "easy phase" of import substitution industrialization. If transitions from military rule during the 1970s and 1980s can be seen as the creation of an expanded domestic political market through the extension of suffrage, the urgent political question today that this analogy raises is how to deepen citizenship and democratic politics. The response may be the same in politics as it was in economics, that is, state-led development.[4] Latin American economists recognized the need for state-led industrialization in late development generally, and particularly the need to deepen industrialization through creation of capital goods production after the end of the "easy phase" of import substitution industrialization. After the creation of domestic markets through national-populist policies and a period of growth led by direct foreign investment, newly industrialized countries in Latin America shared similar problems that were described by the need to deepen their industrial parks.[5]

A central argument of this volume is that posttransition experiences in Latin America may provide similar arguments for political development through deepening democracy. If gradual, negotiated, open methods of governance can resolve long-standing problems, then the new civilian administrations of Latin America may provide examples of state-led representation and executive leadership that endow citizenship with substance while respecting the rule of law. In sum, deepening democracy is a concept that attempts to capture the political creativity of post-transition executives in Latin America. Caution is clearly in order to avert embracing the centralization of power by executives, a risk and reality that is neither the political intent nor conceptual content of deepening democracy.

In this respect, Latin Americans share a post-transition legacy of excessive centralization. A critical legacy of military rule in the 1960s and 1970s in the region arises from the institutional changes introduced by military elites to remove policy making from popular pressures. New constitutions, central banks, constitutional tribunals, electoral laws, and formal guardianship roles for the military were often designed by the military to isolate economic and public policy from voters, parties, and political elites. Military elites believed that populist politics produced deficit spending, inflation, and the radicalization that led to democratic breakdown in the 1960s and 1970s. Like progressive-era reformers in the United States who sought to create good government and reduce party and popular control over policy, military rulers in Latin America designed state institutions with a substantial degree of autonomy from social and political pressures.

To the extent that transitions to civilian rule in Latin America failed to reverse the concentration of executive power by military rulers, a new kind of hybrid regime darkens the region's future.[6] In this hybrid regime, democratic politics remains restricted to more or less competitive elections, while isolated executives tend toward exclusive patterns of technocratic policy formulation and implementation, especially regarding critical economic matters. Whether competitive electoral politics can produce Latin American governments able to build democratic institutions and surpass economic crisis, or whether volatile plebiscitarian appeals and futile electoral exercises will be grafted onto centralized and authoritarian policy styles, is a critical concern of this volume. In this regard, a new version of what Alexis de Tocqueville first described as a trend toward democratic dictatorship in modern times looms over contemporary Latin America.

To reverse a potentially vicious cycle of policy failure and democratic neglect, new conceptions of democracy must reflect the region's political creativity. Executives and their technocratic policy teams must learn from their successful colleagues in the region that both competitive party-electoral politics and pluralistic modes of policy making are needed in order to produce effective governance and deepen democracy. The tasks of Latin American politics are telescoped: New civilian governments must simultaneously rebuild power capacity into state agencies (weakened by both departing military and transition governments) and democratize state-society relations while they deploy power to surpass economic crisis. The urgent normative question is whether open, pluralist, and participatory patterns of state-society relations are compatible with these tasks of statecraft. In other words, can competitive elections and inclusive, pluralistic policy-making styles be combined, thereby building problem-solving capacity into state institutions capable of being deployed by governments "empowered" to speak in the state's name? Economic problems may divert new governments from the complex constitutional issues involved in building the power capacity of a liberal-democratic state and regime.[7] But this only tends to undermine governmental capacity to sustain viable economic policies.

While these tasks may appear daunting, the opportunities for change are considerable. Indeed, linking competitive party-electoral politics to new, open patterns of governance may resolve long-standing problems of governmental capacity and democratic stability in Latin America. The cyclical alternation between authoritarianism and democracy in Latin America throughout the twentieth century is, in part, linked to the inability of either regime form to produce an enduring capacity to govern. Instead, weak civilian governments have provoked authoritarian responses during periods of competitive democratic politics, while the centralization of state power by military elites tends to produce pressures for liberalization and democratization. If competitive party-electoral politics and liberal-democratic modes of policy making can produce effective government throughout the region, the haunting sequence of polarization, power vacuum, democratic breakdown, military intervention, and the terror of military rule may give way to sustainable democratic politics.[8]

The need to deepen democracy by linking electoral representation to open, inclusive, and pluralistic patterns of governance also arises because of universal tensions in liberal and democratic politics. The liberal-democratic tradition views representation in two recurrent and quite different moments: first, the selection of representatives through competitive elections, and second, a more vaguely shaped process whereby representatives transact with social interests to produce the substantive content of government, public policy. During elections, representation is conceived of in geographical terms as the articulation of individualized citizen-electors through votes and the realities of mass party-electoral politics. After elections, questions of representation shift to functional images of pluralism; of a mobilized civil society, of organized interests, and of groups that attempt to impact state bureaucratic politics and policies.

Emphasizing both party-electoral politics and pluralistic means of governance challenges prevailing positions in democratic theory. Since the work of Schumpeter, self-declared mainstream theories of democracy have focused on the selection of elites through competitive elections as the core characteristic of mass democracy.[9] In opposition, participatory theories of democracy criticize competitive theorists for omitting broader values that they claim are central to the liberal and democratic tradition, and they explore diverse mechanisms for the expansion of participation, citizenship, and the empowerment of civil society.[10] But neither perspective fully develops arguments about democratizing relationships between organized groups of civil society and the bureaucratic politics of formulating and implementing policies.

This insistence on expanding definitions of democracy to include problems of governance also pursues a central concern in recent debates about democracy in post-transition Latin America. O'Donnell, Cavarozzi, and other political scientists argue that contemporary Latin American politics present new problems for theories of democracy and typologies of democratic regimes primarily because of the tenuous relationship between electoral outcomes and government policies over time. For O'Donnell, the absence of control mechanisms or checks and balances on executives who claim to act for some unitary general will or national interest suggests that a new form of delegative democracy is emerging in Latin America. Delegative democracy fails to provide opportunities for access, feedback, and political negotiation with executives after elections. For Cavarozzi, this serves only to recreate the passivity and dependency of traditional personalistic and populistic ties between government elites and Latin American masses.[11]

In sum, hybrid or mixed regimes have emerged throughout Latin America during the 1990s. Although each country is crafting its own institutions, these national variations can be seen to pivot around a central theme, that of a marked tendency of folding insulated, executive-based patterns of technocratic (even authoritarian) policy making into outwardly liberal democratic constitutional structures.

Democratic politics thereby tends to be restricted to periodic elections, while pluralistic notions of ongoing access to policy making are abandoned. Executives often justify centralized policy styles by describing both legislatures and social groups as illegitimate political pressures that place particularistic interests above national interests. Executives thereby seek to embody this national interest and to legitimize their predominance through provocative direct popular appeals. These direct popular appeals that seek to legitimate the conduct of isolated economic policy teams clash with the liberal and pluralist tradition and threaten the future of democracy in the region because they provide alternative means of representing the nation.[12]

Deepening Electoral Representation in Latin America

The vast majority of Latin Americans have now voted in competitive elections to choose local, state, and federal governments for over a decade. Given the reassessment of scholarly assumptions about public opinion, voter rationality, and party-electoral politics in the long-standing democracies of Europe and North America, closer examination of Latin American experiences may provide new perspectives on classic problems of electoral representation and democratic politics. The analyses presented in this volume suggest that understanding electoral representation in Latin America implies recognition of considerable diversity and complexity across region and nation, as well as common experiences and perceptions of statecraft and governance during the first decade of civilian rule in the region.

The central problem that emerges from ten years of post-transition electoral politics in Latin America is the power of direct appeals to voters by executives. While efforts to simultaneously build democratic institutions and surpass economic crises abound, volatile new forms of direct popular appeals have also appeared that bypass traditional political institutions and other mediating links between voters, social groups, and political elites. The direct election of presidents and other executives combined with new styles of modern media campaigning tend to encourage direct appeals to voters. Meanwhile, more durable attachments to party, class, region, or political ideology that structured public opinion and electoral representation in the past have given way to greater transparency, immediacy, complexity, and flux.

Given the volatility and effectiveness of direct popular appeals, a critical task for deepening electoral representation in Latin America today is to restrain the authoritarian bent of executives by diffusing and dispersing power among diverse institutions of liberal, democratic, and federal politics such as provincial officials, state and municipal legislatures, courts, and newly empowered interest group organizations from civil society. These challenges are not unique to Latin America or our century. Indeed, since Napoleon used plebiscites to confer imperial and consulate powers upon himself in 1799, the power of popular appeals in mass politics has haunted liberal-democratic theory and practice by providing alternative means of national representation.[13]

Indeed, recent Latin American presidents have won office by bypassing traditional partisan attachments and appealing directly to voters. In Brazil, Fernando Henrique Cardoso reduced inflation and vaulted his splinter party, PSDB (Partido da Social Democracia Brasileira) into the presidency. In Argentina, both Presidents Alfonsín and Menem won by crosscutting the traditional Peronista/anti-Peronista cleavage that had dominated politics since the 1940s. After the monolithic PRI (Partido Revolucionario Institutional) was shaken by electoral challenges on the left and right in the 1988 and 1994 presidential elections, Presidents Salinas and Zedillo convinced Mexican elites to pursue new vote-getting strategies through a National Program of Solidarity (PRONASOL) that appealed directly to voters. In the most troubling example, Alberto Fujimori came from outside traditional party organizations to unexpectedly win the Peruvian presidency in November 1991, only to close Congress and impose a state of emergency in February 1992.

The importance of these direct popular appeals by executives suggests that analysts of Latin American public opinion need to avoid reflexively applying theories based on simple liberal assumptions about voters. Indeed, while accounts of Latin American public opinion still cling to traditional liberal models, which assert that electoral behavior is unilaterally determined from the bottom up,[14] recent studies of public opinion in North America and Europe now emphasize dynamics in public opinion at odds with traditional liberal theories. In fact, researchers of public opinion now emphasize the importance of top-down appeals, the reality of feedback mechanisms that make those in power popular, and the existence of other reciprocal patterns among voters in an increasingly volatile political and electoral context. In sum, the traditional liberal view of electoral representation as the bottom-up articulation of individual preferences fails to account for the diversity, complexity, and volatility of public opinion and the power of direct popular appeals in contemporary Latin America.

Indeed, in comparative perspective, Latin American public opinion tends to be direct, unmediated, fluid, and tied both to political personalities and conceptions of substantive justice. The populist tradition in the region that endowed state-society relations with this greater transparency and immediacy suggests that public opinion in the region, although more volatile than rigid electorates in established democracies, can nevertheless also be closely linked to conceptions of substantive justice.[15] These characteristics are not simply a consequence of the region's past. The recent trend toward direct popular appeals by executives and media-oriented electioneering in Latin America means that voters now tend to judge candidates, issues, economic performance, and political parties *directly*, without the moderating influences of European ideologies, American notions of group interest, or other long-term identifications with party or class.[16]

Understanding public opinion and electoral representation in Latin America also has implications beyond the region because recent evidence of flux, volatility, and top-down effects in Europe and North America has seriously impaired existing theories. Since the first social scientific accounts of voter choice, it has been widely recognized that classic ideas such as mandate, authorization, accountability, and virtual representation fail to adequately describe how representation works in mass politics.[17] Furthermore, theories of geographical and demographic representation are no longer sufficient because public perceptions crosscut traditional cleavages of class and region.[18] Finally, popular identification with parties no longer provides the critical link it once did. Because both the direct appeals of electoral campaigns and the traffic of interests afterward bypass the party identification of voters, party organizations no longer retain the near monopoly on representation typical of competitive party systems for much of the postwar period.[19] In sum, new realities have overturned traditional conceptions of electoral representation.

Scholars of European and North American electorates tend to explain top-down influences by referring to elite leadership, to irrational psychological processes among voters, or to the manipulation of public opinion through techniques of marketing, public relations, and polling. Competitive theories of democracy are accurately labeled elite theories because scholars believe that the proper role of elites is to shape public opinion and organize voter alignment. Landmark contributions from Adorno, Lane, and Noelle-Neumann suggest that the excessive influence of elites and other top-down realities in public opinion are caused by irrationalities among voters, whether from low ego-strength, repression, displacement, or other underlying psychological mechanisms.[20] Recent critical accounts of public opinion argue that party elites in centralized campaign organizations increasingly manipulate voters through improved technologies of political marketing.[21] While these perspectives are certainly insightful and relevant for understanding Latin American electorates today, emphasis on elite leadership, mass psychology, and technologies of manipulation fails to fully develop the *political* implications of recent trends toward direct popular appeals by executives and mass media electioneering.

New comparative perspectives on representation and democracy are also required to counter liberal-reformists who seek to produce strong party systems and adopt parliamentary government in Latin America. During and after transitions from military rule, the presidential systems of Latin America allowed the direct nomination of party professionals to executive posts and administrative offices, thereby producing a rapid and sweeping reorganization of parties in alliance with diverse local patronage machines. But because scholars retained theories and concepts from European experiences with parliamentary institutions and their rigidly organized party systems, they failed to perceive these mechanisms of political change typical of presidential and federal systems in the Americas. Scholars who criticize presidential institutions in Latin America today for exacerbating populism, patronage, party indiscipline, corruption, and weakening Congress (like advocates of the responsible party system model in the United States over four decades ago) fail to recognize the fundamentally different trajectory of political development in the presidential and federal systems that predominate in the Americas.[22] Indeed, from the classic observations of Weber and Bryce to the "new political historians" of the United States,[23] it is widely recognized that precocious political development in the nineteenth-century United States occurred because the direct popular appeals of presidential campaigns mobilized voters and because presidents, once in office, could freely nominate party professionals to administrative posts (thereby negotiating alliances with the patronage systems of senators).[24]

Far from seeking to substitute one model for another, this volume suggests that sustained analysis of both similarities and differences across the Americas is needed. Shifting comparative perspectives from Europe to the Americas may also provide more realistic goals for institutional reform. The political risks and opportunities presented by direct popular appeals and fluid alliances with patronage machines cannot be met by simply adopting parliamentary institutions. Proponents of liberal democracy in Latin America must confront the reality of direct plebiscitarian appeals and pursue practical means for their institutionalization. Both experiences within the region and from North America suggest that political reform of presidential and federal systems is possible by combining social movements, legislative work, presidential initiative, and the separation and diffusion of power.

In sum, the first decade of competitive politics in Latin America after transitions from military rule suggests that voters, parties, and electoral representation in the region share both universal problems of liberal and democratic government, and a series of risks and opportunities grounded in the post-transition realities of the region. Latin American experiences certainly have much to tell about classic tensions between the direct plebiscitarian appeals and indirect representative government, as well as a series of classic issues in the study of public opinion, voter choice, party organization, and other matters that the region now shares with established democracies. However, the transparency, immediacy, and substantive content of direct appeals between executives and popular sectors in Latin America provide a new context for these classic issues of electoral representation.

Deepening Democratic Governance in Latin America

How can elected elites convert the potential of existing institutions and political practices into a deployable ability to define, implement, and sustain viable policies? Given this general problem of liberal democratic governance, how can Latin American political elites confront the dual tasks of building democratic institutions and implementing viable economic policies of adjustment, restructuring, and modernization? Perhaps the central argument about governance in this volume is that until economic policy making is both linked to competitive party-electoral politics and accessible to groups from civil society after elections by means of institutionalized practices, isolated technocrats in executive agencies will not only truncate democracy but also fail to govern effectively. This emphasis on deepening democratic governance in Latin America also attempts to provide new perspectives on a basic tension between neoliberal economic ideology and pluralist democracy. The formulation and implementation of neoliberal economic packages and policies appears to require the concentration of power in an executive capable of closing access to the policy process, thereby negating the debate and participation implied in both democracy and political liberalism. The Pinochet government in Chile demonstrated the affinity between neoliberal economic restructuring and authoritarianism. Contemporary Latin America reveals a more complex, multilayered reality in which centralized, authoritarian styles of governance often tend to be folded into democratic politics understood almost exclusively in terms of elections. Despite this complexity and diversity, neoliberal programs tend to universally cut labor and other groups out of the policy process and hand them a substantial bill in short-term austerity, which often provokes violent confrontations. Popular demonstrations and military coup attempts in Venezuela provide graphic evidence of this tension.[25] And other cases like Bolivia show that even business groups that backed neoliberal ideological pronouncements can subsequently be cut out of the policy process.

In sum, the central theme that emerges from recent experiences of governance in Latin America is the profound tension between technocratic and exclusive policy-making patterns deemed imperative by "rational" neoliberal economic restructuring and the ideals of broad-based participation of both citizens and associational groups historically implied by liberal and pluralistic conceptions of democracy, ideals publicly ascribed to by governments and key political players throughout the Americas. This theme of contradiction combines with the accumulated legacies of specific historical contexts to produce the specific hybrids and unsettled regimes characteristic of post-transition realities in the region today.

Contemporary Latin America illustrates that leadership or statecraft, often ignored by theorists bent on developing scientific, nomotheoretical, or predictive models, becomes particularly important in moments when more routinized ways of government and politics give way to more open and volatile moments of transit to or founding of new regime forms. The open nature of such moments of transition and founding suggests that outcomes cannot be predicted in advance and that explanations will perforce have an after-the-event quality to them. On the other hand, while statecraft or leadership has an idiosyncratic dimension, there is no reason why one cannot examine strategies of leadership after the fact and draw from them, not nomothetic generalizations, but generalizations in the form of prudential rules of action that could serve leaders and analysts confronting analogous situations. This type of analysis has been done to great effect by theorists from Machiavelli in *The Prince* to Richard Neustadt in *Presidential Power*.

Indeed, in *The Machiavellian Moment* Pocock argues that the new understanding of politics forged by Machiavelli and his contemporaries five centuries ago fed into subsequent political thought and practice in the West because it provided critical guidance to political leaders confronting similar moments of crisis during the foundation of republican regimes.[26] Such moments have recurred in various times and places (Pocock looks specifically at Renaissance Italy, seventeenth-century England, and eighteenth-century America). The concept of a Machiavellian moment provides new perspectives on statecraft and the prospects for deepening democratic politics in Latin America as the region prepares to enter the twenty-first century. Indeed, contending forces throughout Latin America describe their national experiences as ones in which economic and political contingencies threaten to overwhelm not only democracy but nation and statehood as well. In the electoral contests of the 1980s and 1990s the central issues were not so much the programs or policies of presidential candidates but the sense in which leaders had the requisite capabilities to impose some order on the situation and confront economic crisis within a framework that bore at least some resemblance to constitutional democracy or republican government.

For Machiavelli and his contemporaries the central problem of such a moment was described as a confrontation between *virtu* and *fortuna*. These concepts attempted to reveal how universal principles, institutions, and practices could emerge from the particularity and contingency inherent in the uncontrolled behavior of contending political forces. To govern was to assert human mastery, however temporary, over the inherent fragmentation and contingency of ungoverned human nature and its predisposition toward a Hobbesian state of nature. In terms of recent discussions about democracy, the problem is to reduce the uncertainty of contingent political events and contending interests by means of abstract institutions and principles embodied in concepts such as the "rule of law" or "rules of the game." The task of statecraft in such a context is to introduce a set of formal and informal rules or practices that can become a common framework for political contestation in a game of rationally calculable probabilities rather than the uncertainty of institutional breakdown or arbitrary authoritarian rule.

Following the analogy further, the strategic task of Machiavellian moments is to transform the initiatives of personalized leadership into more permanent institutional structures, which are implied in conceptions of republican or rule-bound government. Personality, leadership, or statecraft can create a set of formal institutions through the creative deployment of "practices" that can be repeated or built upon as problems are resolved and new ones confronted over time. Past patterns of leadership can thereby become the accumulated customs, traditions, or informal rules that underpin a formal constitutional structure of rules and institutions.

The centrality of leadership or statecraft has been recognized to a considerable extent by the custom of associating particular presidents with the success or failure of specific programs. Notable experiences widely perceived as failures would include President Fernando Collor de Mello in Brazil and Presidents Belaunde Terry and Alan Garcia in Peru. Presidents Paz Estenssoro in Bolivia, Carlos Menem in Argentina, and Fernando Henrique Cardoso in Brazil are widely perceived as success stories both nationally and internationally.

While this is not the place to analyze these presidencies, it would be helpful once again to highlight certain themes and trends to keep in mind while reading the contributions to this volume. Current options in Latin America are shaped by the problematic institutional legacies of attempts throughout the nineteenth and twentieth centuries to institutionalize constitutional democracy in the region. One such legacy, perhaps the most important, has been a marked tendency throughout the region toward immobilized standoffs between executives and legislatures. This central institutional problem of governance has attracted a good deal of attention among theorists and prompted many to call for discarding presidential systems that have long predominated throughout the region in favor of formal models of parliamentary government. However, we would caution that in their striving for rationalized constitutional engineering as a way of solving problems of statecraft, recent advocates of parliamentarism echo the theoretical idealism of constitutional debates in Weimar Germany.

It is striking that while Presidents Menem, Cardoso, and Paz pushed rationalized economic packages, none engaged in broad theoretically derived programs of constitutional overhaul to confront political obstacles. Instead, these presidents adopted incremental strategies of statecraft designed to find ways out of specific dilemmas rather than big-bang resolutions of all political problems. Moreover, these presidents did not seek to design new institutions or single principles. Rather,

both took extant institutional practices and mechanisms of power and put them together in new and creative ways to overcome long-standing impasses. These presidents have advanced their societies toward new forms and practices fashioned from
the old. Whatever novelties have emerged from within these countries in terms of
regime form and practice have taken shape out of the accumulated weight of skillful statecraft, which finds its way from one problematic situation to the next.
Grand solutions based on theoretical design, strategies derived from formal instrumental rationalities, and broad constitutional engineering have fallen far short of
this creative statecraft of muddling through.

These experiences also suggest that leaders cannot maintain mastery over
events indefinitely in a democratic context. For example, President Paz realized
that a specific combination of circumstances carried within it a substantial power
potential. His statesmanship lay in seizing the moment and converting potential
into institutional and policy realities; yet he also knew that circumstantially generated authority had limits and that after a certain point bold new initiatives become
less possible. In the present context of seeking to define and give shape to effective
democratic systems, governmental authority must be continually built and rebuilt;
particularly as one moves from one government to another, from one often inde-
cisive election to another. Each new moment confronts governments not only with
the need to rebuild their own authority, but also to contribute by elaborating new
institutions and rules of the game out of the old. This task remains so difficult because of the persisting contradictions inherent in the situation and the fact that
each problem-solving move involves problem-creating tensions in other areas.

Another classic theme among analysts of modern Venezuela, Colombia, Bolivia, and Mexico is the assertion that political pacts can avert violence, overcome
political impasses between executives and legislatures, and facilitate economic adjustment. But social pacts or formal party agreements to share power also have serious downsides. From the perspective of liberal-democratic governance, pacts between parties can convert legislatures into rubber stamps for an isolated
policy-making style on the part of executives and their technocratic teams. Indeed
pacts, along with other factors like the economic crisis itself and the logic of a tech-
nomanagerial view of government, tend to reinforce a marked tendency for a de
facto authoritarian style of executive-based governance and the monopolization of
power by parties.

In our view, each positive move in one direction can and most probably will
create problems in another direction. For example, while pacts might help to reduce the electorally rooted political side of the problem of governance they might
do so at the cost of undermining the capacity of governments to assert authority
and control over the state apparatus. Most neoliberal stabilization programs are

predicated on reducing the size of government. The creation of a leaner, meaner state is seen as the best instrument of a technically sound program. However, the logics of patrimony, patronage, and negotiation, which are essential to forging a party-based pact, run counter to the rational legal logic of administrative downsizing and reform. Indeed, pacts tend to put more pressure on public employment because they reinforce the patrimonial logic within state apparatuses. As Baloyra's analysis of Venezuela demonstrates, pacted democracy over time tends to create the perception of tyranny by a corrupt party oligarchy that can undermine the legitimacy of the entire system. This particular contradiction between pacts and governance still pervades the region and will continue to surprise those seeking an easy solution or formula for reconciling neoliberal economic programs, democratic politics, and effective policy performance.

The tasks of deepening democracy in Latin America are further complicated by the marked tendency to see economic management as the primary task of government. This perception holds even where governments are called upon to downsize through the privatization of state firms, the liberalization of markets, and a general retreat of the state from economic life. These policies are predicated less on a disengagement of the state from the economy than a restructuring of the state's relationship to the economy. In effect, the goal is a leaner, meaner state overseeing and guaranteeing an ostensibly free market. Unfortunately, the model for economic liberalization in the region remains Chile under the Pinochet dictatorship and the Chicago Boys who surrounded him.

An ironic outcome of this emphasis on government as economic management in Latin America today is that business groups who pushed for democracy because they were shut out of policy making under military government now often find themselves shut out by their civilian democratic successors; policy processes built around technocratic economic policy teams often turn out to be as exclusive as those fashioned around military-technocratic alliances. Substantively, neoliberal programs call for the goring of some well-established business oxen as well as those of the popular sectors. For example, reducing tariffs does not set well with national manufacturing interests. Hence, national business interests are often not consulted when the programs are formed and their protests often fall on deaf ears as the programs are implemented.

Indeed, a new political cleavage often appears to have split neoliberal coalitions throughout Latin America. Business elites whose understandings of capitalism have been forged in the day-to-day experiences of running firms tend to oppose technocrats with their abstract theoretical constructions of market capitalism on the macroeconomic level. Tensions arise in part because technocrats remain attached to government-designed programs and concerned with aggregate performance targets such as monetary, fiscal, import-export, investment, and GNP (gross national product) figures, which fit into their economic models, rather than with the fate of any given firm or sector. A more important source of tension is that the decision style of the new political-technocratic policy alliance tends to exclude bargaining with business groups. In the current scene technocratic policy makers follow what one might call a logic of economic packages; once programs are derived from economic theory they are presented as a package that must be implemented as a whole. Therefore, the kind of bargaining and policy compromise long associated with a liberal, pluralistic, and democratic policy style is precluded by the holistic logic of economic packages.

This political cleavage reveals deep differences about governance and democracy in Latin America. Executive-based policy teams offer images of governance and democracy that counterpose their presumedly apolitical efforts with other more traditional types of policy process that they often seek to describe as reflecting mere politics and particular interests. Surely this constitutes a novel construction of liberal democracy.[27] Indeed, technocratic policy elites tend to present their programs (a) as carrying the legitimacy of an apolitical theoretical and scientific grounding and (b) as being articulated in the name of the economy and the nation as a whole. From the perspective of isolated technocratic teams, the concerns of business and other groups are consequently viewed as reflecting a lower order of particularistic interests fighting to preserve short-term privileges at the expense of the national interest.

The reality of these issues may well have surfaced in the recent Peruvian elections where substantial segments of national business feared Vargas Llosa's uncompromising holistic and technocratic vision of market capitalism and the likely effects of further policy packages and shock treatments to reduce inflation. Having lived through Belaunde Terry's (1980–1985) orthodox and uncompromising neoliberal program that devastated local manufacturing, hot on the heels of the military regime's 1968–1980 technocratic tinkering, Peru's capitalists are clearly skeptical of grand schemes hatched by technocrats dressed in either authoritarian or democratic garb. Finally, the criticism of traditional political parties and legislatures by technocrats and executives in these countries encourages the emergence of volatile new political contenders and novel sources of support from outside traditional electoral patterns and organizations.

In sum, new types of liberal-democratic governance will be required to meet the dual tasks of building democratic institutions and surpassing economic crisis. If executives continue to pursue technocratic solutions to political problems, not only will democracy and representation be gutted, but ineffectiveness will also continue to pervade new civilian governments.

Deepening Democracy in Latin America: A Look Ahead

By focusing both on emergent characteristics of electoral representation and on how interest groups, bureaucratic politics, and economic factors constrain the policy process, the contributors to this volume seek to identify critical problems for democratic politics in Latin America in this post-transition and post–cold war fin de siècle. Chapters 1 and 2 provide cautionary tales from Mexico and Venezuela about the impediments to democratization in party-electoral politics. For Roderic Camp, Mexico during the 1980s and 1990s presents an extreme case of a hybrid regime, one in which executives retain power at the center while more or less competitive elections on the local and state level serve as a type of escape valve for social and political pressures. Camp argues that the tenacious party monopoly of the PRI (Party of the Institutionalized Revolution) and its corporatist organizations of representation confined processes of political liberalization to the local and state level, while precariously securing neoliberal austerity throughout the 1980s and into the 1990s.

Corporatism, that is to say the monopoly of representation through functionally defined groups recognized by the state,[28] is antithetic to the liberal tradition of dispersing power through a variety of independent social groups and political institutions. Given this distinction, Camp's analysis of Mexico in chapter 1 suggests that the organization of three functionally defined organizations of labor, business, and peasants within the umbrella state-party of the PRI rigidly controlled by state elites sets difficult barriers to deepening democracy in Mexico. In this respect, Camp's analysis concurs with Aldo Vacs's comparative analysis of Uruguay and Argentina in chapter 8. Like Mexico, Argentine president Menem imposed neoliberal policies of austerity by relying on long-standing corporatist organizations of labor and business.

Although Venezuela has been seen as a paradigm of pacted democracy since 1958, Enrique Baloyra's analysis in chapter 2 suggests that the exclusive hold of Venezuelan parties on power ensures neither stability nor democracy. Baloyra argues that since a series of revolts on the left were put down in the 1960s, oil revenues and effective party organizations did ease social tensions until the late 1980s. However, since policies of economic adjustment were first introduced in 1983, the Venezuelan party oligopoly has faced new challenges from a society and military dissatisfied with corruption, scandal, and austerity. Baloyra's analysis of the legacies of popular and military revolts that wracked Venezuela's traditional party politics in the late 1980s provides new perspectives on party politics, economic policy, and the content of democracy in the region.

In chapter 3, Julio Carrión presents a causal analysis of support for Peruvian presidents that reveals the primacy of economic performance and the risks of direct appeals by executives to the populace. The Peruvian experience provides further grounds for caution when discussing the role of executives in deepening democracy. While the contributors to this volume recognize the importance of the populist tradition in Latin America, and the continued need to include and represent popular sectors in post-transition politics of the region, the risk of executives overstepping the rule of law is also a central concern. In this respect, the Peruvian experience with President Fujimori represents the most recent variation on a classic problem, that of the threat posed by democratic dictators and the power of direct plebiscitarian appeals to individual liberty and the rule of law.

In chapter 4, Eduardo Gamarra argues that neoliberal policies were implemented in Bolivia through the creative statecraft of President Paz-Estenssoro. The unique features of the Bolivian presidential system and the skilled leadership of Paz-Estenssoro permitted the organization of popular expectations, the negotiation of party coalitions, and the implementation of tough measures of economic adjustment. However, Gamarra argues that external constraints and domestic austerity programs have consistently hampered the building of democratic politics during the 1980s. The Bolivian system, because it requires that first-round elections producing no absolute majority be settled in the legislature, has forced presidential candidates to balance the popular appeals needed to get votes in the first round with realities of forming party coalitions in the legislature and renegotiating obligations with foreign creditors.

In chapter 5 Borzutzky suggests that although the party-electoral dimension of Chilean politics has returned since the transition from military rule, the social functions of state have been drastically reduced in favor of its economic functions. For Borzutzky, the preceding period of modern democratic government in Chile from 1924–1973 depended on a balance between executive and legislature, a multiparty system, and extensive social investments on the part of the state. The Pinochet dictatorship ended political contestation, atomized society, and imposed neoliberal policies. Borzutzky argues that the critical dimension about politics in Chile after the return to civilian rule in 1989 is not the widely recognized reduction of state intervention into the economy, but the defeat of left groups and the reduction of state social services. For Chileans, democratic politics today lacks the social dimension of the pre-1973 system.

In chapter 6, Montecinos argues that understanding democratic politics in Chile and the region requires recognition of the exceptional degree of influence that economists have developed during and after transitions from military rule. From this perspective, the causal mechanisms of political economy have changed. Economic policies are no longer imposed by international financial institutions such as the International Monetary Fund, nor are they dictated directly by market forces. Instead, the experience of Chile suggests that a new policy consensus has emerged among a new generation of economists who occupy not only critical posts in economic ministries, but also, in the case of Chile, direct control of party organizations and platforms. Given this rise of economists, the development of open and pluralistic conceptions of governance becomes even more critical for deepening democracy in Chile and the region as a whole.

In chapter 7, von Mettenheim argues that the election of President Fernando Henrique Cardoso in 1994 combines new movements for political reform with traditional mechanisms of competitive mass politics in Brazil. Indeed, the 1994 presidential campaign brought two candidates to the fore—Luis Inacio da Silva and Fernando Henrique Cardoso—who represent the major intellectual and political innovations in Brazilian and Latin American politics of the last decades. Indeed, the successes of President Fernando Henrique Cardoso's gradual, inclusive, and transparent approach to policy making suggest that open and pluralistic styles of governance can both deepen democracy and produce viable economic policies.[29]

The analysis of party-electoral politics by von Mettenheim leaves little room for doubt: Westminster ideals of well-organized ideological parties, disciplined political elites, and gradual evolution within parliamentary institutions are simply not relevant in Brazil. Instead, understanding the prospects for deepening democracy in Brazil requires shifting comparative perspectives away from idealized images of Europe to new concepts that reflect the trajectories of political change in the presidential and federal systems of the Americas. Recent political change occurred in Brazil because direct popular appeals mobilized voters during executive elections and because presidents, governors, and mayors were able to deftly renegotiate electoral alliances and legislative coalitions by nominating professional politicians directly to administrative posts. The rapid sequence of creative economic packages and unexpected party-electoral outcomes in Brazil since 1985 suggests that scholars will need open concepts to accompany the new risks and opportunities for deepening democracy through pluralistic governance and competitive politics.

In chapter 8, Vacs compares experiences with neoliberal policies in Argentina and Uruguay, as leaders in these countries seek to develop economic policy alternatives after the decline of import substitution industrialization. For Vacs, the successful implementation of neoliberal policies in Argentina and their failure to take root in Uruguay is determined largely by domestic factors. Specifically, the corporatist institutions of Argentine politics permitted President Menem to split and defeat labor and popular opposition. In comparison, in Uruguay the separation of legislative and executive powers, the autonomy of its social organizations and party factions, and the holding of a national referendum on privatization permitted steadfast resistance to the imposition of draconian measures of neoliberalism. President Sanguinetti had no recourse to decree powers and was forced to negotiate policies in the legislature.

The conclusion returns to the questions posed at the outset of this volume and attempts to review and synthesize the various contributions contained in the essays on particular national experiences. The diversity and wealth of national experiences implies that understanding both the risks and opportunities for deepening democracy in Latin America will require analysis well beyond the bounds of this volume. By shifting debates about Latin American politics from questions of military rule, transition politics, and stability, the hope is that elites and citizens may deepen both competitive electoral politics and open pluralistic governance as the region enters the twenty-first century.

Battling for the Voter

Elections, Parties, and Democracy in Mexico

RODERIC CAMP

Introduction

Normally, the conceptualization of democratic politics and political liberalization incorporates elections as an integral component of the political process.[1] Indeed, it would be impossible to find in the academic literature a definition of political democracy that did not include a reference to the electoral process.[2] Theorists are careful, however, to specify that such elections must be competitive. Moreover, they generally include the caveat that the primary test of a functioning democracy, and the level of electoral competitiveness, is an exchange of leadership in the governing process, implying the defeat of the incumbent party.[3]

The 1990s have witnessed, for better or worse, an Americanization of electoral processes worldwide. Features of the American electoral process have been imposed willy-nilly on structural and cultural patterns often incompatible with, or different from those complementary to democratic electoral politics.[4] Despite the influence exercised by international political liberalization, the United States' closest neighbor, Mexico, remains resistant to change. The irony of a nondemocratic Mexico, a stubborn island of authoritarianism in a sea change of democratization, has not been lost on political observers.

Democratization has, however, affected the institutional and cultural fabric of Mexico since the early 1980s, especially since 1988. Mexico, unlike most countries in the region, has not gone from the extreme of authoritarian politics, where parties are eliminated altogether and elections suppressed, to competitive party elections. Instead, it has gradually expanded political participation among opposition parties, while giving up power at the local and state level only. At the same time, the economic and political context in Mexico has generated a plethora of nongovernmental organizations, many of which have the potential to act as interest groups and to strengthen competitive parties. Mexico has the potential to increase political participation, but it will not happen suddenly, as in Nicaragua. While the political culture remains cynical about the veracity of elections, and exercising a voice in the political arena, there are growing signs that Mexicans expect more out of their electoral process and that they are willing to use nontraditional techniques to influence political outcomes.

Will Mexico be the newest experiment in western democracy in the next several years? The answer is likely to be no. What, then, explains Mexico's ability to resist such changes? And second, to what extent has Mexico, in spite of its leadership's resistance, been the recipient of recent influences? Two sets of variables play a significant role in the relationship between elections, parties, and democratization. The first of these are structural. A second set of variables, which have structural consequences, can be seen as cultural.

The PRI and Political Parties

When Mexico established the National Revolutionary Party (PNR), the antecedent to the Institutional Revolutionary Party, in 1929, it immediately introduced a peculiar distortion to the party system and electoral process.[5] It is critical to understand that the party was founded by a leadership already in power. Yet, the classic definition of political parties spells out the primary goal as one of winning power. Mexico's postrevolutionary political history establishes a fundamental contradiction in the party's role, function, and origins. The party's purpose, then, has not been to seize power through the electoral arena, but to consolidate and retain political control.

It is fair to say that the PNR's establishment gradually eliminated smaller regional political organizations, many of which had emerged in response to the diversity of political opinions in the postrevolutionary era. Although the 1920s witnessed considerable political ferment, representatives of these political movements were eventually co-opted by the leadership's electoral vehicle, the PNR, or the state bureaucracy. Those who resisted were suppressed; those who were not a threat were ignored.

A second characteristic of Mexico's dominant party, differing from United States parties, concerns members' origins. Until 1991, membership in PRI and its antecedents involved belonging to an affiliate organization such as a union or pro-fessional group. The party did not go out and recruit individual members; rather, it served as an umbrella organization to other groups. This characteristic deter-mined PRI's structure and again influenced its political functions. Structurally, the party developed three sectors—agrarian, labor, and popular—although for a brief period under President Lázaro Cárdenas (1934–1940), the military provided a fourth category.[6] These sectors formed part of a semicorporatist structure encour-aged in the 1930s.[7] The concept of individual versus group membership, a funda-mental quality of western political parties, remained unchanged until 1990, when the PRI 14th Annual Assembly amended its basic bylaws.[8]

Unlike the Soviet Union, where the Communist Party remained firmly in con-trol, Mexico's PRI and its antecedents never served as the institutional vehicle for recruiting, training, socializing, and promoting top politicians.[9] The state bureau-cracy substituted for the party as the primary institution performing these func-tions.[10] This is not to say that the PRI serves none of the typical personnel func-tions, but that most top political leaders in Mexico typically have risen up through the government, not the party bureaucracy.[11]

Characteristics peculiar to Mexico's dominant party have modified opposition party behavior, contributing to certain features in the electoral process. Over the years, the vast majority of Mexican political parties appeared and disappeared in the electoral arena. Most shared the following characteristics: 1) they were led by dissident members of the governing elite;[12] 2) they were short-lived, often lasting only for a single election; or 3) if they survived, they often did so as appendages of the government party;[13] and 4) they never were able to achieve widespread support sufficient to give them status as a national party. Until 1987, only one party, the Na-tional Action Party (PAN), founded in 1939 by prominent political figures, pro-vided a consistent, national alternative to the PRI.[14]

In the 1988 elections, and subsequently, PAN continued to offer competition to the government party in traditional strongholds: the north, the western state of Jalisco, the central state of Guanajuato, and Mexico City. A careful analysis of its support for congressional candidates reveals clearly the unevenness of its strength. It continues to remain an urban party, drawing its support largely from middle-class city residents. It has won gubernatorial elections in Baja California (1989) and Chi-huahua (1992) and contested the fraudulent results in Guanajuato (1991), leading to the appointment of a PAN politician to the governorship. PAN, beginning in the reform era of the Miguel de la Madrid administration (1982–1988), also won nu-merous mayoralty races, including those in important state capitals.[15]

Following the historical pattern of nearly all Mexican opposition parties, the Democratic Revolutionary Party (PRD) emerged in 1989 from a dissident move-ment within the governing leadership. Essentially, an important faction of government leaders in 1987, anticipating the presidential succession, found their ideological positions, and their representatives, excluded from contention.[16] They favored strong state economic intervention, nationalism, and since the 1980s, rapid political liberalization. When this group viewed their access to government power as closed, they bolted the party and formed their own political movement. Too late to establish their own political party in 1988, instead they formed a coalition of parties already on the presidential ballot. To the surprise of most political observers, this populist-leftist coalition, led by Cuauhtémoc Cárdenas, attracted widespread sympathy and support at the ballot box, winning the largest percentage of opposition votes ever reported in Mexican presidential elections since the Revolution.

Instead of disappearing, typical of most incipient political parties in the past, these dissidents institutionalized themselves in the PRD and proceeded to contest elections widely. Although Cárdenas and the PRD won the mayorship of Mexico City in 1997 and have influenced the role of political parties and the electoral process in Mexico, they have not yet achieved success comparable to 1988, in part due to electoral fraud and to their own failures.[17]

Political parties need patronage not only to survive, but to grow. Although other, smaller parties exist, the viable party spectrum in Mexico in the 1990s is confined to three alternatives, PRI, PAN, and PRD. The intensity with which the PRD battled for political office, and the even greater intensity with which the PRI sought to prevent PRD from achieving political success, introduced some important influences into the function and conception of Mexican political parties. Instead of the PRI providing the only model of a successful political party, one guaranteeing absolute control over political offices, both the PAN and even the PRD offer real possibilities of winning power in the legislative branch nationally, and in state-level executive and legislative branches. Their successes declined *nationally* from 1988 through 1993, but expanded at the state level, increasingly forcing the PRI to master the functions of a normal political party. In short, PRI has had to compete for political office. As PRI's president admitted: "For the first time in history, our party faced a different situation. Part of society withdrew its support from the PRI and threw it behind other parties. In July 1989 we lost the governorship of Baja California. These two experiences triggered the emergence of a new political culture within the PRI: *we had to learn to win votes in a more competitive party system*" (emphasis mine).[18]

Finally, until the 1970s, the PRI rarely provided a mechanism for choosing the best candidate for political office. Party leadership did not choose candidates for elective office, nor were they necessarily selected for their political abilities. Instead, the party became a closed, national electoral arena, open only to PRI loyalists who rewarded politicians with nominations to national and state offices. Since the PRI nomination was tantamount to electoral victory, intense competition for political office occurred *within* the party. Increasing opposition successes, even as early as the Luis Echeverría administration (1970–1976), forced the party in selected circumstances to carry out traditional functions, including selecting the best candidate possible.

The historic role of elections in Mexico complimented the truncated functions of Mexico's leading party.[19] Like the party itself since 1988, the electoral process began to change. This role of elections was firmly established since the era of Porfirio Díaz (1884–1911), who reinforced his legitimacy by holding elections every four years.[20] Again, as was true of the formation of Mexico's government party, the purpose of elections was not to determine *who would govern* but to reinforce the incumbent governors' powers. Despite the showcase nature of these elections, occasionally they were hotly contested at the state and local levels.[21] In the postrevolutionary period, dissenting elites contested several major presidential contests before 1988, especially the 1929, 1940, and 1952 elections.

The process of governance and decision-making has also distorted Mexican elections. Ideally, elections function as formalized channels through which individuals and interest groups select political leadership, giving the individual voter or group access to the political process *after* the electoral outcome. Elections thereby can establish a constituency relationship between the elected and the electorate. In Mexico, however, no such relationship emerged. Mexico's executive branch, especially the presidency, is all-powerful.[22] In the decision-making process, the presidency both formulates and initiates legislation. The legislative branch exercises little influence over the policy process. Thus, the electorate cannot rely on the legislator to provide them with a linkage to executive political leadership, and more importantly, to have input in public policy formulation.[23] The interested individual or interest group bypasses the legislative branch and deals directly with the executive branch.[24] Naturally, it is not in the interest of politically astute groups to support legislative candidates as a means of achieving policy influence. Politically savvy individuals do help PRI candidates as a means of obtaining favors from government leadership generally, but they must go directly to state or national executive branch leaders to accomplish their lobbying efforts.[25]

The Mexican legal system has further distorted the electoral process.[26] It not only gives the executive branch much more authority than the legislative branch, but it actually insures the legislature's dependence on the executive branch. Legislators cannot hold office consecutively in either the Senate or Chamber of Deputies. Consequently, an individual cannot build up a clientele of constituents, giving the person an electoral political base. On the national level, changing this law potentially could do more to strengthen the electoral system than nearly any other legal statute. For Mexican elections to become more important, a linkage needs to occur between influencing policy, electing officials, and the electorate's perception of their representatives' functions. The system is presently structured in such a way as to hamper these linkages.

The dramatic increase in opposition strength since the late 1980s has led the political leadership to renegotiate a new set of electoral laws. In January 1994, an indigenous uprising in Chiapas, in southern Mexico, organized by the Zapatista Army for National Liberation (EZLN), as part of their demands prompted even stronger changes in anticipation of the 1994 presidential elections.[27] Overall, they function to simultaneously encourage and control opposition growth. In 1976, the leading opposition party, PAN, decided to boycott the presidential elections, bluntly illustrating the sham quality of Mexico's electoral process. Their decision, combined with a decreasing interest in elections generally, and a concomitant increase in voter abstention, forced the government to take action.[28]

It is important to remember that until 1989, the government did not permit the opposition to win any state executive office. Thus, the most important political posts conceded to the opposition were seats in the national Chamber of Deputies. It is no accident that the Chamber of Deputies is a weak policy-making body, which explains why electoral reforms primarily affect the legislative branch. The reforms expanded the size of the legislature, increasing opposition party patronage, establishing an allegedly more independent body to approve the election results (Federal Electoral Institute), and revamping voting credentials. Before the advent of the reforms, Mexico's legislative system paralleled that of the United States, based on single-member districts. Presently, Mexico has three hundred such districts. However, since the opposition could not win, or, was not allowed to win a sizeable share of those seats (never more than 10 percent), the government added an additional one hundred seats (plurinominal) allocated on the basis of each party's national vote count, doubling those seats to two hundred after 1988 (see table 1.1). However, when the party witnessed its vote totals reaching only slightly over 50 percent in the 1988 elections, it introduced a governability clause. The majority party not only can now obtain some of the plurinominal seats, but even if it wins only 35 percent of the votes, it automatically receives a sufficient number of those seats to guarantee it a simple majority.

The government did not anticipate the amount of votes both major opposition parties received in the 1988 election. Although PRI maintained a simple majority in the Chamber of Deputies (most observers believe through electoral fraud), it did not have a two-thirds majority necessary to approve constitutional amendments. Traditionally, the government used this technique to legitimize major legislation. From their perspective, then, the only valuable role the legislative branch plays is to reinforce their legitimacy. The government's weakened representation pushed them to engage in high-level political bargaining with one of the two major

TABLE 1.1

Seats in the Chamber of Deputies by Party, 1964–1991

Legislature	Parties										
	PRI	PAN	PPS	PARM	PDM	PSUM	PST	PRT	PMT	PRD	PFCRN
1964	175	2	1	–	–	–	–	–	–	–	–
Party	–	18	9	5	–	–	–	–	–	–	–
1967	177	1	0	0	–	–	–	–	–	–	–
Party	–	9	10	5	–	–	–	–	–	–	–
1970	178	0	0	0	–	–	–	–	–	–	–
Party	–	20	1	0	5	–	–	–	–	–	–
1973	189	4	1	–	–	–	–	–	–	–	–
Party	–	21	10	6	–	–	–	–	–	–	–
1976	1	95	2	–	–	–	–	–	–	–	–
Party	–	20	12	9	–	–	–	–	–	–	–
1979	296	4	–	–	–	–	–	–	–	–	–
Plurin	–	39	1	12	10	18	10	–	–	–	–
1982	299	1	–	–	–	–	–	–	–	–	–
Plurin	–	5	0	10	0	1 2	17	11	–	–	–
1985	289	9	2	–	–	–	–	–	–	–	–
Plurin	–	32	11	9	12	12	12	6	6	–	–
1988*	233	38	4	5	15	5	–	–	–	–	–
Plurin	27	63	27	23	11	46	–	–	–	–	–
1991	290	10	–	–	–	–	–	–	–	–	–
Plurin	31	80	12	14	0	23	–	–	–	–	–

*Three deputies in the 1988 legislature were classified as independents, and one deputy among the PRD majority transferred his loyalty to the PRD after being elected on the PRI ticket.

Source: Adapted from Héctor Zamitiz and Carlos Hernández, "La composición política de la Cámara de Diputados, 1949–1989," *Revista de Ciencias Políticas y Sociales* 36, no. 139 (January–March 1990): 97–108; and Roderic Ai Camp, *Politics in Mexico,* 2d ed. (New York: Oxford University Press, 1996), 177.

parties. For various reasons, the government chose to negotiate with the PAN, which, in return for some of its demands, supported the new electoral law.

Unlike the rest of Latin America, Mexico's proximity to the United States has fostered a host of special relationships. Although the consequences are too numerous to enumerate here, important influences have affected the electoral process.[29] Given the two countries's close proximity, it seems strange that their political systems could be so different, and that Mexico's semiauthoritarian system could survive its northern neighbor's liberalizing influences, a testament to the strength of Mexican nationalism.

This is not to suggest, however, that the Mexican regime's longevity indicates no influence from the United States, but rather that it has persevered in spite of those influences. A historic feature of Mexican politics, one that national leadership has viewed as a threat to national political stability, is regionalism. It is no accident, for example, that some of the stronger opposition movements in the twentieth century occurred at the geographic appendages of Mexico's national territory, including the Yucatán peninsula, Guadalajara in the far west, and along the northern border. The latter states have come under the influence of the United States, not merely from overt economic penetration, but more importantly from shared cultural experiences and a resentment toward Mexico City specifically.[30] Numerous surveys suggest that Americanization has leached indirectly into the political culture. For example, when Mexicans were asked if their country should advance toward a more democratic government, all regions, except the north, which gave an even stronger, favorable answer, responded equally.[31] Northerners also believe that voting can be an important vehicle in effecting change, much more so than their sophisticated counterparts in Mexico City.[32]

Northerners have also understood for some time their geographic advantages in the electoral process. The dominant opposition party in the north, PAN, began since the mid-1980s to use geography as a vehicle for political protest. PAN adopted the occasional strategy of blocking international bridges or roads between the two countries, thus attracting media and governmental interest from the United States. Even more threatening to the Mexican government, PAN members have requested political asylum, alleging physical threats. A large number of Mexicans making such requests would have serious consequences on United States-Mexican relations, jeopardizing many other commercial and financial linkages.

Interestingly, the type of Americanization of Latin American elections that Alan Angell and his colleagues describe elsewhere in the region, particularly the use of electronic media in campaigns, has not taken place in Mexico.[33] Again, the structure of the political process imposed a different set of criteria on media, censorship, and their relationship to the state.[34] While the average Mexican, like his counterpart in Latin America, is exposed to American television, Mexican television does not permit the free-wheeling political advertising found in other parts of the region. Television and radio advertising are strictly controlled, as is intellectual programming involving political discussions and interviews. Many Mexicans claim to be most influenced by television, but the blandness of television and radio programming could only help the incumbent party, not the opposition.[35] Therefore, techniques developed in North American campaigns, including negative advertising and debates, have not appeared in the Mexican political arena.

Proximity to the United States generates another consequence peculiar to the Mexican electoral process. The United States government, and even more important, its media, takes on greater significance in the electoral campaigns. All sides use the United States, and media sources, to legitimize their role in Mexican elections. One special feature of Mexico's proximity to the United States is the number of Mexicans who reside across the border, who have relatives living in the United States, and who have traveled to and from the United States.[36] The Mexican government is sensitive to the attitudes of their citizens living abroad, fearing that they could become a powerful interest group for or against Mexican public policy in the American political arena. Opposition parties, believing that the millions of Mexicans temporarily living abroad would be more sympathetic to their programs, free from electoral coercion and fraud, have campaigned to allow them to vote. The Mexican government, fearing their assessments are correct, steadfastly has refused to allow their participation. Instead, government representatives, particularly PRD leadership, have sought to politicize Mexicans residing in the United States to support their programs and electoral activities in Mexico.

Even if no Mexicans resided in the United States, the government and the opposition would pursue an active interest in the U.S. media's posture. Although such media attention sometimes focuses on controversial policy issues, such as the drug trade, border problems, or the implications of the North American Free Trade Agreement (NAFTA), most coverage over time involved Mexican elections. The United States media provides insightful and critical articles on election fraud. To some extent, the media actually contributed to opposition parties' efforts to achieve clean electoral vote counts. The *Washington Post*, the *New York Times*, the *Los Angeles Times*, and the *Wall Street Journal* frequently comment on the state of Mexican democratization and the fairness of its electoral process. When a North American media source cites progress in Mexican political development, the Mexican government is quick to report it in state-controlled media. On the other hand, editorials critical of the government's handling of the elections are immediately reported in independent publications.

The importance of the United States's influence increased significantly with Salinas's government commitment to a free trade agreement. There is little question that editorials appearing in the *Wall Street Journal* influenced President Salinas to annul Guanajuato election results in 1991, preventing the PRI gubernatorial candidate from taking office. Critics have made President Salinas sensitive to charges that the United States and Canada should not form a trade pact with an antidemocratic political system.[37]

Since 1973, one of the additional features of electioneering Latin America borrowed from its northern neighbor is public opinion polls. Again, Mexico has taken a back seat to the rest of the region. Although the PRI financed some unpublished polls, their results were never made public. It was not until the 1988 presidential elections that polls became part of the election process. The North American media financed some of these polls, the most widely cited of which is the *Los Angeles Times* poll.[38] The growth of independent pollsters, led by Miguel Basáñez, produced a plethora of surveys, not only national, but in hotly disputed state and local elections.[39] Responding to the publication of these polls, the government hired its own pollsters. It also began using polls to target electoral efforts.[40] The publication of *Este País*, an independent monthly publishing the results of various surveys on all aspects of Mexican life, highlights public opinion polls' importance. As might be expected, the government claims that survey results are politicized. The government has used the same censorship techniques against pollsters as it has against the media generally, to dampen enthusiasm for independent surveys.

Polls do affect electoral observers' opinions, providing a benchmark from which to assess actual results. This applies to domestic critics, foreign analysts, and government officials. Even in cases where government officials commit electoral fraud, their own, unpublished polls make them aware of the actual vote. It may even indicate to PRI alchemists where and what type of fraud needs to be committed. As polls increase in number and sophistication, they provide independent verification of *actual* versus *alleged* changes in the electorate's behavior.

The ability of the electoral system to achieve its full potential is limited by the level of intimidation applied to members of opposition parties. Although the Mexican political system has often resorted successfully to co-optation, using financial or political rewards to eliminate individual threats to its leadership's hegemony, it has not been averse to using far more repressive techniques. Intense electoral competition always has led to some political violence in Mexico, but in recent years, before and after the 1988 elections, supporters of Cárdenas and later the PRD disproportionately have been victims of human rights abuses and murder. Political assassination targeting PRD members is well documented by international and independent Mexican human rights organizations.[41] Emphasis on these violations is due, in part, to how the Mexican government perceives itself being viewed in the United States.

Complementary to Mexico's proximity to the United States, but exercising an influence independent of some of the other political and social variables, is the role of economic liberalization.[42] As suggested above, economic liberalization in anticipation of a free trade agreement introduced a number of consequences for Mexican elections.[43] Until 1993, such consequences were essentially confined to Carlos Salinas's savvy political efforts to placate United States critics, so the negotiations themselves would not be sidetracked.

The more intriguing structural question to be raised is does economic liberalization influence political behavior? Will political consequences be associated more strongly with economic liberalization after the treaty goes into effect in 1994? This relationship has elicited considerable interest among pundits and academics alike, but most of it is speculative at this point.[44] Nevertheless, some concrete economic policies have been associated with changes affecting electoral behavior. For example, Luis Rubio believes that more intensified economic competition will be translated into more competitive political behavior. He argues that a stronger, economically independent workforce, out of the grasp of government-controlled unions, will exercise greater independence in the voting booth.[45] Given Mexico's major economic crises since December 1995, and its severe economic and political consequences, it would be difficult, it not impossible to isolate the role of economic liberalization. Other analysts suggest that until entrepreneurs' behavior changes, specifically that their own interest groups' decision making is decentralized, their electoral influence will remain limited.

Geography not only exercised an important influence on Mexican political development because of proximity to the United States but also served as an internal variable. Mexico, like many parts of Latin America, evolved along two different axes: rural and urban. The pace of urbanization and the internal transfer of migrants from rural to urban Mexico has been phenomenal, as is true elsewhere in the region. The differences in the level of development between urban and rural regions, measured by standard of living, level of education, and the sophistication of the economy, is much more pronounced in Mexico than in the United States.[46]

These sharp geographic divisions have important consequences on electoral behavior, specifically on the potential for enhancing democratization, measured by competitive elections. The evidence shows that at least since 1970 political opposition achieved much greater success in urban compared to rural districts. Mexico City, for example, the most urbanized center in the country, always has allocated a large percentage of the vote to opposition parties, long before vote counts suggested their influence nationally.[47] There are both developmental and structural reasons for this pattern. On the developmental side, explanations include a higher level of education, a greater level of political sophistication, and higher levels of income, all of which are positively associated with greater political independence. On the structural side, PRI is the only political party in Mexico with an organizational depth reaching down to the grassroots. No other political party yet has achieved their level of breadth or depth. This not only has implications for getting out the vote, which PRI used to its advantage in the 1991 congressional elections to recover from its staggering losses during 1988, but for its ability to engineer election fraud. It is the only party that can still muster its own poll watchers at every single polling station in Mexico.[48] As a result, opposition parties are susceptible to manipulation, especially in more isolated, rural voting booths.

The Mexican Presidency

Another structural variable important to consider is the centralization of political authority in Mexico. Centralization not only has strong political roots in Mexico extending back to precolonial and colonial times, but it is legitimized in many practices in contemporary Mexico. President Carlos Salinas was perhaps the most unpopular recent president when elected in 1988. The presidency itself lost considerable sheen as a consequence of serious economic conditions in the 1970s and 1980s. Yet, to revive his popularity and that of the presidency, Salinas skillfully resorted to a series of deft, forceful decisions in the first year in office. He selected his targets carefully, and his exercise of presidential authority, often in contravention to established legal norms, made him popular in the eyes of the Mexican public. This suggests that the Mexican people expect a president to exercise such authority, and they may well be impressed with a presidential figure's decisiveness, distinct from the policy implemented. It also demonstrates that the legal culture takes a distant back seat to the exercise of political authority.

President Salinas translated presidential authority directly to the electoral process in two ways. First, centralization of political authority was part of an overall trend during his administration in spite of promises of political liberalization. The degree of political liberalization introduced by the government since 1988 is the work of the president.

Presidential political development dominates Salinas's administration. The ability of the opposition to convert electoral contests to ultimate victory often has been as much a result of presidential intervention as deserved electoral success. In four important cases, San Luis Potosí (1991), Guanajuato (1991), Tabasco (1992), and Michoacán (1992), where the PRI claimed to have won important state or local election victories, the president intervened personally in response to demonstrations orchestrated by opposition groups. In three cases the governor or governor-elect was removed, replaced by a Priista or Panista substitute, and in the fourth case, another PRI governor replaced the incumbent, who was not running for reelection. Whatever motivations the president may have had for intervening, the important consequence to keep in mind is that the president made the decision to alter the electoral outcome, ignoring available legal procedures. As Javier Garrido has suggested, the president exercises metaconstitutional powers as the ultimate authority in electoral matters, delineating "organizational forms and procedures for supervising elections. He also has priority use of election resources."[49]

Such presidential interference has significant symbolic implications for the structure of the political system, for the political culture, and for the electoral process itself. First, it encourages all political groups, PRI and the opposition alike, to look to the president to resolve political conflicts. Second, it devalues the legal system in the eyes of the political leadership, and the populace generally, compared to the political power of the president. Third, electoral integrity relies heavily on the acceptance of the rule of law, and the application of the rule of law to the voting process and the results. Presidential intervention, even when the political goal may be commendable, negates the prestige of law in Mexican society and culture. Fourth, it distorts the function, once again, of elections. For both the opposition and the PRI, "elections are not to elect, but to set the terms of post-electoral negotiation."[50]

President Salinas also has involved himself, and the presidency, in a second facet of the electoral process. Much of the revenues the government obtained through the resale of large state-owned enterprises, including major banking chains, has gone into the National Solidarity Program, established personally by the president. The thrust of this program is to use federal funds to support grassroots development projects ranging from education to public works. Critics immediately charged that the government designed a program to influence the outcome of elections, providing huge influxes of monies to areas that previously voted for the opposition. (In 1991, 60 percent of federal investments in the states were through Solidarity.) Of course, any government providing benefits to the populace would be rewarded with higher vote counts in the polling booths. The question here is what criteria are being used to distribute the funds, and second, are the funds distributed through this program, which has since become a cabinet-level agency (Social Development), actually used for the proposed projects?[51] More importantly, even if we were unable to determine the truth of these accusations, the fact is that the president, and the executive branch, increased, not decreased their control over economic disbursements, contrary to the president's decentralizing rhetoric.[52]

The remaining variable not inherent to Mexican electoral behavior is the structural consequence of opposition electoral victories. These victories have been so recent, and so selective, that little analysis has taken place.[53] Election successes at the national level, in the legislative branch, as suggested above, have limited consequences, even in terms of patronage. Congressmen in Mexico, especially from opposition parties, are not in a position to provide employment to other Mexicans. By contrast, governors and mayors have numerous positions to fill, thus creating much more potential for sustaining their parties over time. In addition to the more obvious consequences of political rewards to the faithful, which all parties rely on, winning the posts have led to other, important repercussions.

During the 1992 elections PRI spent extravagant amounts of money funding gubernatorial and mayoralty races. For example, in the gubernatorial race in Chihuahua, the PRI spent $52.00 per vote compared to $2.60 spent by PAN. In Michoacán, PRI spent an estimated 32 million dollars, which translates to $80.00 per vote compared to $2.30 for the opposition.[54] In the past, such campaigns have not involved significant outlays of funds. Now, however, in an effort to retain or even win back lost support, funding in many cases has been excessive. Previously, given the government's unilateral control over the political system, it obtained many businesses' donations, not in actual pesos, but in services and products ranging from meals, to transportation, to brochures. In turn, these businesses expected to be repaid with political favors or lucrative state and local contracts. Once PRI no longer can win these elections, then the businesses will demand actual payment for their services, money the party does not have.

This will have two significant consequences. First, it will force the party to seek other means of financing. The finance secretary for PRI in 1992, Miguel Alemán, Jr., son of the former president and a wealthy entrepreneur, is exploring independent revenues for the party, including investing in a credit card system.[55] Second, it will give other parties the opportunity to compete for private sector resources. Once a crack appears in PRI's monolithic dominance over executive office holding, it has long-term consequences on electoral behavior among the parties and the ability of the government party to rely on unequal sources of funding. Decentralization of political control, therefore, will have a salutary effect on the liberalization and competitiveness of financing electoral campaigns.

Mexican Political Culture

Other variables contributing to specific characteristics of the Mexican electoral process are cultural in scope. Mexicans are not immune to the internationalization of many issues ranging from ecology to loss of confidence in political institutions. In many categories, Mexicans have expressed views similar to those found in the United States, Canada, and Europe. Three important values have important consequences for political behavior, specifically participation. Since voting is the most common form of participation in societies where elections are held, it is useful to examine Mexican attitudes toward participation or political activism, trust in others, and tolerance of opposing viewpoints.

When Mexicans were asked if they view favorably an increase in opposition parties, the majority responded favorably, as the figures in table 1.2 suggest. Only a fourth of the Mexicans polled believed the PRI should remain strong, about the same percentage who sympathized strongly with PRI. But as I have argued elsewhere, believing theoretically in the growth of opposition parties, essential to a competitive electoral culture, and accepting someone whose views you dislike are two different issues, even to North Americans. What little data is available on Mexicans indicates that they are much more intolerant toward someone expressing opposing views, when they might have to come in contact with such a person, than when asked theoretically about their tolerance of opposing views.[56] When urban Mexican voters were asked if they approved of critics of the Mexican government having the right to run for public office, their answers placed them in an authoritarian, not a democratic category.[57]

Finally, Mexican trust in the political system has declined over the last

TABLE 1.2
Attitudes of Mexicans Toward Increased Political Opposition

Response	Percent Responding
Other parties should increase strength	55.1
Only PRI should remain strong	24.5
Not sure	13.2
No answer	7.2

Adapted from Roderic Ai Camp, ed., *Politics in Mexico* (New York: Oxford University Press, 1993).

decade, as has been the case in the United States and Canada. In the 1990s, only one out of five Mexicans expressed confidence in their government, and only 12 percent respected the political process. Although Mexicans' appreciation for institutions declined, their trust in their fellow citizens advanced substantially. In 1981, only 18 percent of the population expressed confidence in their fellow human beings, a figure that increased 83 percent to one-third of all Mexicans in the 1990s.[58] This is a very positive sign for democratization.

Conclusion

It is apparent that many characteristics of a country's political structure can affect the nature and importance of the electoral process. Mexico is no exception; indeed, cultural and structural variables explain many facets of its election behavior. It is necessary to question what role elections play in the Mexican process, because for most of the postrevolutionary history, elections functioned to legitimize the continuity and control of a political elite and not as the essential means of determining who governs. Mexicans have responded pragmatically to this reality, with cynicism and absenteeism. In the 1988 elections, fewer than one in five Mexicans believed their vote would be counted fairly. Given the promises of President Salinas, and the more competitive nature of elections since 1988, the number of Mexicans who believed their votes actually count doubled (to approximately 40 percent) by 1991, in spite of alleged fraud in many elections. This suggests that despite continued electoral problems, more Mexicans are hopeful of a new, electoral era, where elections can perform their prescribed functions.

Mexico's electoral process is very much in a state of flux. However, the degree of democratization occurring in elections, measured by an exchange in leadership, is most prevalent at the state and local levels. What happened in 1988 is not likely to be repeated soon, unless a party with a stronger appeal can confront the PRI.

Several recent analyses suggest that no major voter realignments occurred between 1988 and 1991.[59] In short, the voters who cast their ballots for Cárdenas in 1988 defected from PRI. Those voters who newly voted for PRI in 1991 were mostly the original defectors in 1988. Second, careful examination of voter sympathies suggests that voters are most interested in the individual candidate, and in change, not in specific economic or political platforms.

The strength of the opposition parties lies in their abilities to win electoral victories on the local and state levels. These victories, in the long run, establish a firm basis for grassroots support, and greater breadth among opposition organizations. They can gradually break down the government party's monopolization of executive power at these levels. On the other hand, given the control the executive branch exercises, and the president's involvement in determining election outcomes, opposition parties must have the real potential to wrest control from *national* political leadership.

The president's persistent interference in the electoral process delegitimizes the process further, reinforcing the traditional Mexican view of elections as not determining who governs. President Salinas has placed the presidency in the dangerous position of resolving serious electoral conflicts by replacing government candidates or the incumbent governor. As suggested above, respect for the legal system is an essential ingredient of democratization. When the legal system is ignored, or executive authority is superimposed over the legal process, it is difficult for the culture of law to become a respected and significant ingredient of the political system.

Under President Salinas the government appears to have pursued a blatant political strategy toward the opposition. Essentially, it has made the decision to co-opt the National Action Party, even allowing that party to win several gubernatorial elections. PAN, as of 1992, controlled three states: Baja California, Chihuahua, and Guanajuato.[60] PAN candidates defeated their PRI opponents in the first two states, and the president replaced the governor-elect in Guanajuato with a PAN appointee. The president has not allowed the PRD to win any state elections, nor has he replaced a governor in a disputed state election with a PRD politician. The PRI under President Salinas conducted all-out war against the PRD, considering them traitors rather than loyal opposition. Fortunately, President Zedillo appears to have changed somewhat by congratulating Cuauhtémoc Cárdenas and the PRD for their victory in the 1997 mayoral election in Mexico City.

The United States continues to exert considerable influence on the election process, and on democratization trends. However, the United States government has taken a different posture in the post-1988 era. Under President Reagan, some government sources were highly critical of PRI, of election fraud, and of Mexico's lack of democratic opening, although not to the degree found elsewhere in the world.[61] Once the 1988 elections demonstrated the possibility of a center-left coalition returning to power, the United States government associated itself much more strongly with the establishment leadership. George Bush, determined to obtain a free trade agreement, essentially ignored "Salinas' track record of election fraud and political violence."[62] Not only did his posture assist in legitimizing Salinas's administration, implemented when the United States quickly recognized Salinas's disputed 1988 election victory, but it made it more difficult for the PRD to be heard in United States government circles.

Since 1988, the U.S. influence on electoral democratization crystallized around the North American Free Trade Agreement negotiations. Instead of the executive branch expressing concerns about Mexican elections, Congress generated most of the criticisms, charging antidemocratic practices and human rights abuses.[63] With its approval, the treaty may become a focal point for continued U.S. pressure on Mexico.

The dynamic nature of the electoral process since 1988 does open it up to stronger democratic influences.[64] But reforming the electoral institutions and the process itself is not sufficient to achieve democratization in Mexico. Fundamental changes in attitudes are essential for structural change. Intolerance of opposition parties by the leadership in power, even if selective, and intolerance of opposition views generally among the electorate makes it difficult, if not impossible, to develop a political mentality conducive to democracy in practice.[65] The democratic process requires negotiation and bargaining, based on the essential concept of compromise. These properties are essential among both elites and masses in all sectors of society and not just within the political realm. Political compromise, likely to be exercised in the legislative arena, requires relatively high levels of political tolerance and individual trust. Thus changes in cultural attitudes, some of which are already in process, must accompany changes in function and structure if democratization can establish a strong foothold in Mexican elections.

Deepening Democracy with Dominant Parties and Presidentialism

The Venezuelan Regime in a Period of Turbulence

ENRIQUE A. BALOYRA

Para Arístides Torres, *in memoriam.*

The contemporary Venezuelan regime is the work of professional politicians who utilized a plentiful fiscal base provided by oil revenues to postpone having to make tough choices between equity and growth. They created a party-based democracy that, like others in Latin America, has fallen short in a number of respects. Traditionally, Venezuelans irritated with democratic shortcomings seldom went beyond complaining, and challengers repeatedly failed at mobilizing them and providing alternatives to populist reformism. But increasing dissatisfaction with parties and politicians and grievances about receiving less than a fair share of the spoils of the system progressively darkened the mood of the public. Public discontent and criticism billowed when fiscal austerity had to be implemented, amid scandals and inefficiency that frayed the public's patience and turned words into actions.

Such actions and their consequences cover four important areas of discontinuity: political violence, electoral abstentionism, a new political party equilibrium, and new autonomous political organizations. The most serious instances of violence were the failed military insurrections of February and November 1992. Less organized outbreaks have included student demonstrations and popular protests, and widespread urban riots in February 1989. Electoral nonparticipation has increased dramatically: between 1979 and 1989, absenteeism doubled from 27.1 to 54.8 percent in municipal elections and reached an unprecedented 41.7 percent in the general election of 1993, more than double the previous high. The electoral dominance of the Social and Christian Democrats was broken in that election, when a number of adverse trends apparently converged. Finally, a truly positive development is the autonomous organizations emerging at the state and local levels.

These four are very strong indications of crisis and discontinuity but they are and must be kept separate from other aspects of crisis in Venezuela. To be sure, the last years have been very hard on ordinary Venezuelans but it is erroneous to blame all the social and even moral problems enveloping the Venezuelan democratic regime on the depressed export prices of petroleum. What a depressed economy does is exacerbate the frequently lethal combination of public discontent with policy outcomes and impatience with continued high levels of official corruption. But the distinction must be maintained to determine which remedies are likely to become useful vectors for reform: the plebiscitarian aspects of presidentialism (on behalf of the society), effective popular representation in all legislative bodies (on behalf of the political community) or judicial rectitude (in the name of the rule of law). Then comes the question of whether the country is moving into the "new form of politics" or if a new party system is emerging in Venezuela.

From Duo-Centric Dominance to Multipartyism: Party Alternatives

Strong presidentialism and strongly articulated parties have been the key referents of contemporary Venezuelan politics.[1] These were the ramparts that kept military domination out and that contained the centrifugal tendencies of populism, enduring the avatars of military insurrections and guerrilla warfare in the sixties and helping consolidate the contemporary democratic regime in the seventies.[2] Elite agreements and distributional policies anchored in clientele politics helped the parties to thoroughly penetrate the society and organize the political community as an ancillary network of competitive, party-based loyalties.[3] This strengthened the stability of the regime but at the expense of a more open system of representation and, in turn, of personal accountability and of effective redress of grievances through the judiciary.

Despite a system of proportional representation, frequent splits, and personalistic challenges, Venezuelan multipartyism gravitated toward a duocentric system dominated by the Social Democrats of Acción Democrática (AD) and by the Social Christians of the Comité de Organización Política Electoral Independiente (COPEI).[4] This dominance is notorious and easily detectable in the electoral trends of the last thirty-five years. During 1973–1988, the combined presidential vote for the two parties was never less than 85 percent; their combined congressional vote averaged about 75 percent of the valid total (see table 2.1). This dominance was all the more impressive because it rested on very high levels of popular participation in elections. Apparently, compulsory voting was taken seriously by a large majority of eligible voters: in the seven national elections between 1958 and 1988, approximately nine of every ten of those eligible registered to vote and about the same proportion actually voted. Venezuela ranked sixth in electoral participation in the world. But this dominance weakened, as the opposition took advantage of increasingly higher levels of abstention to make inroads in Congress and in state and local governments during the 1980s, and then, in 1993, to produce a new and uncertain configuration featuring AD, COPEI, and two populist coalitions, Causa R and Convergencia Nacional.

The drawing power of the dominant parties was particularly impressive considering that Venezuela's legislative elections are not predicated on winner-take-all, single-member districts but on a system of proportional representation (PR). While PR supposedly improves minority representation, only seven parties enjoyed more or less permanent representation in Congress.[5] Between 1958 and 1988, the number of parties offering congressional candidates jumped from 8 to 78 and the number offering their own presidential candidates increased from 3 to 23. However, of the 159 new parties created during the period only 11 competed in at least half of the national elections. This suggests that Duverger's Law, attributing different structural outcomes to electoral competition, based either on simple majority or on proportional representation (two-party or two-party dominant versus genuine multipartyism), may have operated with very pronounced interactive effects in Venezuela.[6]

Between 1968 and 1988, party-based challengers systematically failed to engage the loyalty of voters.[7] With the exception of Cruzada Cívica Nacionalista (CCN), the more successful challengers were the parties of the Left, which tried to replicate the strategy of the major parties. They tried to get the Venezuelan masses to see the "electoral carnivals" for what they were and to refocus them on the daily struggles of social confrontation.[8] Leftist optimists viewed elections as mechanisms of the legitimation of conservative reformism that could gradually open itself to genuine transformism.[9] A dearth of access to patronage forced them to engage in a different blend of presentational and participatory techniques than those available to the major parties.[10] They stood for change and sought the support of wide sectors of the electorate by insisting that AD and COPEI were basically the same thing.[11] The more successful of these were the Movimiento al Socialismo (MAS) and the Movimiento Electoral del Pueblo (MEP). More recently, Causa R became the most obvious antisystem alternative.

Although generally effective in campaigns, MAS was supposedly unable to overcome the logic of the so-called economy-of-the-vote and never reached 20 percent of the vote.[12] More likely, MAS was constrained by the distrust of the elec-

TABLE 2.1
Venezuelan Electoral Trends: National Elections of 1958–1993

	1958	1963	1968	1973	1978	1983	1988	1993
Nonparticipation:								
Not registered	12.3	17.3	2.5	7.2	−.6	5.0	2.3	–
Abstention rate	7.9	9.2	5.6	3.5	12.4	12.3	18.1	41.7
Null votes	4.1	6.1	7.0	4.3	2.1	2.5	2.8	3.6
AD-COPEI dominance:								
Presidential	65.4	53.0	57.0	85.4	90.0	91.3	93.3	46.3
Congressional	64.6	53.6	49.6	74.7	79.5	78.7	74.4	54.7a
President's party:								
Senatorial seats	62.5	46.8	30.8	59.6	47.7	63.6	47.8	34.6
Chamber seats	54.9	37.1	27.6	51.0	42.2	56.5	48.3	26.9
Pres. candidates	3	7	6	12	10	12	23	17
Parties competing:								
in Presidential	7	9	16	24	15	27	34	49
in Congressional	8	11	33	37	29	52	78	92b
Represented	4	8	11	10	11	11	11	5

a. Percentage of AD-COPEI seats in Chamber of Deputies.

b. Includes 49 national and 207 regional organizations, and 235 so-called groups of electors.

Note: All figures in percentages, except numbers of parties competing, listed in the last four rows. Nonregistered estimated from estimated eligible population. Dominance refers to combined AD-COPEI vote. For 1993, congressional seats for the president's party refer to AD and Carlos Andrés Pérez, not Ramón J. Velásquez and his interim presidency.

Sources: Juan Carlos Rey, *Continuidad y cambio en las elecciones venezolanas: 1958–1988* (Caracas: Instituto Internacional de Estudios Avanzados, 1989), charts 1–5, 7, 10, 11, 12, 13; using data from Consejo Supremo Electoral (CSE). For 1993, *El Universal*, 5 de Diciembre 1991, 1–12; CSE, *Boletín # 6*, 10 December 1993, and *El Nuevo Herald*, 27 January 1994, 5A.

torate and undermined by the eternal curse of the "unity of the Left" but, by joining the Convergencia Nacional of Rafael Caldera, MAS helped break the AD-COPEI dominance in 1993, assisted by a strong showing by Causa R.[13]

In general, it does not appear that party-based challengers have benefitted greatly from electoral reforms. In June 1979, in the first separate elections held for municipal councils, the four parties of the Left presented a common slate. In addition to MAS and MEP, these included the Movimiento de Izquierda Revolucionaria (MIR), and the Communist Party of Venezuela (PCV). Compared to 1978, the total vote for the Left increased by less than one-half of one percent of the electorate, while the combined AD-COPEI vote reached 79 percent of the total valid vote. Even more significant was a much higher rate of abstention, 30 percent of the eligible or almost 1.9 million staying away or nullifying their vote. Widespread disenchantment with the AD, not public discontent, was perceived as the main determinant of this spurt in abstentionism.[14] But, in 1984, the rate of abstention in municipal elections jumped to almost 43 percent, a very sizeable figure under any standard. Disinterest and increasing public discontent were identified as the most relevant operative causes.[15] The combined Left vote was about 13 percent, slightly less than in 1979; the combined vote for AD and COPEI, 74 percent, with AD receiving 52.6 percent. Therefore, the duocentric dominance was reproduced in municipal elections but in a context of much-diminished public interest. Apparently, to the discontented, abstaining was a more attractive option than voting for party-based challengers.

In the general election of December 1988 the abstention rate went to 18 percent (see table 2.1). The main reasons advanced by nonvoters included in a very large national sample survey of January 1989 were that they did not like any of the candidates (22 percent) or had lost faith in the democratic system (18 percent) or knew that Carlos Andrés Pérez was going to win anyway (14 percent).[16] Another survey of early 1989 showed that 65 percent of abstentions had resulted from political (48.7 percent—primarily, distrust of politicians [23.5 percent] and a sense of futility [16.1 percent]) and from motivational consideration (disinterest, 16.7 percent).[17] The first direct elections for governors, mayors, and municipal councilmen, held on 3 December 1989, confirmed this trend: the rate of abstention went through the roof, to 54.8 percent, but the combined AD-COPEI vote remained above 70 percent—AD with 40 and COPEI at 32 percent. A study of abstentionism, comparing the general elections of 1988 and 1983 and the municipal elections of 1989, showed an increase in political (distrust of politicians, futility of the vote) and motivational (disinterest) reasons for nonvoting.[18] This marked a qualitative discontinuity.

In 1992, with only 50 percent of the electorate voting in state and local elections, AD and COPEI dropped to about 68 percent of the vote—31 and 37 percent, respectively—and saw three governorships go to MAS with Bolívar's remaining under Causa R.[19] Compared to 1989, MAS, the recognized challenger during 1973–1988, dropped from about 18 to 13 percent and Causa R advanced from 2.5 to about 8 percent. Aristóbulo Istúriz, a forty-four-year-old black schoolteacher and candidate of Causa R, was elected mayor of Libertador Municipality in Caracas. Mr. Istúriz prevailed in a field of fifteen candidates, including Claudio Fermín, the AD incumbent, and Teodoro Petkoff, a former presidential candidate of the MAS. But this major victory of Causa R was tarnished by the abstention of 59 percent of the eligible voters in the district. The high rate of abstention was a steep price to pay for a more competitive party system.

In December 1993, Rafael Caldera was elected with about 30 percent of the 58 percent who bothered to vote.[20] The base of support of his Convergencia Nacional was primarily composed of COPEI defectors, as COPEI identifiers split almost evenly in their voting intention between Caldera and COPEI's own candidate, Oswaldo Alvarez Paz.[21] Causa R made an impressive showing, with about 21 percent of the popular vote, thereby contributing to establish the bases for multiparty competition in a reduced electorate.[22] Even though they barely surpassed 50 percent of the legislative vote, AD and COPEI retained a majority of seats in Congress.

Therefore, the first unmistakable pattern of change that must be reported is not of replacement or disappearance of the traditionally dominant parties but a new configuration produced by two drastic simultaneous declines: one in their level of support and another in the level of popular participation in elections. During 1973–1992, the gains of the challengers were not really spectacular since they really did not profit from the misfortunes of the dominant parties. Whatever is said about the elections of 1988–1992 must be qualified by the fact that they were accompanied by very high abstention rates. The result of this process of gradual change, which may have reached a critical threshold in 1993, is the anomaly of a more competitive party system emerging from a marked public disinterest in elections and in party politics.

From Corporatism to Grassroots and NGOs: External Challengers

Challenges directed against the dominance of AD and COPEI that have come from civil society have always been ineffectual, particularly if they were in the guise of "civic" forays into the electoral arena promising national unity, effective government, more widespread patronage, and more flexible pacts outside the control of party elites.[23] Many of these came across as efforts at plebiscitarian, direct democracy. Usually, the vehicle was the presidential campaign of a self-recruited notable who posed as the leader of a "bottom up" movement of national renovation.[24] Some tried to ride on widespread dissatisfaction with urban life.[25] Others were launched as crusades against corruption and venality, and the hermeticism of the hegemonic circle of *cogollos* (top party elites).[26] A long parade of independent movements that followed this route never left the ground, either at the electoral moment or beyond.[27] In style and substance, their leaders did not resemble the Fujimoris and Menems who heralded the so-called "new form of politics" (NFP) of the 1990s.[28]

Still other challenges came from aspiring interests trying to enter the process of policy making or at least acquire a voice by being able to influence policy implementation.[29] These were predicated on the assumption that there was no area or issue to which the state could not dedicate resources and on the recognition that the political parties always interfered with and practically regulated associational life.[30] What these challengers faced was a peculiarly Venezuelan version of corporatism in which latent or poorly organized interests came together voluntarily, as part of a process of pluralization affecting a changing society, and received judicial assent as a formality and not as an interference of the state.[31] But, once duly recognized, such efforts were frequently overwhelmed by the established parties, which tried to infiltrate, co-opt, or create rival organizations in order to preserve their control of the process of interest intermediation.

Although relatively hapless as electoral competitors, it is probable that new social groups and movements seeking space in the dynamics of state-society relations mounted the most formidable challenge to the manner in which the dominance of the largest parties translated into public policy. They challenged not only those parties but also the interests that had learned to accommodate to their dominance, the better-organized and more powerful Venezuelan interests that took their matters directly to the executive or had their interests accommodated through the vast network of state institutions. It is generally acknowledged that, being more independent from the state, those established interests had greater leverage in the *concertación* of interest intermediation.[32]

According to critics, the status quo was a false model of conciliation that engendered government inefficiency and rent-seeking behavior, a consultative means of elite participation that was isolated from a changing society and that once in place became very difficult to reform.[33] Beginning with the first government of Carlos Andrés Pérez, organized interests received representation in a vast network of commissions and decentralized public agencies. As attempts to democratize the relatively tight, party-controlled structure provided by the Pact of Punto Fijo of 1958, these decentralized institutions initially contributed to open the legislative process to interest groups. But they were quickly dominated by the political class, which was represented in them by party factions and delegates of organized labor, and by private capital, and gradually became more and more exclusionary.[34]

Critics and observers agreed that enduring party loyalties, the electoral margins into which they translated, the rarity of divided government, the autonomy of political entrepreneurs who monopolized control of the state, the sustained emphasis on distributive policies driven by oil revenues, control of the centralized bureaucracy, and an overwhelming presence in the media enabled the party hegemony to reproduce itself.[35] More or less guaranteed reproduction allowed presidents and the leaders of the dominant parties a wide berth, and neither they nor the business associations did much to alter this arrangement. The parties maintained their vertical structure of command and a democratic-centralist style of decision making that was "Leninist."[36]

The political class, as well as the powerful and the not-so-powerful, assumed that the price of petroleum would hold steady and that this pattern of state-society relations could be maintained. They all erred together in this. As the economy worsened in 1983 and beyond, incumbent presidents and the dominant political parties engaged in persistent efforts to postpone the profound policy changes that would have to be made.[37]

Political reforms came first. Yielding to continued public dissatisfaction with their performance, leaders of the dominant parties begrudgingly engaged in incremental and, according to critics, timid changes. Beyond their comprehensiveness, lofty rhetoric, and grandiose design, the main problem with these reforms may have been the insistence on creating a new regime pact.[38] In December 1984, following a wide consultation, the Presidential Commission for the Reform of the State (COPRE) was created. The COPRE concluded that reforming the state would have to include the conduct of elections and the modus operandi of the parties, public administration and the administration of justice, and the exercise of economic freedoms.[39] The parties came under heavy criticism since these views agreed with the prognosis that the more forward-looking critics had been making for some time.[40] Political leaders apparently hoped that, by making it more representative and responsive, the democratic regime would be reinvigorated. They wanted to control the substance and implementation of the reforms. After all, these were the cautious men who had taken politics seriously and who had strained to avoid polarization.[41]

In addition to the classical challenges of structural reforms, these leaders confronted other difficulties. According to an astute observer, the first was a political environment of weakened party elites, endemic factionalism, and loss of prestige, which made it unlikely for the parties to remain at the center of a new political pact.[42] Another was the growing divergence between the demands of the public and what the political class was willing and able to deliver. For example, in August 1988, Congress passed two organic laws on municipal and state organization providing for the direct election of mayors and governors. In January 1989, on the eve of the riots that followed the dramatic turnaround in economic policy by President Carlos Andrés Pérez, almost 60 percent of the public did not know about the reforms and practically the same proportion said that full employment was the problem that should receive the most urgent attention by the newly inaugurated Pérez.[43] Similarly, in September 1989, the Organic Law of the Suffrage was amended to allow for the direct election of one-half of the Chamber of Deputies in single member districts, beginning in 1993. Despite these changes, the rate of abstention continued to increase.

From Discontent to Insurrection

Venezuelan voters have remained loyal to the regime but frustrated by its shortcomings. In 1973, despite much discontent with the outcomes of the policies of the governments of the democratic era and with the performance of political parties, the bureaucracy, and the politicians, the level of support for the intermediary institutions of democracy remained very high.[44] Citizens were particularly incensed by widespread official corruption and by the deteriorating quality of urban life beset by crime, inflation, poverty, housing shortages, and decaying public services.[45] But a low regard for parties and politicians did not seem to erode their high appreciation for the institution of elections.[46] While high levels of criticism were anchored in partisanship and ideology, cynicism was rooted in the social circumstances of individuals, beyond the constraining influence of organized politics. Increased criticism and cynicism led to a diminished sense of personal efficacy and withdrawal from politics, not to radical protest behavior.[47] This mechanism may help explain the massive defections and absence of violent protest during 1979–1988.

In 1983, more people believed that the governments of the democratic era had wasted public resources, that their policies had been harmful to their interests and had really served the interests of the powerful and not those of the people, and that many public officials had been corrupt. While the democratic regime continued to be preferred to any dictatorial alternative, there was increased public concern with official corruption and its consequences. Political discontent was more pronounced among the young, those in adverse social circumstances, and radicals.[48]

In 1983 the country had a rude awakening to the need to impose fiscal discipline and to absorb economic austerity. In February COPEI president Luis Herrera Campins had to devalue the bolívar and establish exchange controls. For the first time since the inauguration of the democratic regime, Venezuelan reformist populism could no longer pretend that there were public resources to match all imaginable problems nor afford the luxury of continuing to avoid choices between equity and growth. Increased public discontent favored the Social Democrats and restored them to the presidency in 1984, with great expectations of improvement. Unfortunately, the costs of adjustment were unevenly distributed and public discontent increased; this despite efforts on the part of the administrations of Herrera and of *adeco* (AD) president Jaime Lusinchi to make austerity more bearable to the lower strata of society.[49] Not only the marginal urban sectors but the broad middle class felt the direct impact of inflation and austerity. Well-publicized corruption of high government officials compounded long-running criticism of government inability to control public spending. Scandals involved friends and protégés of President Herrera as well as President Lusinchi and his secretary. The courts failed to sanction the alleged principals.[50] Equally important, the macroeconomic variables remained unbalanced, and the two dominant parties kept accusing each other of mismanagement but did little to think through a new scheme of political economy.

In the mid and late 1980s, tendencies that had been afoot for a while became more pronounced: dissatisfaction that had been channeled outside the party system and become rooted in civil society found new opportunities to express itself at the political level, outside the control of the parties. New, truly independent movements and voluntary associations were organized that challenged the party monopoly over mechanisms of intermediation, such as labor unions.[51] Causa R emerged from within the dissident ranks of the steelworkers' union of Bolívar state defeating well-established trade unionists linked to the major parties. Andrés Velásquez, its leader and founder, became state governor in 1989, was reelected by an overwhelming margin in 1992, and ran a very respectable campaign for the presidency in 1993. Other new independent movements were able to subsequently stake out their own turf, as in the case of the Federation of Associations of Urban Communities (FACUR), which represented the majority of the neighbors' associations of greater Caracas. A host of symbolic and normative orientations continued exerting a powerful influence on broad segments of urban labor, whose diffuse support for the regime remained high despite setbacks in material gratification.[52] But more popular sectors apparently felt differently. On 27 February 1989, shortly after Carlos Andrés Pérez returned to the presidency and staged a complete reversal on the economic platform on which he campaigned, popular discontent really exploded into a series of riots in some of the major cities.[53] The armed forces were ordered to put an end to the rioting, which they did with a high number of civilian casualties.

A cycle seemed to be closing. In the early 1960s, it had been assumed that party-based politics was the only antidote against militarism. In the early 1990s, military plotters saw themselves as the only ones capable of disciplining corrupt party politicians and restoring democracy to the people. Midlevel officers struck first. Chafing at what they viewed as a sellout of national and institutional interests by an oligarchy in uniform, they began to plot an exemplary punishment and launched their coup on 4 February 1992. More senior officers regrouped and tried again on 27 November 1992. Both movements miscalculated as loyal military and police units defeated the two insurrections.[54]

From Criticism to Absenteeism

Since 1983, many proposals have been advanced for reforming the Venezuelan regime and its system of parties, but opinions have been divided, particularly at the level of the elite. Intellectual leaders of the dominant parties favored solutions mixing a democratization of their own party structures with a series of incremental measures: creating the office of mayor, institutionalizing neighbors' assemblies, changing the system of closed party slates in legislative ballots. They found it ironic that the crisis had worsened precisely when political reforms were implemented to deepen democracy.[55] They were dismayed that many enlightened citizens would have nothing to do with parties, by the declining quality of leadership, and that more people were abstaining despite measures to keep them engaged.[56]

Some critics blamed the parties for allowing the state to become an obsequious servant of the entrepreneurial bourgeoisie.[57] Others thought that conservative and entrepreneurial interests were underrepresented in the dominant parties.[58] Even the success of the parties at defeating left and right radical alternatives, and the absence of any other comparable threat, were lamented for having allowed the parties to focus on clientele and patronage politics and thereby to diminish public confidence in them.[59] There were direct accusations of fraud leveled at the *cogollos*.[60]

In 1985 COPRE concluded that the dominant parties were falling short of the democratic ideal within their own organizations, in their relations with minor parties, and by interfering with the associational life of civil society.[61] The more discerning party leaders were aware of these shortcomings but continued insisting on the indispensability of parties and on making them the fulcrum of reform. They argued that other factors were also complicating matters; for example, the clash between party structures designed to resemble those of European parliamentary systems and the requirements of the presidential system, and the absence of a democratic civic culture.[62] Regardless of how the issue was framed, the intellectuals of the dominant parties insisted on keying the reforms to renewing and reinventing them.[63]

The party intellectuals may have been partially correct but it was impossible to ignore how adamant the public was about the need to ensure full employment, cleanse the system, curb urban crime, alleviate poverty, and stop the widening gap between those who unfairly or unlawfully benefitted from the abundant resources of the state and those without the proper party connections and social credentials. People wanted to see some results. There was a very big difference between 1983 and 1993: people had moved from words to action. Not only had the tone of the criticism intensified but, more important, sectors of the public had resorted to violence, a traditional Venezuelan reaction to frustration.[64] Military interventionism had become a clear and present danger. Then there was the disappointment of the general election of December 1993. Despite voters being able to select individual candidates from mixed congressional slates for the first time ever, and despite the

highest number of organizations ever to have participated in a Venezuelan election, only 58 percent of the eligible bothered to vote.

To be sure, the public continues to prefer democracy and those who would
like to experiment with a different type of regime are decidedly in the minority:
surveys conducted in 1977, 1983, 1987, and 1988 showed that those who wanted to
substitute the system were 15, 25, 14, and 17 percent of the public, respectively.[65]
While, according to a May 1992 survey, only 8 percent preferred a strong military
government, 40 percent wanted a democracy without the dominant parties, very
close to the 43 percent who wanted to retain them.[66] Critics have always questioned the extent to which democratic norms have been enculturated in
Venezuela.[67] The insurrectionists of 1992 may or may not have been aware that,
even after three decades of democratic continuity, large segments of the Venezuelan public still harbor utilitarian attitudes about military coups. In 1973, roughly
one half of the public agreed with the proposition that, in general, there are occasions in which military coups are justified. In 1983, the same identical question
generated the acquiescence of 53 percent, with about 34 percent of all respondents
believing that conditions actually justified a military coup.[68] On the eve of the insurrection of 4 February 1992, 31 percent of the public believed that a coup was imminent and 34 percent approved. Shortly thereafter, the level of support for *that*
coup had dropped to 24 percent, with 60 percent opposed. A DATOS poll of
March 1992 suggested that 63 percent of the public continued to prefer democracy
over a military regime, favored by 26 percent. While still decisively in favor of
democracy, this margin represented a decline from the 82 percent for [a] democracy [such as Venezuela's] versus 10 percent for dictatorship recorded by a survey
conducted in 1983 (see table 2.2). According to DATOS, only 12 percent of the
public identified dissatisfaction with the performance of President Pérez as a cause
of the coup, while 42 percent attributed it to discontent with corruption.[69] In 1983
corruption was the aspect concerning which respondents in a national survey rated
the Venezuelan regime as worse than a dictatorship.[70]

In early 1993, an embattled President Pérez remained in office despite demands for his resignation, intermittent street violence, protests about unprecedented inconclusive results of the December 1992 state and local elections in
Sucre and Barinas states, rumors about still another military insurrection, and formal attempts at removing him by constitutional means. Pérez's approval rate took
a nosedive between April 1989 and January 1992 (see table 2.3). Even in historical
perspective, his ratings were very poor: Luis Herrera Campins, hitherto the most
unpopular previous president, received a negative rating of 52 percent during his
last year in office.[71] But this did not mean that most Venezuelans wanted Pérez to
leave office before the end of his term. During 1992 the two most reliable polling

TABLE 2.2
Opinion About Coups, 1973–1992

	(a) Dec. 91– Jan. 92	(b) Feb.– Mar. 92	(c) Oct.– Nov. 83	(d) Oct.– Nov. 73
1a. Coup likely now				
Yes	31	na	36	na
No	59	na	23	na
Not Sure	10	na	21	na
Depends	na	na	17	na
1b. Response to coup				
Support	34	24	na	na
Oppose	49	60	na	na
Neither	10	11	na	na
No Response	7	5	na	na
2. Current situation justifies a coup				
Yes	na	na	34	na
No	na	na	52	na
Not sure	na	na	9	na
Depends	na	na	4	na
3. Coups sometimes justified				
Yes	na	na	53	50
No	na	na	32	32
Not sure	na	na	10	8
Depends	na	na	5	10

Sources: (a) MERCANALISIS, reported by Orlando Utrera, *Diario de Caracas,* 7 February 1992, 25, from FBIS-LAT-92-045 (6 March 1992), 54–55; (b) MERCANALISIS, reported by Vladimir Villegos Poljak, "The Image of the Government is Deteriorating," *El Universal,* 28 March 1992, section J; from FBIS-LAT-92-087 (5 May 1992), 38–40; (c) and (d) Baloyra (1986: 196, 211, tables 10.1 and 10.3).

organizations in the country could find no more than 35 percent of the public agreeing to this course of action. As a matter of fact, a GAITHER poll released in July 1992 showed 62 percent opposed to a Pérez resignation (see table 2.4).

Levels of discontent with party politicians and national political institutions, such as Congress and the judiciary, were high but comparable to those of the 1980s.[72] However, party preferences were taking a beating. Between 1973 and 1983, the percent of nonidentifiers had fluctuated between a high of almost 35 percent

TABLE 2.3
Presidential Approval Rate, 1989–1992

				Pérez Image	
Dates	Approve	Disapprove	No Opinion	Pos.	Neg.
Apr. 89	46	44	10	56	44
Dec. 89	51	40	9	64	36
Jun. 90	39	50	11	52	48
Sep. 90	48	43	8	63	37
Mar. 91	53	39	7	67	33
Aug. 91	43	49	8	56	44
Nov. 91	35	56	9	47	53
Jan. 92	26	65	9	35	56

Source: Alba Sánchez, "Poll Respondents Reject CAP, Support Caldera," *El Nacional,* 26 Jan. 1992, section D, from FBIS-LAT-92-037, 25 February 1992, 25–28.

TABLE 2.4
Opinions About Perez's Resignation

Date of Poll	Should Resign	Should Not	Do Not Know	No Opinion
Mar. 1992	31	30	2	37
Jul. 1992*	33	62	NA	NA
Sep. 1992*	35	23	39	—

* Date Published

Sources: "Corruption and Abuse of Power Caused the 4 February Coup," *El Nacional* 25 May 1992, section D; from FBIS-LAT-92-128 (2 July 1992), 49–51. GAITHER Poll, from FBIS-LAT-92-135 (14 July 1992), 30. DATOS Poll, from FBIS-LAT-92-183 (21 September 1992), 43.

(in 1973) and a low of 27 (in 1983). GAITHER figures showed an increase from 18, in October 1988, to 32 percent of the public, in November 1991, refusing to acknowledge any political party as "best" (see table 2.5). Specific questions on party identification, included in surveys of October 1988 and May 1992, showed the *adecos* (AD identifiers) dropping from 35 to 26 percent, the *copeyanos* (COPEI identifiers) more or less stable at about 25 percent, MAS below 10 percent, the combined figure for all other parties at 1 percent, and the percentage of independents increasing from 33 to 38 percent.[73] Just as the loss of electoral support for the dom-

TABLE 2.5
Opinions About Best Party, 1983–1991

	Oct '83	Oct '88	Dec '89	Jan '90	Sep '90	Mar '91	Aug '91	Nov '91
AD	48	52	36	28	35	39	35	31
COPEI	21	20	16	19	17	16	18	17
MAS	7	6	14	9	11	7	6	7
Causa R	-	2	5	5	4	5	5	8
Others	4	3	6	9	6	5	5	5
None	19	18	23	30	27	29	31	32

Source: GAITHER, reported by Alba Sánchez, *El Nacional*, 26 Jan. 1991, section D, in FBIS-LAT-92-037, 25 February 1992, 25–28.

inant parties did not favor party challengers, declining numbers of identifiers with dominant parties did not engross other party options but merely fattened the ranks of the independents. Nevertheless, there has been a very serious erosion of support for the dominant parties.

Conclusion: The Venezuelan Crisis in Perspective

Cynics familiar with similar situations in other latitudes may be far less than surprised at hearing of the vicissitudes of the dominant parties in Venezuela. They may ask, Are parties not in crisis everywhere? Are they not out of step with the times? Have they not allowed media consultants and campaign specialists to take over and relegate even their more reliable and engaged militants? Where, other than in the defunct regimes of the former socialist bloc, did the idea of "party government" manage to survive?

Political parties have been in trouble for some time in Latin America. They were asked to deepen democracy when, following years of military authoritarianism, economic restructuring severely narrowed the scope of the state, and class and ideological referents were in flux.[74] Important aspects of this scenario did not apply in Venezuela but, as shown above, the dominant parties have failed several important tests prescribed by the public. First, at least for the last twelve years, there has been a sustained demand to eliminate corruption and to govern more responsibly that the traditional parties have failed to satisfy. Second, as witnessed in the campaign of 1993, the Venezuelan parties have not resolved the riddles of how to win elections without a populist program that becomes an albatross that any incumbent government has to get rid of, and how to campaign with a responsible platform that may have too much of a neoliberal flavor and cost them the election altogether. AD and COPEI may have opted for the latter in 1993. Caldera and Causa R followed more or less populist styles of campaigning. This is not just a matter of campaign tactics but of a more transparent style across the board in all transactions between the parties and the public.

Third, whether or not sophisticated or rational, and despite changes that have given greater impact to the voting act, ordinary citizens have found it less useful to vote and to identify with political parties. It may come down to not voting being the best manner in which to punish one's party for past transgression, given the lack of clarity toward the future, and unattractive candidates. Fourth, whether political, that is, evaluational, or motivational aspects of nonvoting prevail remains to be seen. According to previous findings, if the proportion of cynics has truly increased we are likely to continue to see elections with about 50 percent turnout.

Fifth, as a result of this, the definite configuration of the Venezuelan party system is very difficult to predict from the results of the 1993 election. To all extents and indications, the basically new element is a stronger Causa R, which is but one of four basic pillars in a configuration where dominant and challenger parties and populist and neoliberal options follow a cumulative grid and seem to be in equilibrium. Basically, what this may be is a transition from one system of parties to another. What remains unclear is how many poles the system will consist of and what, if anything, these poles shall represent.

Looking at the results of the elections of 1989–1993, one may be able to put the success of the challengers, primarily Causa R, in proper perspective, and ponder whether this transition is from a two-party dominant, or moderate pluralism, as some analysts used to call it, to a genuine multiparty system resulting primarily from a reshuffling of existing loyalties.[75] It truly is hard to cast the winner, Rafael Caldera, as an outsider. After all, President Caldera was the founder of COPEI and practically inseparable from the image of that party. The more anti-system parties of the Convergencia are marginal players at best. In addition, it has been shown that, despite their criticisms, and while moving away from the polls and from the dominant parties, Venezuelan citizens have not adopted extreme attitudes.

What is novel about the multiparty context of the 1990s in Venezuela is that it is the result of the crisis of *two* dominant parties. For the moment, therefore, the outcome may hinge on the ability of the formerly dominant AD and COPEI to recapture the voters' imagination, with or without decreases in abstentionism. This obviously is intimately related to the efficacy and efficiency with which the traditional political and business classes manage the economy. As for other elements supposedly affecting parties everywhere, even if, in a postmodern context, a "new form of politics" has thrust the broadcast media forward, altering intermediation, and threatening party linkages,[76] media politics has been an important feature of the Venezuelan regime for some time and media figures have not done particularly well in politics. If anything, part of the problem has been that such party linkages were too tight in Venezuela and that they were asphyxiating the society. Probably more than in other countries where parties were not so dominant, corruption *is* the crisis and failure to address it to the satisfaction of the majority has been compounded by the inability to adopt new styles of decision making to cope with economic crisis. Failure to solve the latter, that is, to improve the economy, fuels speculation that the former continues unabated and that crooks continue to steal the state and the people blind.

But notices of imminent demise may always prove slightly premature. Parties do not necessarily have to roll over and die: "Failure has rarely involved the permanent decline or disappearance of a particular major party or the basic realignment of a party system."[77] Even Leninists have managed to survive. The Mexican perestroika has been going on since 1977 without regime breakdown, and the Partido Revolucionario Institucional shows no signs of surrender. Fidel Castro is still president of Cuba, amid truly horrendous economic circumstances.

The coup attempts of 1992 may have finally awakened the Venezuelan political class to some basic realities. One is that tokenism and more of the same will not do.[78] Another is that the so-called nominal or "preferential" system of candidate slates will have to be implemented in all Venezuelan elections. There simply is too much pressure behind it for this demand to be ignored. Third, it is inevitable that the reform begin and end with the parties but highly unlikely that it may succeed without them. Finally, the high levels of abstention and the advent of a multiparty system are not, in and of themselves, a crisis. They may be the outcome of very complex processes that may or may not be related to the details of the present juncture. To be sure, enough has transpired in Venezuela to suggest that we better look very hard at several different aspects of the performance of the democratic regime. But complex outcomes are not necessarily divorced from parsimonious explanations, and two things remain very clear: the voting citizenry has shrunk and, at the same time, the party system has become more competitive. Herein lies the focal point of any serious analysis of the Venezuelan politics of the last two decades and of any serious attempt to make it more democratic in the future.

Partisan Decline and Presidential Popularity

The Politics and Economics of Representation in Peru

JULIO F. CARRIÓN

Introduction

Among observers of Peruvian politics, initial optimism about the prospects for democratic consolidation has frequently turned into disappointment. Indeed, recent history advises us to be cautious in our predictions. In 1963, after a one-year military regime, Fernando Belaunde took office with a program of moderate social reform and respect for political liberties. His program of social and economic modernization faltered, however, when the Alianza Popular Revolucionaria Americana (Popular Revolutionary American Alliance, APRA) and conservative forces in Congress decided to block or dilute the most progressive proposals, such as land reform. By 1967, the failure of the Belaunde administration to deal with the pressing issues of land reform and popular unrest was compounded by internal strife in the governing alliance. Acción Popular (Popular Action, AP), Belaunde's own party and the dominant partner in the coalition, was affected by the defection of its secretary-general, who formed a new organization named Acción Popular Socialista (Socialist Popular Action, APS). The Partido Demócrata Cristiano (Christian Democratic Party, PDC), the minor coalition partner, was also badly shaken by the emergence of a rightist spin-off, the Partido Popular Cristiano (Popular Christian Party, PPC). To make matters worse, Belaunde devalued the currency by 50 percent in late 1967, only a few weeks after he declared emphatically that he would not do so, generating a great deal of discontent among voters.[1] Thus, the administration that began with great hope and popular support in 1963 was in great disarray by 1968. When General Juan Velasco Alvarado seized power as head of a military junta on October 3, 1968, nobody was greatly surprised, and no meaningful opposition to the coup d'etat was organized.

The military junta that ruled this country from 1968 to 1980[2] implemented a vast program of social and economic reforms, with land reform as the most lasting accomplishment. These reforms were well received by the population, and although no survey data exists to back this claim, most observers agree that at the beginning the military regime had an important degree of popular support.[3] By the mid-1970s, however, the compounded effects of economic crisis and lack of political liberties had dramatically eroded the bases of support for this regime. After a couple of years of great upheaval—whose peak was a massive national strike in 1977—the military announced a Constitutional Assembly for 1978 and general elections for 1980. Alter twelve long years of military rule, a widespread sentiment in favor of democratic rule seemed to have taken hold of elites and masses alike.[4] Optimism about the future of democracy was high. Even the marxist Left, albeit reluctantly, was playing the democratic game, with unexpected success. Alfonso Barrantes, leader of the electoral coalition Izquierda Unida (United Left, IU), was elected mayor of Lima in 1983, and other leftist candidates won important cities of the interior, such as Arequipa.

The 1980s, unfortunately, turned out to be troublesome years for democratic rule. Hard economic times made extremely difficult the enactment of much-needed policies of income redistribution. The emergence of an unusually violent terrorist group, Sendero Luminoso (Shining Path, SL),[5] as well as the significant increase in urban crime, provoked widespread feelings of personal insecurity. Last, but not least, governmental corruption fostered a feeling of mistrust in officials and government in general.

The major parties had a taste of the degree of citizen dissatisfaction when an independent figure, Ricardo Belmont, was elected mayor of Lima, defeating easily all the parties' candidates. The real blow to the parties came, however, when Alberto Fujimori, another independent personality, came from behind to challenge Mario Vargas Llosa, the well-known novelist, forcing a runoff that Fujimori eventually won in June 1990. To the surprise of many, the constitutional regime inaugurated in 1980 was interrupted when Fujimori decided to close Congress, dismiss the Supreme Court, and rule by decree on April 5, 1992. Another experiment in constitutional rule was thus broken, this time by a civilian staging an auto-coup.

This chapter seeks to explain the process of voters' alienation with the traditional parties represented in Congress, which probably contributed to Fujimori's decision to rule by decree. I argue that a number of factors undermined or prevented the consolidation of the emerging party system. The political inexperience of the electorate, due to Peru's extremely weak electoral tradition, hindered the development of strong partisan identities. In addition, presidents elected in the 1980s made repeated efforts to undermine their parties' strength in Congress, in order to consolidate their own power positions.[6] Both Belaunde and García decided to govern with a close-knit set of personal advisors bypassing their own parties. They both acted as if their congressional representations were obstacles to the smooth application of their policies. This seriously affected Congress's capacity to become an efficient policy-making institution, which translated into negative evaluations among the mass public.

While the first part of this chapter deals with the more political nature of representation, the second emphasizes the impact of economic conditions on people's perceptions of their chief executives. There is now irrefutable evidence that the situation of the economy affects a president's standing with the public.[7] To be sure, disagreements remain as to the extent of this influence and the weight of specific economic variables. Analyses of presidential popularity in Latin America, however, remain scarce.[8] In this study I conclude that the impact of economic variables on presidential popularity, although present, is tenuous. Only inflation appears as a significant economic influence on the levels of popularity, and in this sense a president who is able to control inflation accumulates important political capital.

All things considered, I argue that the pattern of political representation that slowly emerged in 1980—a style that seemed to resemble class-based politics—was fatally shaken by the combination of economic crisis, a politically inexperienced electorate, and a decision-making style that reduced the role of Congress in the formulation of policy. The new pattern of representation that was originated in 1990, and affirmed in 1995, is characterized by the relationship between an authoritarian but popular leader and a nonpartisan electorate.

The Politics of Representation: Parties and Electoral Politics in the 1980s

By accepting the constitution drafted by the Democratic Constituent Congress, the Peruvian electorate gave its formal seal of approval to the authoritarian solution implemented by Fujimori on April 5, 1992. In the referendum held on October 31, 1993, about 53 percent of the electorate checked the yes box on the ballot, while 47 percent chose the opposite alternative. Legitimated with this electoral victory—despite the widespread allegations of electoral fraud raised by the opposition—Fujimori continued with his restructuring of Peruvian politics and economics. Moreover, the immediate reelection of chief executives having been approved in the new constitution, Fujimori turned rapidly from being technically a dictator to becoming a candidate for reelection. His unprecedented landslide victory on April 8, 1995, gave him the right to continue a government that has already left a historical imprint in Peruvian politics. In this election, Fujimori obtained 64.4 percent of the vote while his closest contender, former UN secretary-general Javier Pérez de Cuellar, reached only 21.7 percent of the vote.

Back in 1990, political observers were astounded by Fujimori's strong electoral showing in the first round of election, and his eventual victory in the runoff against Vargas Llosa.[9] Even more surprising was the steady, albeit modest, popular support he gathered in the first two years of his first administration, especially when compared against the backdrop of previous governments. Fujimori's continuous confrontation with the major political parties represented in Congress during this period was eventually resolved when he decided to assume full legislative powers and establish what he labeled an "emergency government of national reconstruction," on April 5, 1992. Again, to the astonishment of many, this clearly authoritarian action was received with widespread popular support in Peru. Polls registered levels of approval for this action ranging from 75 to 85 percent.[10] This high level of support for the autocoup was a final confirmation that Peruvian voters had indeed become deeply alienated from their traditional political representatives. To understand how this process came about, we first need to take a quick glance at Peru's electoral politics in the 1980s.

Between 1980 and 1990 four major parties dominated the political arena: AP, APRA, PPC, and IU. Since the 1978 election for a constitutional assembly and up to the municipal elections of 1986, these parties—or, as in the case of the Left, the organizations that would later form the United Left—monopolized most of the political representation. In the 1980 presidential elections, for instance, these four parties obtained 97 percent of the vote. Six years later, in the 1986 municipal elections, these parties continued commanding more than 90 percent of the preferences. By the 1989 municipal elections, however, their vote share began to fall. In this year, APRA, PPC, AP, and the Left (IU and its spin-off, Acuerdo Socialista de Izquierda [Socialist Pact of the Left, ASI]) obtained slightly more than 70 percent of the national vote. The declining electoral appeal of these organizations was more accentuated in the first round of the 1990 presidential elections, when they reached only 68 percent of the electoral preferences. Fujimori's eventual victory in the runoff of June 1990 sanctioned this decline. The 1993 municipal elections further confirmed the predominance of independent candidates, when they obtained two-thirds of the national vote. Figure 3.1 shows the exponential growth of the independent vote, against the decline of the partisan vote (added vote share of AP, APRA, PPC, and the leftist parties).[11] Let's examine in more detail the electoral fortunes of each of these organizations.

APRA underwent a dramatic change in the 1980s. From being the bedrock of

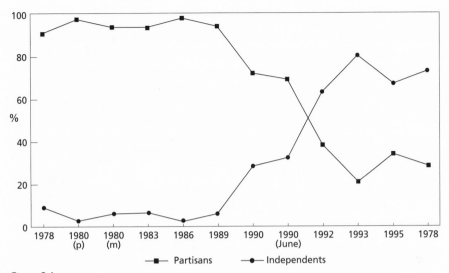

Figure 3.1

the oligarchical regime in the period 1956–1968, APRA became the Peruvian expression of international social democracy in the 1980s.[12] This transformation was
accelerated after the death in 1979 of Victor Raúl Haya de la Torre, its traditional
leader and ideologue. In a party convention convened in 1980 to renovate the leadership, the fractional tension between social democrats and conservatives was resolved when Armando Villanueva del Campo, leader of the Social Democrats, was
appointed both secretary-general of the party and presidential nominee. Villanueva, however, projected an image of intolerance to most voters, which eventually cost him the election, obtaining only 27 percent of the preferences. When
the young leader Alan García replaced him as party leader and presidential nominee for the 1985 elections, the process of social democratization was further accelerated. García moved the party to a clear center-left position and modernized its
symbols and program. García soon became an outspoken critic of Belaunde's economic policies, and the party established itself as a solid contender for the presidency. García won easily the 1985 presidential elections with 53 percent of the
vote[13] and became the first Aprista president in the history of this seventy-year-old
party. After a disastrous performance in office, however, APRA was ousted out of
office in 1990, after obtaining 22 percent of the vote.

Acción Popular, founded in the mid-1950s, followed in the 1980s a different
trajectory than APRA's. After being the party of moderate social change in the
1960s, AP gradually became more conservative. Fernando Belaunde, founder and
leader of this organization, deeply resented the 1968 military takeover—which de-
posed and sent him to exile—and the statist economic policy pursued by Velasco

Alvarado, head of the military junta. Both Belaunde and the party grew increasingly suspicious of anything that smacked of state planning or intervention in the economy, and they developed a technocratic and market-oriented ideology. After AP won the 1980 presidential election with 43 percent of the vote, Belaunde enacted a number of economic stabilization programs to control inflation and, following the International Monetary Fund's advice, tried to dismantle the state apparatus inherited from the military regime. He was not successful on either account, however.[14] Belaunde's dismal performance in office caused AP to lose its bid for reelection in 1985, when the party nominee obtained a highly disappointing 7 percent of the vote.

The Partido Popular Cristiano (PPC) became a national actor in the period 1978–1980 due to AP's decision not to participate in the elections for the Constituent Assembly of 1978. This decision enabled the PPC to occupy exclusively the center-right side of the political spectrum, getting 25 percent of the national vote, the second largest. Nevertheless, PPC was not able to repeat this impressive electoral performance. For the 1980 elections, PPC returned to its real electoral level, reaching 10 percent of the vote. Since AP could not achieve control of the Senate in 1980, AP and PPC formed a governing alliance, and PPC was granted three cabinet posts in exchange for its voting support in Congress. In the 1985 elections, PPC's vote share was basically similar to what they obtained in 1980. In the 1990 elections, PPC ran in the same ticket with AP and Mario Vargas Llosa's Movimiento Libertad (Freedom Movement, ML), winning a plurality in the first round but losing in the runoff against Alberto Fujimori.

The Left, in its various incarnations, had a very important political presence in the 1980s. After the unexpectedly good performance that the various leftist alliances had in the 1978 elections, the Left approached the 1980 elections with great hopes. Ideological and turf disputes, however, prevented the Left from presenting a single candidacy to this election, and as a result their total vote share fell to 14 percent from the 30 percent obtained in 1978. Deeply shaken by this clear defeat, almost all of the major leftist parties decided to sum forces for the municipal contest of 1983, thus creating the electoral alliance Izquierda Unida (United Left, IU). The alliance performed extremely well in this election, winning many important cities, including Lima. In the 1985 elections the Left remained an important contender. Alfonso Barrantes, leader of IU, finished in second place with 24 percent of the electoral preferences. One year later, in the 1986 municipal elections, the Left lost Lima's mayoralty, but its electoral strength remained very strong, with 31 percent of the total vote. IU's wide base of electoral support was unprecedented for the Andean area and the Latin American region in general.[15] An unabashedly marxist organization, IU expressed the dissatisfaction of Peru's working class with the effects of the severe economic crisis and Belaunde's program of stabilization.

Its electoral appeal declined, however, when the leftist parties were unable to keep the alliance together.[16] In the 1989 municipal elections the Left ran two separate tickets, and consequently its voting appeal declined to 20 percent of the national vote. In 1990 that share fell further to 13 percent, as they remained divided.

The Decline of the Partisan Vote: An Interpretation

A clear pattern emerges from this rapid description of electoral politics in the 1980s: the notable fluctuation of the vote. Between 1978 and 1990 the four major political parties obtained at one point or another impressive levels of electoral support, only to see that support decline dramatically after disappointing performances in office (either at the national or local level). The Left, for instance, went from a high of 30 percent in 1978 to 13 percent in 1990. AP, similarly, went from 43 percent in 1980 to 7 percent in 1985. APRA, the party with the most stable vote share, had an electoral support that fluctuated from a high of 53 percent in 1985 to a low of 22 percent in 1990. Clearly, Peruvian voters were skipping from one party to another, shifting allegiances as the parties failed to fulfill voters' great expectations.

The electoral performance of the traditional parties in the 1990s was even worse. In the 1992 municipal elections, AP, PPC, APRA, and the Left had a total vote share of only 33.8 percent. For the 1995 presidential election, PPC and a fraction of the Left decided to support Pérez de Cuellar's bid for the presidency. The other traditional parties (APRA, AP, and IU) obtained a paltry 6.3 percent of the total vote. The collapse of these parties was unmistakable.

The volatile nature of the Peruvian electorate was indeed remarkable. This collapse of the representational capacity of the parties is even more surprising given the nature of the electoral patterns that were developing in the first half of the 1980s. Many analysts suggested that strong identities were emerging between labor and popular sectors with the parties of the Left, on one hand, and between the middle class and APRA, on the other hand, with AP and PPC catering to the upper-middle classes and the affluent.[17] In 1990, however, the popular and lower-middle classes embraced Fujimori with enthusiasm, and in 1995 even the upper-middle class decided to vote for him.[18]

Some have attributed this decline to the parties' inability to respond to the demands of the increasing number of people involved in "informal" activities — streets vendors, petty manufacturing, personal services.[19] Others have suggested that this inability was rooted in the antidemocratic and patrimonialist nature of party leadership.[20] A third line of interpretation prefers to stress the disruptive role that the demise of ideologies of social transformation has played on the parties' capacity to mobilize the electorate.[21]

All these interpretations hold some validity, but they omit some important historical and political factors that help explain the rapid disintegration of the emerging party system of the 1980s. First of all, Peru lacks a tradition of long attachments to political parties and leaders. The only probable exception to this rule was APRA, which was able to develop a strong regional allegiance in the northern part of Peru. This loyalty, however, seems restricted to older voters, as the electoral performance of this suggests.

As many studies in the United States have shown, the development of party identification begins at an early age, when the child is exposed to the values and preferences of their parents.[22] As the process of political socialization proceeds into the adolescent years, the identification with a party solidifies, setting the basis for a more conscious decision in the adult age. In the Peruvian case, long processes of party identification have not been possible due to the transient nature of parties and the sporadic periods of electoral politics.[23] Most voters find it relatively easy to shift party loyalties, since strongly held attachments are not there in the first place.

Carlos Franco refers to the same phenomenon in his analysis of mass political loyalties in Peru.[24] He argues that what characterizes mass political allegiances is a transient loyalty to specific "populisms" rather than a strong attachment to populism as such. Since the 1930s, Franco contends, working and middle-class voters have aligned themselves behind populist leaders on many occasions. Nevertheless, when these leaders have failed to deliver, they were abandoned in favor of a new populist leader or party. This is quite a contrast with other countries' experiences with populism, where the popular sectors remained loyal to the populist party that incorporated them into the political arena.[25]

In addition, the shutdown of electoral politics in the 1970s, due to the existence of the military regime, produced an inexperienced electorate in the 1980s. In the 1978 elections, the first national electoral contest since the 1966 municipal elections, more than half of the registered voters (53.4 percent) had never voted before. In the 1980 general elections, that proportion was certainly much lower, but still remained a significant proportion of registered voters (19.8 percent). The number of first-time voters remained high in the ensuing years. Thus, in the 1985 elections almost one-third of the registered voters (31 percent) had never voted before in a *presidential* election. In 1990, that fraction dipped to 16.5 percent.[26]

To these already dismal conditions for the consolidation of a stable party system, parties became almost irrelevant policy makers as a result of the marginalization of the legislature by authoritarian executives.[27] Once parties won elections, they immediately lost all political importance. Presidents and their entourage of technocratic teams and personal friends rapidly locked mid- and high-level party leaders out of the decision-making process. Thus, while presidents retained the rights of making and implementing policy, parties were confined to petty battles in

Congress. Voters rapidly became disaffected with Congress's performance as a policy-making institution.[28]

The Economics of Representation:
Understanding Presidential Popularity

Economic crisis and the management of the economy dominated Latin American politics in the 1980s and early 1990s, replacing old themes associated with development and social reform. Although this was hardly a Latin American pecu-
liarity, for in many industrialized countries the economy became the central
preoccupation at the time, in this region economic issues permeated the political
debate to an extent unseen before. There was a good reason for this seeming obsession with economics. Across Latin America, the 1980s were the years of deep recession, high inflation, rampant fiscal deficits, high levels of unemployment, and
decreasing wages. Not without reason, the 1980s have been characterized as the
"lost decade" in Latin America.

Peru was no exception to this trend. Between 1980 and 1990, this nation went
from high inflation to hyper inflation; from economic slowdown to full-fledged recession; and from deterioration of real wages to the most dramatic fall in real wages
of the last decades. In policy terms the changes were no less drastic, since all possible variants of both orthodox and heterodox stabilization programs were implemented at one point or another.[29]

The severity of the economic crisis can be appreciated in table 3.1, where key
economic indicators for the period 1980–90 are shown. The gross national product
had a negative growth from 1988 to 1990, and the average real income in 1990 was
a third of what it was in 1979, the baseline year. By the same token, employment
in the industrial sector declined since 1983. Inflation, probably the most graphic
indicator of the severity of the economic crisis, grew dramatically since 1980, and
between 1988 and 1990 Peru was in a situation of hyperinflation (if we define it as
an accumulated yearly rate of one thousand percent or more). To put these figures
in comparative perspective, let us say that while the cumulative variation of the per
capita gross domestic product for all Latin America and the Caribbean was a negative 7.5 percent for the period 1981–1990, that figure for Peru was a negative 28.9
percent.[30] Only Nicaragua and Trinidad and Tobago did worse than Peru in those
years.

The dismal performance of the economy, as one might expect, had a negative
impact on the president's standing with the public. As the economy deteriorated,
so did the levels of presidential popularity. Both Belaunde and García, for instance, began their terms with high levels of popularity, but after one year or so in

TABLE 3.1
Peru: Evolution of Selected Economic Indicators, 1980–1990.

Year	GNP Growth (Percent)	Index of Employment[a]	Index of Wages[a]	Inflation Dec./Dec. (Percent)
1980	2.9	101.9	107.6	60.8
1981	3.1	103.0	109.2	72.7
1982	0.9	101.6	118.2	72.9
1983	-12.0	96.2	101.3	125.1
1984	4.7	86.1	93.0	111.5
1985	1.9	85.0	85.5	158.3
1986	8.5	90.1	105.1	62.9
1987	6.9	97.7	108.8	114.5
1988	-8.3	95.6	67.8	1,722.3
1989	-11.7	85.1	43.6	2,775.3
1990	-5.1	82.9	33.8	7,649.6

a.1979 = 100. Metropolitan Lima. Index of Employment is only for the industrial sector.

Source: Economic Commission for Latin America and the Caribbean, *Preliminary Overview of the Economy of Latin America and the Caribbean* (Santiago: United Nations-ECLA, 1995).

office their rates of approval declined dramatically and kept falling until the last semester of their administration, when they recovered slightly.[31] This cyclical pattern—initial high support, posterior decline, and then slight recovery—has been originally identified in the United States.[32]

The Peculiar Experience of Fujimori's First Administration

Fujimori's popularity curve during his first administration did not conform to this pattern. It began at a low level, and even though the economy did not improve noticeably during the first year of this administration, his approval rate did not decline as one might have expected, given the previous experiences with Belaunde and García. Fujimori started with an approval rate of less than 50 percent as he decreed, in August 1990, the harshest stabilization program in recent times, which jumped the inflation rate to 397 percent for that month alone. From that low baseline, Fujimori's popularity rates improved gradually as 1990 came to an end. In 1991, however, those levels declined, reaching a low of 32 percent in September 1991. Suddenly, Fujimori's popularity jumped to 58 percent in November 1991, and to 65 percent in January 1992.

Undoubtedly, the important reduction of monthly inflation rates achieved in those months explains some of this sudden popularity. For instance, in the first half of 1991 the lowest monthly rate was 5.8 percent (April) and the highest was 17.8 percent (January). In the second half of 1991, however, the lowest rate was 3.7 percent (December) and the highest was only 7.2 percent (August).

But an additional explanation of this surge is more political in nature. In the second half of 1991 Fujimori initiated a campaign against Congress, accusing it of being a hindrance to the development of the country. The attacks were so harsh that *Caretas*, the leading news weekly magazine in Peru, ran an article alerting against those attacks, suggesting at the same time that Fujimori was trying to distract public opinion and gain popularity points by attacking a discredited institution.[33] Indeed, polling data showed at the time the correctness of this analysis: seven out of ten respondents declared their agreement with Fujimori's harsh attacks on Congress.[34]

Fujimori's subsequent decision to close Congress and rule by decree came to solidify, somewhat unexpectedly, his standing with the mass public. On April 5, 1992, Fujimori appeared on national television to announce that due to the obstructionist stance of Congress, the rampant corruption of the judiciary, and the high level of terrorist activity, he had decided to close Congress, dismiss the Supreme Court, and assume all legislative powers. Despite the wide international repudiation to this clearly antidemocratic action, the reaction of domestic public opinion was highly favorable. Almost 80 percent of those interviewed in Lima declared to favor the autocoup, and Fujimori's approval rate jumped to 82 percent.[35] Fujimori's high popularity rate received an additional boost when security forces captured Abimael Guzmán, Shining Path's undisputed leader. In the last month of this administration, Fujimori's popularity rate was still in the low sixties, in a marked contrast with Belaunde's low twenties and García's low teens at similar points in their administrations.

Understanding Presidential Approval: Model and Estimation

While the behavior of the popularity curve under the Belaunde and García administration hints at the existence of a strong influence of economic factors, the data from Fujimori's first administration suggests a much more complex relationship. To ascertain the real impact of economic conditions on presidential popularity, I develop a model that incorporates both economic and noneconomic variables.

Samuel Kernell has shown that voters tend to respond sluggishly to environmental influences.[36] He argues that presidential popularity (P) at time t will be affected by economic conditions present at time t-1, where 1 usually stands for one month. In Peru, however, not all the economic data is available on a monthly basis. For this reason, I am forced to use bimonthly and quarterly economic data. Given this constraint, we cannot specify a uniform time lag for economic variables to affect presidential popularity.

Nevertheless, there is one way to take into account some of the effect of previous economic conditions into current levels of presidential approval. As some studies have shown, voters' evaluation of current presidential performance takes into account their previous judgments (in other words, P is affected by P_{t-1}).[37] This "political memory" term includes the effects of past economic conditions on current levels of presidential popularity.[38]

In addition, it has been established that presidents can count upon, during their first months in office, a particular goodwill from the electorate.[39] This "honeymoon" effect (labeled EARLYTERM in our model), gives presidents a higher standing in the polls than would be expected if only economic conditions were to be considered.

Thus, our general model of presidential popularity (P) in Peru includes economic (ECON) and noneconomic (NONECON) influences, political memory (P_{t-1}, and "honeymoon" effects. In formal terms,

$$P = a + b_1(ECON) + b_2(NONECON) + b_3(P_{t-1}) + b_4(EARLYTERM) + e$$

where a is a constant term, and e an error term for random influences on P.

The variables used to measure the economic influences on P are four: index of growth of the Gross National Product (GNP), the average index of employment in the manufacture and commerce sectors, index of real wages, and monthly inflation. Due to the nature of the economic information, data from November 1980 to January 1986 is quarterly, and from February 1986 to July 1993, bimonthly. Since monthly inflation rates fluctuated widely in the period under study, from 5 to more than 300 percent, we use here the natural logarithm of the original series, in an effort to have a more normal distribution.

The noneconomic variables are already identified. The "political memory" measure is given by previous levels of presidential popularity. To measure the "honeymoon" effect I employ a dummy variable with a value of 1 for the first twelve months in office, and 0 for the other months.

The model was initially estimated using Ordinary Least Squares regression. An examination of the plots of standardized residuals and the partial autocorrelation function (not shown here to save space) showed the presence of autocorrelation, a common problem in models of presidential popularity. When autocorrelation is present, the estimation of the standard error of the slope is not reliable, and therefore the t values for the predictor variables could be overestimated.[40]

To overcome this problem, the model was reestimated using Exact Maximum-Likelihood regression, a procedure that controls for first-order autocorrelation, and appropriate when one of the independent variables—as is the case here—is the lagged dependent variable. The goodness of fit for the model is given by the Akaike Information Criterion (AIC) and the Schwartz Bayesian Criterion (SBC). The results are shown in table 3.2.

The results reported in table 3.2 indicate that the influence of economic conditions on presidential popularity, while present, is very tenuous. Of the four economic variables in the model, only inflation emerges as a statistically significant influence. Moreover, not all economic indicators behave in the way one would expect. For instance, employment in the manufacture and commerce sectors emerges with the wrong sign. Although one might be surprised to find that unemployment does not play a significant role in the determination of presidential approval levels, the same has been found in other national contexts.[41]

The two noneconomic variables, the honeymoon effect and the political memory effect, came out with the right sign, but only the former achieved statistical significance. This finding suggests that Peruvian presidents can rely on a favorable disposition from voters in the first year of their administrations to pursue policies that might not be very popular. The experiences of Fujimori's first administration lend support to this conclusion. Despite the enactment of a very harsh stabilization program that meant a severe deterioration of income, employment, and the national product, Fujimori's levels of approval remained basically stable in his first months in office.

TABLE 3.2
Exact Maximum-Likelihood Regression of Presidential Popularity on Selected Variables

Predictor Variables	B	SE of B	T-ratio	p. of T
Growth National Product	0.40	0.30	1.34	0.18
Employment Index (maf + comm)	−0.91	0.51	−1.81	0.08
Index of Wages	0.23	0.23	1.00	0.32
Natural Log of Inflation	−8.45	4.22	−2.00	0.05
"Honeymoon" Effect	19.79	5.32	3.72	0.00
"Political Memory" Effect	0.20	0.12	1.70	0.09
Constant	72.50			
Standard Error	10.96			
Log Likelihood	−244			
AIC	503.9			
SBC	521.3			
Number of observations: 66.				

Sources: Economic Commission for Latin America and the Caribbean, *Preliminary Overview of the Economy of Latin America and the Caribbean* (Santiago: United Nations-ECLA, 1995). For presidential popularity, sixty-six polls from Apoyo S.A.A. and Datum.

The initial support that all presidents have, however, is quite contingent to a certain effectiveness in curtailing inflation. The political effects of inflation levels cannot be underestimated. In the period under study, presidents came to be judged basically on their ability to keep inflation at bay. Monthly inflation figures (which constituted front-page material for many years) were for many voters an easy and accessible way of summarizing the state of the economy. Those who have lived through periods of high inflation can fully understand the disruption that this economic phenomenon can cause on people's everyday lives. The sense of lack of control over one's own life that high inflation generates, not to mention its devastating economic consequences for those living on a salary, give this economic indicator a high political content. Fujimori's ability to keep a high level of presidential popularity in the last two years of his first administration can be certainly attributed to his success in drastically reducing monthly inflation rates.

Fujimori's Reelection and the Prospects for Deepening Democracy

Fujimori ended his first administration with an unprecedented level of popularity, with no less than 60 percent of respondents declaring their approval of the way Fujimori was doing his job. The economy was in the midst of a notable recovery, with the GDP growing at 12.8 percent during 1994, the highest rate in the region for that year. In 1995 the economy grew an additional 7.5 percent, the second highest in the region for that year.[42] Inflation rates are low (10.2 percent in 1995), and although employment and income levels had not recovered their 1980 levels, people are optimistic about their economic prospects.[43] To give again a comparative perspective of this economic performance, the cumulative variation of the per capita GDP in the Latin American and the Caribbean region between 1991–1995 was 5.1 percent. In Peru that figure was 19.3 percent. Only Argentina, Chile, and Guyana did better than Peru in the same period.[44]

The opposition, on the other hand, lost the opportunity to offer a viable alternative to Fujimori's bid for reelection in 1995 due to its inability to present a single candidate. Although Javier Pérez de Cuellar had been able to form a coalition consisting of independent personalities, former members of Vargas Llosa's Movimiento Libertad, and sectors of the Left, the other opposition parties (APRA, AP, and IU) refused to support his candidacy. In the end, fourteen candidates vied for the presidential sash, something that clearly worked to the incumbent's advantage.

Fujimori was reelected in a landslide. A little bit more than six out of ten voters decided to cast a vote for him (64.4 percent), while Pérez de Cuellar failed to obtain more than 22 percent. The combined vote for the APRA, AP, and IU candidates did not reach 7 percent. These three parties, major players in the 1980s, lost their right to compete automatically in future elections when they failed to reach the threshold of 5 percent of the vote.[45]

However, neither this new electoral victory nor the improved situation of the economy has softened Fujimori's penchant for authoritarian politics.[46] He has used his majority in Congress to block serious investigations into human rights abuses during the fighting against Sendero Luminoso.[47] He has continued with his efforts to control the judiciary, and most recently, he has used his clout in Congress to appoint a mostly sympathetic Constitutional Court. Moreover, he has proceeded with his program of privatization of public enterprises, even in the face of wide public opinion opposition.[48] Thus, the electoral origin of his new administration has not translated into a commitment to democratic governance. In this, he has been aided by the frail condition of the political opposition in Congress.

It remains to be seen to what extent Fujimori can keep his influence beyond the end of his term, in the year 2000. It has already been proved that he cannot easily ensure strong electoral support. For the 1996 municipal elections, Fujimori was unable to get his candidate, Jaime Yoshimaya, elected as Lima's mayor. Alberto Andrade, another independent figure who is friendly to political parties,[49] ran a successful campaign based on his successful performance as mayor of Miraflores, defeating Fujimori's candidate 53 to 47 percent.

Final Remarks

I show in this chapter that Peruvian voters grew highly unsatisfied with political parties in the 1980s and turned to independent personalities. This process, which can be traced to the 1989 victory of Ricardo Belmont to Lima's mayoralty, reached international attention when Alberto Fujimori defeated Mario Vargas Llosa in the 1990 general elections. Since then, Fujimori has increasingly asserted his control over the state apparatus and has weakened already weak institutions such as Congress and the judiciary. Fujimori's landslide reelection has confirmed the dramatic demise of political parties in Peru. I argue that this rapid disenchantment with parties can be explained by the combination of an inexperienced electorate, a weak electoral tradition, and a policy-making process that tends to diminish the role of parties in Congress.

Unlike past presidents, Fujimori has retained a sizeable degree of popular approval. His relentless attacks on traditional parties and his decision to close Congress and reorganize the judiciary in 1992 (institutions that most voters do not trust) have probably contributed to this sustained popularity. In a pattern resembling that of Louis Napoleon, Fujimori has tried to paint himself as the true representative of the nation, against particular and private interests supposedly represented by

Congress. In this, he has been successful. This sustained popularity, however, is also based on some tangible achievements, particularly in the economic arena. A major finding of this study is that the ability to control inflation plays an important role in the determination of presidential popularity.

Fujimori has been further aided by the capture of Abimael Guzman, leader of Shining Path, and the subsequent reduction in political violence. Fujimori has tried to show this amelioration of political violence to be the result of his decision to assume full legislative powers in early 1992.

Does the previous discussion imply that parties in Peru no longer have an important role to play? It is clear that the parties that dominated Peruvian politics in the 1980s do not face a bright future. Javier Pérez de Cuellar's efforts to create a new type of political organization, loose on ideology but firmly committed to the development of democratic institutions, may well turn out to be successful, but at the time of this writing those prospects do not look promising. Nevertheless, the idea, or hope, that the best elements of the traditional parties might be able to reconstruct their organizations, or create new ones, should not be summarily dismissed. A true democracy cannot be established without strong and democratic political parties. Fujimori will probably try to get reelected for a second time, against the letter and spirit of the 1993 Constitution. In fact, a bill has recently been passed that allows for that possibility, and although the opposition has rejected it on legal grounds, it remains to be seen if the Constitutional Court will overrule it.

Fujimori's efforts to get a new term may well face a more difficult obstacle. Peru's recent history shows that political representation in this nation is basically an open field. Voters could turn away from Fujimori as easily as they turned away from other popular leaders in the past. Let us hope that if this time comes, the new allegiances will be to institutions, not to persons.

Facing the Twenty-First Century

Bolivia in the 1990s

EDUARDO A. GAMARRA

Introduction

A dozen years have elapsed since Bolivia completed its transition to democracy. In the intervening years, and under four different democratic governments, the country has experienced significant changes in its economic, political, and social structures. Under democratic rule, Bolivia defeated hyperinflation in 1985, imposed neoliberal measures, and experienced profound political reforms in the mid-1990s. By most minimal standards, democracy appears to be firmly in place.

The mid-1990s also represents the end of an era for Bolivian politics. The leadership of the Movimiento Nacionalista Revolucionario (MNR), which dominated political life since the early 1940s, gradually passed away with the deaths of the old stalwarts of the 1952 Revolution, such as Walter Guevara Arce, Zuflo Chávez Ortíz, and Hernán Siles Zuazo. Víctor Paz Estenssoro, the last remaining titan of the Movimiento Nacionalista Revolucionario, who led the turnaround of the mid-1990s, neared the ninth decade of his existence. Juan Lechín Oquendo, the old labor chieftain, was the only one left to accompany Paz to his final days.

As the country prepared itself for the 1997 elections to elect the first president of the twenty-first century, a new generation of leaders was barely flexing its political muscle. Political parties searched vainly for younger generations, and as Acción Democrática Nacionalista (ADN) demonstrates, whenever possible they reach into the past for guidance and leadership.

In this general context, this chapter provides a brief analysis of Bolivia's democratic experience since 1982. In a second section the government of President Gonzalo Sánchez de Lozada is analyzed. Finally, the chapter explores the principal issues facing Bolivia in the next decade.

Transition, Governance, and Economic Reform

The transition to democracy in Bolivia came only after three decades of profound turmoil sparked mainly by the dynamics unleashed by the 1952 revolution. Between 1952 and 1964, the Nationalist Revolutionary Movement (Movimiento Nacionalista Revolucionario, MNR) nationalized the mining industry, declared universal suffrage, and approved an agrarian reform law. Moreover, the MNR initiated a state-led development strategy that, despite its overthrow by a military junta in 1964, lasted until the mid-1980s.

Throughout most of the 1960s and 1970s, Bolivia was ruled by a variety of military rulers. While these military governments generally followed the contours of the state-centered development strategy introduced by the MNR, they were distinct from one another in terms of mainly ideological and generational differences. Between 1978 and 1982, seven military and two weak civilian governments ruled the country. Coups and countercoups characterized one of the darkest and most unstable periods in Bolivian history. The unsolved dilemmas of the MNR-led revolution, worsened by decades of military dictatorships, accounted for Bolivia's convoluted transition to democracy.

Not surprisingly, the transition to democracy came during Bolivia's worst-ever economic crisis. Hernán Siles Suazo, the first civilian elected president to assume office, could do little to control hyperinflation, respond to pent-up social demands, overcome an opposition-controlled Congress, put down military coup attempts, and satisfy a hostile private sector. Even his own ruling coalition, the Unidad Democrática y Popular, turned on the president. Among the many conspirators against the government was one led by then vice president Jaime Paz Zamora who entertained the opposition's offers to topple Siles in a so-called congressionally sanctioned "constitutional coup." The hapless Siles government was also trapped by demands from the international financial community for greater economic austerity and from the United States to carry out a controversial interdiction-based counternarcotics strategy. Considering the magnitude of the crisis facing Bolivia, in the mid-1980s the challenge for any government was first and foremost to control the spiralling economic crisis. But the political challenges were equally pressing. Institutions, such as legislatures and parties, were undisciplined and constantly conspired to end prematurely Siles Zuazo's mandate. Whoever came to power faced the impossible task of producing a government with both an executive and legislative force.

President Siles Zuazo took tenuous steps to resolve the crisis that contributed only to a deepening of the economic debacle. In 1984–1985, the situation peaked with a catastrophic hyperinflation rate of 26,000 percent and a huge foreign debt burden. Bolivia appeared to have reached profound depths and a bottom was not in sight. The coming to office of Víctor Paz Estenssoro, the leader of the MNR and the man who directed the 1952 revolution, set the stage for the Bolivia's dramatic recovery.

Bolivia's Dramatic Transformation

When Paz Estenssoro was sworn into office in August 1985, the state-centered development strategy he and his MNR had initiated in the 1950s reached its outer limits. Apart from hyperinflation the country also faced a total collapse of the world tin market, a foreign debt burden, and no international creditworthiness. More-over, as Bolivia sank into the depths of the economic crisis, the country also experienced a tremendous boom in the coca-cocaine industry; as this industry grew so did U.S. pressure to combat the War on Drugs on its own terms. In short, the new government faced the herculean task of maintaining democratic rule, restoring economic stability, and preventing the expansion of the coca-cocaine industry.

Less than a month later, on August 29, 1985, via Decree 21060, President Víctor Paz Estenssoro introduced the Nueva Política Económica (New Economic Policy, NPE), a program that effectively restructured the country's development strategy. The NPE sought three basic objectives: liberalization of the economy, ascendance of the private sector as the central actor in economic development, and recuperation of control over key state enterprises. The NPE shock therapy included reducing fiscal deficits, freezing wages and salaries, devaluing the currency, and drastically cutting public-sector employment. Over the long term the NPE aimed at reducing the role of the state in the Bolivian economy.

Within one year NPE measures were credited with reducing inflation from the record-breaking level of 26,000 percent in 1984–1985 to a mere 11 percent in 1986. By most accounts the foundations for economic recovery were firmly established. Bolivia's NPE became a showcase as financial institutions and foreign governments praised it extensively. In 1986, for example, Bolivia signed an agreement with the International Monetary Fund, which opened the path for negotiations with the Paris Club and other groups.

Bolivia sought international assistance to maintain stability and reactivate the economy. The initial phase of the plan called for a public investment program that would allow the country to bide time to carry out major structural reforms. Although the NPE envisioned a greater role for the private sector, it was in no condition to assume a major proportion of the investment needs of the country. If anything, this is an ongoing long-term objective. To deal with the accompanying high social costs of stabilization, the government established a so-called Emergency Social Fund (FSE) with funding from the World Bank. This plan aimed to provide a short-term remedy to the unemployment generated by the NPE. Thousands of workers who were laid off by the NPE reforms and others who were affected by the overall economic crisis had few mechanisms to overcome their situation. The FSE provided temporary relief. Bolivia's FSE became an example emulated by other nations, such as Panama and Mexico.[1]

Bolivia's economic recovery did not proceed rapidly. The collapse of the tin market in October 1985 and the decline in the price of natural gas, the country's only other legal source of hard currency, threatened to derail the NPE. By sticking closely to the broad NPE guidelines, however, the economy finally showed signs of growth in 1987, the first time since 1980. Dubbed the "Bolivian miracle," from 1987 onward the NPE produced impressive long-term results in controlling inflation, resuming growth, and maintaining overall macroeconomic stability. This achievement became the principal value of this and all future governments who vowed to maintain macroeconomic stability at all costs, including delaying the deepening of neoliberal reforms.

Retaining stability had other costs. It depended on a large dose of foreign subsidies and loans that resulted in a current account deficit that reached 9 percent of Bolivia's GDP in 1993. Moreover, despite the intent of the NPE to promote a greater role for the private sector, two-thirds of all investment was public.

Despite macroeconomic stability the underlying state of the economy was not promising. Although GDP growth averaged 3.5 percent between 1987 and 1993, negative growth rates between 1981 and 1986 resulted in a thirteen-year period in which the Bolivian economy grew at a rate of only 0.9 percent while the population rate increased at over 2 percent. These figures also translated into a per capita GDP rate in 1993 that was 14 percent below that of 1980. In the early 1990s, national poverty rates reached 70 percent; rural poverty rates hit an amazing 94 percent. Clearly, the NPE had achieved stability but the task of alleviating poverty remained.

Reaffirming Democracy

Bolivia's success at maintaining economic stability rested largely on the fact that the country's leaders found a political mechanism to both govern democratically and simultaneously press ahead with the NPE. Between 1985 and 1993 Bolivia had two governments whose style of rule set in motion significant trends, which may not have solved the country's deep structural problems but fundamentally transformed the pattern of governance. The key to maintaining democratic stability was rooted in the forging of a ruling coalition known as the Pacto por la Democracia between the MNR and the Acción Democrática y Nacionalista (Democratic and Nationalist Action, ADN). This pact was primarily a legislative coalition that enabled the government to obtain congressional support for the NPE. As a result, the relatively disciplined coalition passed most government initiatives through the legislature.

More significantly, the Pact for Democracy established a precedent for Bolivian democracy. After 1985 it became plainly evident that to win elections and to govern, all political parties must seek lasting coalitions. This pattern has been fundamental for Bolivian democracy as all actors have accepted the rules of the game and fathom no other alternative. This is clearly a major development in a country where until the early 1980s the major vehicle for political change was the military coup d'etat.

Fighting Drugs

This chapter is not the place to analyze Bolivia's experience with narcotics production.[2] Given the significance of the industry and the fact that it dominates U.S. relations with Bolivia, a brief discussion is warranted. The origins of the industry have been discussed elsewhere. Suffice it to say that in the mid-1980s, Bo-

TABLE 4.1
Bolivia: Democratic Governments Since 1982

President	Term in Office	Coalition Parties
Hernán Siles Zuazo	October 10, 1982– August 6, 1985	MNR–I, MIR, PCB, PDC, among others, Union Demócrática y Popular
Víctor Paz Estenssoro	August 6, 1985– August 6, 1989	MNR and ADN, Pact for Democracy
Jaime Paz Zamora	August 6, 1989– August 6, 1993	MIR and ADN, Patriotic Accord
Gonzalo Sánchez de Lozada	August 6, 1993– August 6, 1997	MNR, MBL, UCS, Governability Pact

livia had become the third most significant producer of cocaine hydrochloride and the second producer of coca leaves in the world. In this general context, U.S. pressures to eradicate coca and to pursue interdiction as part of an overall counternarcotics program were great.

Beginning in 1983, Bolivian governments agreed to both eradicate coca and carry out interdiction in exchange for economic assistance and counterdrug aid. In 1987, the United States and Bolivia signed a framework agreement that tied progress on eradication to foreign assistance levels. By the end of the 1990s, Bolivia had become the largest recipient of counternarcotics assistance in the region and the presence of U.S. personnel was noteworthy.

The Paz Estenssoro government was responsible for the establishment of what quickly became a large counterdrug enforcement complex financed almost exclusively by the United States. The consequences were significant, as U.S. influence was felt not only in terms of a larger presence of Drug Enforcement Administration agents, but also in the design and implementation of policy. While the government was busy with the conduct of the economy and the implementation of the NPE, it largely accepted and implemented U.S.-designed legislation, allowed the DEA and other agencies carte blanche to operate in Bolivia, and more generally surrendered design and control of counternarcotics policy. These decisions proved to have long-term effects as the next two governments were forced to deal with the consequences.

U.S. designs over policy notwithstanding, the growth of the coca-cocaine industry in Bolivia reached serious proportions by the end of the decade. Coca production increased significantly and Bolivia surpassed Peru to become the world's second largest producer of cocaine hydrochloride. Despite the buildup, the policy did little to stop the flow of drugs.

Macroeconomic Stability and Delayed Reforms

Bolivia experienced an important political transition in 1989 with the coming to office of a coalition government headed by Jaime Paz Zamora of the Movimiento de Izquierda Revolucionaria (Revolutionary Left Movement, MIR) who joined forces with the former military ruler General Hugo Banzer Suárez's Acción Democrática y Nacionalista (Democratic and Nationalist Action). Contrary to Paz Zamora's campaign promises the new president did not reverse the NPE; in fact, he stubbornly continued with the policies of the NPE, thus maintaining macroeconomic stability. Beyond that, however, major structural transformations to deepen market-oriented reforms were delayed.

A few reforms were launched aimed at a gradual opening of the economy. In

January 1990, the government introduced Decree 22407 that allowed foreign investment in mining and hydrocarbons. Subsequently, new codes were approved to allow joint ventures in these two key strategic areas of the Bolivian economy. Paz Zamora also pushed through a privatization law that targeted only smaller state enterprises while leaving the so-called strategic sectors intact.

Despite pushing through significant pieces of legislation the Paz Zamora government did not embark on the structural changes many deemed necessary to consolidate the NPE. By the end of his term in 1993, it became evident that, in some measure, the process initiated in 1985 had slowed down considerably. Privatization was largely cosmetic, private investment was low, and the state continued to be the largest investor. In contrast to other nations in the region that initiated similar reforms years after the Bolivian NPE, profound changes in state ownership did not occur as the key state enterprises were left untouched by the reform process. By 1993, only a few very small enterprises were actually privatized, rendering little revenue for the state.

Putting the NPE Back on Track

Despite the gains of two successive governments in maintaining economic stability, Bolivia's economy presented several signs that revealed fundamental flaws in the NPE. Most significantly, Bolivia's fiscal deficit was still approximately 7 percent of GDP and was being financed almost entirely by foreign credit. However one examines the state of the economy in 1993, it was evident that the NPE had been successful in reestablishing economic stability, but because major structural reforms were not carried out, the state was still a key actor in the economy. Contrary to the vision of the NPE, the private sector had not stepped in to satisfy savings and investment needs and the state was still dependent on foreign capital to fund its own operations. More significantly, growth rates of less than 4 percent were not enough to overcome the critical needs of the Bolivian population.

For this reason the 1993 electoral victory of Gonzalo Sánchez de Lozada, one of the principal architects of the NPE, raised a great deal of expectations. To vast sectors of the electorate, "Goni," as he was popularly called, was a man of action who would deliver all of the promises made during the campaign. His campaign platform, dubbed "El Plan de Todos," promised to reduce the impact of austerity measures. To the working class, the MNR platform offered the best hope that, in some measure, demands for higher wages and the alleviation of the levels of critical poverty brought about by the economic crisis of the 1980s would be met. To a good portion of the electorate, but especially the middle class, Sánchez de Lozada was the only one who could also end government corruption.

Sánchez de Lozada and the MNR

The new government took office in August 1993 with the intention of setting the NPE back on track after what it perceived to be four years wasted on simply maintaining economic stability rather than deepening market-oriented reforms. The basic economic logic of the Plan de Todos was "to recuperate time wasted during the previous government" through a "transforming shock" aimed mainly at "accelerating economic growth, reducing poverty, improving human capital, and promoting citizen participation."[3] These three interrelated pillars were translated into concrete policy proposals known as capitalization, educational reform, and popular participation.

The MNR's economic agenda had five broad objectives. First on the government's agenda was the maintenance of economic stability through a combination of short-term and long-term strategies that included reestablishing fiscal equilibrium, controlling salaries, and dealing with burgeoning foreign loan obligations. A second objective was to carry out major structural reforms through a privatization process and through the capitalization of state enterprises as well as the promotion of private and public investment. The third tier of the strategy aimed to modernize the state, including plans to modify the structure of the executive branch, tax reform, privatization of customs, and to secure a new central bank law among others. Fourth, the government's political objectives were to carry out significant constitutional reforms, including popular participation. This objective was met partially in 1994 with the enactment of the Popular Participation Law. Described broadly, popular participation reassigns public resources to the rural areas of the country where poverty is concentrated. The program entails the transfer of administrative authority to municipal governments and communal leaders. In a nutshell, the program forces communities and municipalities to define their priorities and to oversee the spending of public funds. Popular Participation is being hailed as the most significant shift of political power since the 1952 revolution.

The fifth and final objective of the MNR government was a profound process of legal reform to establish a framework that would facilitate the process of structural reform and modernization of the state. Legal reforms achieved during its first three years in office included capitalization, hydrocarbons, mining, electricity, telecommunications, and pension legislation. As seen below, however, these laws did not come without a great deal of confrontation and struggle with labor and the opposition.

Bolivia's Capitalization Strategy

Capitalization is at the core of the government's economic strategy as embodied in the Plan de Todos. The basic premise of the capitalization plan is quite simple. It proposed to increase the capital of the principal state enterprises (Yacimientos Petrolíferos Fiscales de Bolivia—YPFB, Empresa Nacional de Fundiciones—ENAF, Empresa Nacional de Telecomunicaciones—ENTEL, Empresa Nacional de Electricidad—ENDE, Lloyd Aereo Bolivia—LAB, and Empresa Nacional de Ferrocarriles—ENFE) through foreign investment while simultaneously maintaining an equal participation of Bolivian citizens by converting them into the effective owners. At least 50 percent of stock holdings in these enterprises were to remain in Bolivian hands, while foreign partners would own the remaining 50 percent of shares. The following are state enterprises capitalized:

- Empresa Nacional de Electricidad (ENDE) Electricity (Capitalized July 1995)
- Empresa Nacional de Telecomunicaciones (ENTEL) Telecommunications (Capitalized October 1995)
- Empresa Nacional de Ferrocarriles (ENFE) Railroads (Capitalized October 1995)
- Lloyd Aéreo Boliviano (LAB) Airlines (Capitalized November 1995)
- Empresa Metalurgica-Vinto (EMV) Smelting (Pending)
- Yacimientos Petrolíferos Fiscales Bolivianos (YPFB) Hydrocarbons (Pending)

It is not hard to understand why capitalization of state enterprises is necessary. The privatization of smaller state enterprises has had a very small impact on the Bolivian economy. In short, if privatization is to affect the Bolivian economy in any substantive way, then private capital would have to target the six largest public enterprises, which represent over 90 percent of the value of all transactions of the public enterprise sector. This is essentially what capitalization attempted to achieve in Bolivia.

In March 1994, the Bolivian Congress approved the initial legal framework to carry out the government's capitalization program. Under the terms of the new law, the capitalization initiative essentially authorized a joint venture association in which a state enterprise contributes its assets and a private investor contributes an equivalent amount in capital. In theory, this would double the original value of the enterprise. Once an enterprise is capitalized the investor would receive 50 percent of the company's stock and sole management control. As mentioned earlier, the remaining stock would be distributed evenly among the 3.7 million Bolivians over the age of twenty-one. The MNR government hoped that the investment generated by capitalization would provide capital to modernize the six enterprises targeted by the plan.

The legal framework to carry out capitalization also consists of the Sectoral Regulation System (SIRESE) signed into law in October 1994. The SIRESE Law (Law Number 1600) establishes a regulatory and oversight framework for each sector that will be capitalized. The basic objective of the law is to develop a new arbiter of the Bolivian economy. Basically, the notion that drives SIRESE is that the state must only play the role of regulator and abandon any previous producer function. A general superintendent was to be selected to serve as the broad overseer of the telecommunications, electricity, hydrocarbons, transport, and water services. Each sector would also have its own superintendent to guarantee the efficiency of the process and the transparency of their management.

The capitalization strategy also included a plan to privatize the state retirement system by partially funding the establishment of private pension funds. In brief, the shares of capitalization owed to Bolivian citizens—to be held by a fiduciary institution outside of Bolivia until the pension fund can be established through a new law—would be solely administered by an independent trustee outside of Bolivia. As of this writing, a new law has not been approved as organized labor, opposition political parties, and retirees have rallied against the measure.

The Promise and Pitfalls of Capitalization

The premise of turning over the ownership of state assets to Bolivian citizens and workers in exchange for social benefits and the right to participate in the new joint ventures is an important shift from pure privatization. The very notion of workers becoming shareholders of former state companies is a unique innovation in the current Latin American neoliberal era.

Capitalization is an interesting Bolivian innovation that may provide an alternative to the pure privatization strategies that have been employed around the region to dismantle state enterprises. However one examines Bolivia's capitalization initiative, its boldness has caught the eye of outside observers and has even served as a model for other nations faced with the task of dismantling state enterprises. Haiti and the Dominican Republic, for example, have introduced their own capitalization strategy and have established close contacts with Bolivian capitalization officials. Other nations such as Costa Rica and Paraguay are also watching the Bolivian experiment.

Under privatization the government sells state-owned enterprises and applies the receipts for:
- Investment
- External Debt Repayment
- Budgetary Support
- Balance of Payments
- Other

Under capitalization the government increases the share of capital of state enterprises and then sells 50 percent to the private sector investor who signs a management contract to invest in the sector.

- State's shares are transferred to all Bolivian citizens over the age of twenty-one.
- Shares are first deposited in a trust fund until capitalization is concluded. At that point the trustee becomes the global custodian supervising the administration of shares.
- Shares are then transferred to privately administered funds.

Despite all its promises, capitalization faced innumerable problems and suffered a great number of setbacks. Labor opposition was very high: numerous strikes, stoppages, and major confrontations occurred in 1995 and 1996. The most contentious was the attempted capitalization of YPFB, Bolivia's hydrocarbons enterprise. Labor unrest rocked Bolivia for several months in early 1996 as the MNR government introduced its proposed hydrocarbons law. Only after major modifications of the original guidelines was Congress able to approve the law. More significantly, the MNR government was able to cut a separate deal with YPFB workers that insured the approval of the law and an end to labor unrest. While worker unrest continued, labor was split, and the most important sector was co-opted.

The sale of the railroads (ENFE) to a Chilean company also raised nationalist responses from labor and from political parties in Congress, especially CONDEPA, the MIR, and ADN. It did not help matters when the company replaced the Bolivian flag with a Chilean flag on its inaugural trip.

Finally, the government had trouble figuring out a way to implement pension reform without a great deal of political turmoil. Throughout the Bolivian winter months of 1996, the government sought numerous options to implement pension reform despite massive street demonstrations by retirees, organized labor, and others. At this writing, it is likely that the MNR will get its way and secure congressional approval. The road, however, has been difficult and has tested the ruling coalition.

The Politics of the Plan de Todos

Sánchez de Lozada was a very keen student of the problems of governing Bolivia. He sought international advice from well-known political scientists such as Arturo Valenzuela and Juan Linz; he held seminars on constitutional reform with leading Bolivian social scientists; and he developed a very deep understanding of the need to forge coalitions to govern. The experiences of the last decade had made it very clear that to govern Bolivia in the context of an economic crisis and demands from the international community to carry out counternarcotics programs, decision makers had to simultaneously deal with several issues. Perhaps most significant was the necessity of dealing with pressing institutional questions ranging from electoral laws to constitutional reform. A recurring issue—every president since 1982 has had to face and attempt a resolution to executive-legislative impasses—involved relations between branches.

This task translated into a crucial need to build coalitions not only of groups in civil society but also among the political parties who had fought intense and bitter electoral battles. Coalition building in Bolivia has required three aspects: electoral coalitions, required to compete for formal power; congressional coalitions, to achieve control of the executive branch following the vote in Congress, and ruling or sustaining coalitions, to support governments and specific policy lines. The important characteristic of this process has been the ability of some leaders to craft coalitions both to get elected and to govern. Political coalitions, such as the Pacto por la Democracia (1985–1989) and the Acuerdo Patriótico (1989–1993) played several key roles. They linked the domestic arena with international themes, such as neoliberalism, provided support for governments, and enabled these to carry out specific policy initiatives. Since the mid-1980s, the dynamics of coalition formation and competition have driven the process of democratization.

Sánchez de Lozada's search for a governing partner culminated in a surprise. On July 2, 1993, the MNR struck a deal, (dubbing it the "Pacto de la gobernabilidad"—Governability Pact) with Max Fernández, Bolivia's controversial beer baron and chief of the UCS. As in all previous pacts, the distribution of key government posts in exchange for the UCS's twenty-one seats in Congress sealed the agreement.[4] Moreover, Sánchez de Lozada was able to broker the first visit by Fernández with the U.S. ambassador since accusations surfaced of his alleged ties to narcotics trafficking. The MNR's deal making did not end there. On July 7, Sánchez de Lozada signed a Pacto por el Cambio (Pact for Change) with the MBL doling out yet another set of government posts.[5]

In 1993, Sánchez de Lozada faced the critical task of forging an alliance that could resist any challenges from the opposition. Unlike 1985, however, the governing pacts the MNR entered into with the MBL and UCS were extremely fragile. Despite this fragility, Sánchez managed to carry out a great deal of his agenda—albeit at a snail's pace. Most of the government's problems rested with the nature of the ruling coalition. The ruling coalition faced difficulties controlling its ranks as both intraparty and interparty proved destabilizing. A recurring conflict between the president's party and the cabinet was problematic, leading to at least three major cabinet shifts in two years. Sánchez de Lozada's first cabinet was composed of technocrats and businessmen, while Congress was left in the hands of the MNR's old guard. These tensions eventually produced a cabinet crisis in March

1994, forcing Sánchez de Lozada to replace the private sector members with members of the MNR. By 1996, with a few notable exceptions, the entire cabinet was made up of MNR personnel.

The ruling coalition proved extremely unstable. On any given week unsubstantiated rumors abounded about a split or defection. Fernández, who felt excluded from the decisions taken by the government, lashed out often against the MBL and the MNR. He was ushered off the coalition in late 1994 and his party showed serious internal splits. Throughout 1995, Fernández played the same game with the MNR. His early and tragic death in November 1995 did not end the game his party played with the MNR and Sánchez de Lozada. Johnny Fernández, the beer baron's eldest son, took over as UCS party chief and continued the party's idle threats to abandon the government.

By the same token, the MBL found itself in the difficult position of having to defend policies it opposed over the past eight years, such as U.S.-designed counternarcotics programs and deepening "neoliberal" economic reforms. A "national summit" held in January 1994 with Sánchez de Lozada cemented the MNR-MBL relationship, and the coalition held tight for the first two years. Antonio Araníbar, the MBL foreign minister, performed extremely well and, at least according to opinion polls, was the most popular member of the cabinet for a good deal of the MNR's three years in office. A more accurate picture would reveal that the MNR had engulfed the MBL and that its fate may be entirely in the hands of Sánchez de Lozada and the MNR. Despite attempts by members of the MBL to retain their identity independently of the MNR, the future of this small band of well-intentioned former leftists is tied intimately with the fortunes of this government.

In the early phases of the Sánchez de Lozada period it appeared that if these alliances held, the MNR could garner enough power to make all other parties irrelevant and achieve single-party status to close out the twentieth century. Moreover, despite all of its internal problems and squabbles, the coalition held and was able to enact significant measures that have fundamentally transformed Bolivia.

During this period several laws were passed by Congress and signed into law by Sánchez de Lozada, including the Cabinet Restructuring Law; the Capitalization Law; the Popular Participation Law; the Education Reform Law;[6] sectoral laws in telecommunications, energy, and electricity; and the Constitutional Amendments Law. Others, such as the Pension Reform Law and the National Institute of Agrarian Reform (INRA) were still under consideration by the Congress in late 1996.[7] As far as government officials were concerned this body of legislation provided a reform agenda as far reaching as Bolivia's 1952 National Revolution.

The most innovative of these laws was the Popular Participation Law, which was signed into law on April 21, 1994. It may radically change the territorial, economic, and democratic conditions of local government in Bolivia.[8] It provides a relatively large amount of financial resources to municipal governments on a per capita basis. The Popular Participation Law may eventually ensure that central government resources will be disbursed to the newly constituted municipalities. Moreover, it grants legal status to traditional citizens' groups at the grassroots level, arguing that it will facilitate their participation in and oversight of municipal government.

The Popular Participation law proved to be quite popular internationally as extensive media coverage of its implementation painted a very positive picture of a law intended to empower local government and allow citizens to decide how revenues would be spent. Domestically, however, the law was a much more difficult sell. The principal accusation was that the so-called "territorial base communities" and the "vigilance committees" established as "accountability" mechanisms had in reality become instruments of the MNR to control local government. The truth probably lies somewhere in between; however, the opposition used this as a rallying cry against the government. Moreover, the Popular Participation Law appeared to go against the grain of previous administrative decentralization initiatives. In addition, the law bypassed the powerful civic committees in each city and department who considered the new law a potential threat to their vision of decentralization. In April 1995, this debate came to a head with a severe confrontation with regional civic committees from Tarija, Santa Cruz, and elsewhere demanding the implementation of a decentralization law.

Constitutional Reform

In August 1994, thirty-five articles of the constitution were amended through the Constitutional Amendments Law, including direct election of half of the members of the lower house of Congress from single member districts; an increase in the terms for presidents, members of Parliament, mayors, and municipal council members to five years, with general and municipal elections alternating every two and a half years; clear procedures favoring the direct election of the president and all mayors; voting age lowered to eighteen; increased powers to departmental prefects; and departmental assemblies composed of national representatives doing double duty as the only assembly members of the department from which they were chosen by the single member district procedure; the establishment of an independent human rights ombudsman; and the establishment of a constitutional tribunal. These reforms are significant and warrant an extended discussion beyond the scope of this chapter. Suffice it to say, however, that the most significance in the medium to long term may have to do with the way in which members of the lower house of Congress will be elected. If the reform is successful, legislators may indeed become more like the districts they ostensibly represent.[9] Opposition to these reforms is also evident. Charges abound that two types of legislators have been created; those elected through single member districts who will see themselves as true representatives and the rest who will be seen as pure party hacks. Moreover, there is no guarantee that this reform will foster coalition building, the only strength of the Bolivian system.

The Counternarcotics Issue

The Sánchez de Lozada government pursued the same U.S.-designed counternarcotics strategy of its predecessors. Given the fact that the government had to implement outstanding agreements with the United States, this was no surprise. Between August 1993 and January 1994, Bolivia had been one of the principal recipients of civic action missions related to drug control missions; moreover, U.S. presence in the country had increased substantially. Initially, things appeared to go well on the bilateral front. The Bolivian government unveiled a new so-called "Option Zero" that called for industrial projects and mass training programs for coca growers in exchange for the complete eradication of illegal coca leaf crops. These efforts and programs received extensive praise from Lee Brown, the then U.S. government's drug czar. But all was not well on the counternarcotics front.

In 1993 and again in 1994, the cultivation of coca crops expanded and the government failed again to meet established eradication goals. As a result, for two consecutive years the White House recommended to the U.S. Congress that Bolivia be granted only a "national interest certification," a probationary type of certification. Future noncertification could result in a complete cutoff of U.S. economic assistance and a negative U.S. vote on multilateral agency support for Bolivia.

Sánchez de Lozada faced an all too familiar dilemma: comply with agreements with the United States and at the same time, prevent any civil unrest in the coca-growing regions. The government's initial response was forceful; for the first time since the coca-cocaine theme came to dominate U.S.-Bolivia bilateral relations, a Bolivian government recognized that the coca crops in the Chapare region were grown exclusively to provide raw material for the cocaine industry. Predictably this fueled a major confrontation with the peasant unions of the Chapare. The government's policy to eradicate coca forcefully headed toward an all-out confrontation with peasant coca growers. In early March 1994, for example, eradication workers clashed violently with peasants in the Chapare. For the Bolivian government things did not appear to work out at any level.

Then in early September 1994, confrontations with peasants in the Chapare increased as the government arrested prominent union leaders. Coca growers unions staged a march on La Paz demanding an end to eradication policies, police and military actions in the coca-growing regions, and a broader set of issues including greater funding for alternative development programs. The coca growers march stirred a national debate that in some measure prompted a reexamination of bilateral agreements with the United States. This strategy, however, did not pay off, as Washington simply tightened the noose.

The U.S. national interest certification of Bolivia in 1995 stirred numerous other conflicts with coca growers and in some measure contributed to the launching of a state of siege in April. The United States issued an ultimatum that in no uncertain terms stated that the government must reach a specific eradication goal by July 1, 1995, and approve an extradition treaty or face a withdrawal of economic assistance. In its haste to satisfy U.S. demands, the Bolivian government agreed to the eradication terms and negotiated an extradition treaty. The Chapare coca growers, however, were not pleased with the U.S. ultimatum.

In June 1995, Bolivia met the conditions of the U.S. ultimatum and by the end of the year continued to satisfy Washington's expectations. In March 1996, the U.S. State Department's annual certification process granted Bolivia full certification. While Bolivia satisfied the United States, however, its government failed to pass any test with Bolivian coca growers who challenged the eradication policies through demonstrations, marches, road blockades, and in September 1996 a huge march upon the city of La Paz. In reality the March on La Paz was orchestrated by thousands of peasants from all over Bolivia who walked to the capital city to protest the government's proposed agrarian reform bill. The coca growers took advantage of this scenario.

Significantly, Evo Morales, the head of the coca growers movement, attempted to organize a political party and used the march on La Paz as a rallying effort. After several days of violent confrontations with law enforcement, the march ended without fanfare. Morales's efforts had apparently failed, although only the 1997 elections will determine whether this was the case. The government was able to co-opt key peasant leaders, cut a deal with the business sector, and promise to approve the bill. The coca growers and the Central Obrera Boliviana, who attempted to push the peasants into confrontation with the government, suffered a serious defeat.

Overall, the U.S. government appeared pleased with Bolivian efforts in eradicating coca leaf and putting up a fight against narcotraffickers.[10] While the Bolivian government has made every effort to de-narcotize its relations with the United States, this appears to be an impossible task. For the foreseeable future, drugs will be the only important item on the U.S.-Bolivia bilateral agenda.

A Coda on Corruption

In addition to hyperinflation, neoliberal austerity, foreign debt, narco-industry, and U.S. military presence, an explosion of political corruption has plagued Bolivian democracy since the mid 1990s with serious repercussions for the governability of the country. President Sánchez de Lozada faced an all-out battle with opposition political parties from the very day he took office. In the early months of the government the two former ruling parties (ADN and MIR) called for his impeachment and the convocation of early elections. Then in December 1993, when the MNR-controlled National Congress amended the electoral law, the opposition parties charged Sánchez with attempting to rig the rules of the game to favor his party.

But these developments became insignificant as all of these parties faced severe internal crises and scandalous charges of corruption.[11] The unraveling of the opposition warrants more concern because it is intrinsically linked to new problems of corruption.

Since leaving office in August 1993, the ADN party also became engulfed in tremendous internal political battles that forced General Banzer out of retirement. Banzer's return from early retirement confirmed the institutional weaknesses of ADN, especially the inability to name a viable successor. No single individual other than Banzer appears capable of bringing the party together in time for the 1997 elections. In many ways, ADN's internal crisis was fueled by charges of widespread corruption during 1989–1993.

Concern for corruption in office also became the single most significant factor in the almost total collapse of the MIR. Since August 1993 former president Paz Zamora attempted to distance himself from his party and to pursue lofty international objectives that included possible stints at the Wilson Center in Washington, D.C., serving on the International Peace Commission in Chiapas, Mexico, and becoming vice president of the Socialist International. These goals, however, were cut short with the March 1994 accusations by the Special Counternarcotics Force (Fuerza Especial de Lucha Contra el Narcotráfico, FELCN) that widespread linkages between the MIR and narcotraffickers have existed since at least 1987.[12] These accusations extended to the entire leadership structure of the MIR and all but ended the party's quest for a return to political office at mid-decade. In a dramatic sequence of events, drug traffickers outlined in painful detail before a congressional committee the manner in which Paz Zamora and the MIR had allegedly come to rely on the cocaine industry to finance their electoral campaign in 1989. The impact of these accusations was great. On March 25, 1994, Paz Zamora resigned from politics, claiming that "errors were made during his administration but no crimes occurred." In December, Oscar Eid Franco, the party's principal strate-gist, was arrested.

The MNR has not been exempt from charges of corruption. In September 1995, the government was rocked by allegations that several high-ranking members of the party had close relations with a trafficker who shipped four tons of cocaine in a DC-6 to Mexico from the country's principal airport. The planeload of co-caine was intercepted in Lima, Peru, only after DEA authorities in Bolivia alerted Peruvian police. Although the party dodged the accusations, the "narcoavión" scandal, as it was named, had a serious impact on the MNR's popularity in 1997.

The posttransition experience of Bolivia suggests that sustaining market-oriented forms in a small and poor country is very difficult; that executive-centric policy making has relied on legislative pacts and parties quite distant from society; and that international praise of neo-liberal reforms may not produce investment, economic growth, or equity.

Chilean Democracy
Before and After Pinochet

SYLVIA BORZUTSKY

Introduction

This chapter attempts to compare the nature of Chilean democracy before and after the Pinochet regime. The chapter is organized in three sections. In the first I discuss the nature and characteristics of the Chilean political system from 1924 to 1973, stressing the importance of the balance of power between the executive and the legislative branch, the multiparty system, and the social functions of the state. The second section deals with the Pinochet regime and its attempts to eradicate politics from the society while implementing a set of neoliberal economic policies that reduced the socioeconomic role of the state and atomized the society. The final section contains a preliminary exploration into the nature of the current political system and the focus here is both on the structural framework provided by the 1980 Constitution and the actual dynamics generated by the process of transition. The analysis focuses on the first two years of the Aylwin administration, the limited nature of the transition, contraints on democracy from the 1980 Constitution, the impact of electoral laws, the decline of the Left, and the reality of an economic model that has limited the social functions of the state.

The Chilean Political System Before the Coup

The modern political system of Chile is rooted in the 1925 Constitution, which in practice involved the establishment of a populist form of state and the adoption of the import substitution model of economic development.

The 1925 Constitution provided a stable framework for the Chilean political system and created a system in which both the executive and the legislative branch had important powers and prerogatives. The new constitution shifted power toward the executive branch, but Congress was given a central role in the legislative process. The constitution recognized the role of political parties in national politics, establishing an electoral system based on overlapping and varied terms for elected offices which, in practice, ensured that the same political party could not control the executive and the legislative branch at the same time. Elections were governed by a system of proportional representation and in the presidential elections, if no candidate received an absolute majority of the popular vote Congress had the responsibility of choosing the president from among the two candidates who had received the highest number of votes.

The constitution allowed the new social forces to be represented while permitting the old ones to retain a large degree of political and economic power. Political stability rested not only in the establishment of a presidential type of democracy, but also in the existence of a complex legislative process that allowed both chambers of Congress and both branches of the government to intervene repeatedly in the dictation of the laws. While this process facilitated accommodation and compromise among contending parties and interest groups, it also contributed to the inefficiency of the system, creating large amounts of often incoherent and particularistic legislation. In the long run, these checks and balances contributed to the durability of the democratic system, but they also paralyzed effective government, obstructed reforms, and only allowed for incremental changes, at best. However, this process allowed for the conciliation and accommodation of different interests and explains the survival of the political organization for almost forty years. At the same time it explains the growth of the Chilean state.[1]

Underneath the formal political stability there was tension between the two branches of government and the different social groups. Tensions between the branches of government can be traced back to the ability of the political Right to maintain control of Congress through two mechanisms: the control of the rural vote and the apportionment of congressional seats, which created a distortion between representation and distribution of the population. The end result was the underrepresentation of the urban areas and the overrepresentation of the countryside where the Right could, until the electoral reform of 1958, maintain control of the peasant vote.[2] Moreover, the D'Hont system of proportional representation used in municipal and congressional elections also contributed to the conflict between the branches of government since it encouraged the formation of electoral pacts and coalitions on which the president had to rely for the passage of legislation.

In brief, while presidential elections tended to reflect the existing political realities, congressional representation reflected the realities of the past and gave the political Right veto power over political and economic reforms.

The party system covered the entire political spectrum. Paraphrasing Charles Anderson, one can argue that Chile became a paradigmatic case of a "living museum" "because politically pragmatic democratic movements devoted to the Constitution and Welfare State ideals of the 20th century stood side by side with a traditional and semi-feudal aristocracy" and because "new power contenders could always be admitted to the system, as long as they did not jeopardized the position of the established contenders."[3] However, Chile fits only partially in the framework sketched by Anderson since its social struggles took place within the boundaries of the political system.

The ability of the political system to absorb different social groups resulted in large amounts of legislation created to satisfy the needs of the different political contenders and led to a process of expansion of the functions of the state. In a nutshell, the containment of the social struggles within the political system produced the expansion of state activities in the economic and social spheres. This process reached a critical point in the late 1960s and early 1970s when the economic structure proved unable to cope with the demands generated by the increasing number of political contenders.

The political parties, in turn, were basically coalitions of various clienteles, and they established crucial links between given groups and the state. The complexity of the clientelistic system was linked to the nature of the electoral system. As Julio Valenzuela argues, "The intensity of electoral competition led the parties to attempt an expansion of their bases of support by establishing new clientelistic ties. This was done, first, by articulating new demands and interests. . . . Second, clientelistic ties were expanded by capturing the representation of vindicationists' demands of existing groups. . . . These differential attachments offered convenient channels for a party in power to grant benefits which could not be given to all the groups due to the budgetary limitations."[4]

To a large extent, then, the relationships between political parties and social groups were determined by the weakness and uneven distribution of the Chilean economy, which precluded large sectors of the population from obtaining the minimum resources required to subsist. The lack of clear clustering of clientelistic ties created an unstable political system in which parties could not maintain their strength for a long period of time since they could not satisfy the expectations of all the groups co-opted by the party. Dissatisfied groups moved elsewhere within the political system in search of better luck.

Distinctive to the Chilean party system is the combination of ideology and clientelism, but ideology only provided the blueprint according to which the society should ideally function. Clientelism gave the parties political support and clientelistic politics affected legislation more so than ideology. By the end of this period the legislative process had become almost entirely devoted to the solution of particular problems, the concession of special benefits, or exemptions to general obligations. Invariably the process produced the expansion of the social and economic functions of the state.

Although the economic role of the Chilean state can be traced back to the 1850s in its modern form, it was initiated in 1939 with the adoption of the import substitution model of economic development. By the late 1960s the state had acquired a preponderant role, serving either totally or partially some of the most important sectors of the economy, controlling imports and exports, setting minimum wages and salaries, setting prices, investing in infrastructure and utilities, and providing a wide array of social services. The state also had a tremendous importance as an inducer of employment or as a direct employer. By the later 1960s the state controlled 40 percent of total GDP and over 70 percent of Gross Domestic Investment.[5]

Import substitution industrialization was the central economic policy, but in Chile, unlike other Latin American countries, it was carried out with the support of the Chilean bourgeoisie. The policy reinforced the private sector through subsidies and investments and gave the private entrepreneur a large degree of influence in the formulation and implementation of the industrial policies through its representatives in Corfo, the state corporation charged with conducting the industrialization process. In brief, the process of import substitution industrialization neither excluded nor reduced the power of Chile's economic elite; on the contrary, a symbiotic relationship developed in which the state became responsible for the accumulation of capital while private entrepreneurs could control and profit from state activities.[6]

The poor performance and contradictory problems experienced by the economy during this period received much attention. Basic economic problems such as inflation, low rate of economic growth, low rate of capital accumulation, dependency on copper, dependency on foreign capital, and unequal distribution of income persisted throughout the period. Other structural problems such as the low share of the agricultural sector, the continuous growth of the service sector, and the reliance on a highly protectionist set of tariffs and on an overvalued exchange rate were equally refractory. Inflation was, undoubtedly, the source of permanent economic dislocations and constant political crises. Inflation was at the core of the political economy of each administration from 1925 until 1970.

The labor legislation that was enacted in 1924 created a fragmented unionization system characterized by vertical and horizontal divisions and by a large degree of state control over the unions. The law also created an elaborate conciliation system that limited the right to strike. However, these laws did not eliminate labor from the political struggle. Instead they produced a fragmented labor movement. Each of the multiple units that formed the movement developed its own connections with the state through the political parties.[7]

There is little doubt that throughout the period the role and actions of the labor movement were determined by the economic conditions of the working class and especially by the inflationary process. The most pressing problem for labor leaders was ensuring that wages rose at the same rate as the cost of living (52 percent of all the strikes between 1961 and 1970 were geared to obtain improvements in wages).[8] How successful were the unions in their struggle to improve the economic and living conditions of the Chilean workers? Data on overall distribution of income and variations in real wages and salaries indicate a dismal situation. For instance, average per capita income rose 30 percent between 1940 and 1954, while blue-collar-worker per capita income rose only 9 percent.[9] Regarding distribution of income the data also shows pronounced inequalities. In 1967, the median income for a blue collar worker was $100 per month, while the income for a white collar worker was $327 and for an entrepreneur $744 per month.[10] In fact, both blue and white collar workers, but more the former than the latter, experienced a constant decline in real income between the early 1950s and the 1970s.[11] Faced with a divided labor movement, expanding political participation, and a competitive political system, the unions tried to counteract their declining income and their political exclusion by developing what is best described as a symbiotic relationship with the political parties. On the other hand, parties, regardless of their color, were eager to co-opt electoral clienteles and serve as brokers between the workers and the state.

From my standpoint, the 1925 Constitution set the basis for the development of a "policy state," a notion developed in Germany in the later nineteenth century that defines the state as an agency responsible for social welfare.[12] In Chile the state was charged with satisfying the growing needs of a fragmented and rapidly urbanizing society. The two most important policies of the state were industrialization and social security policies.

At a different level of analysis, what one sees developing in Chile is a form of populism. However, here the populist regime did not operate through a large unified coalition as in Argentina or Brazil, but through multiple political parties that formed changing alliances. These alliances incorporated the more articulate sectors of the urban society and they demanded from the state a multiplicity of benefits and services. The incorporation of new political groups produced a constant expansion of the functions of the state. Chile did not have an "Estado de Compromiso," as argued by several analysts,[13] but in fact a lack of compromise, since there was no societal agreement geared to limit the function and obligations of the state. In the long run it generated socioeconomic demands and a further expansion of state functions, which in turn fed the inflationary process.

By the early 1960s Chilean society was experiencing a major crisis due to the exhaustion of the political and economic model created in 1925. Eduardo Frei and the Christian Democratic party (PDC) attempted to deal with these problems through a program based on the notion of the "Estado Comunitario," which attempted to transform the nature of the state and its functions, the relations between state and society, and the main forms of articulation of interests. Essential policies included the regime's efforts to integrate the peasants and those marginal to political society, to change the relations between organized labor and the political system, to adapt the import substitution model to contemporary economic conditions, and to redefine the social functions of the state. Fundamental to the ideology of the PDC were Jacques Maritain's notions of common good, the organic role of the state, and the communitarian society.[14]

President Frei's program attempted to deal coherently with the structural problems of the Chilean economy. The principal actor in the program was the state, which, through a new set of policies and a new group of technocrats, would steer the national economy toward higher rates of economic growth, control of inflation, and a better distribution of income. Following the structuralist approach, the new administration argued that these objectives could be achieved only through a land reform, which would put an end to the lagging impact of that sector in the national economy, and the Chileanization of copper, which would allow the state to control Chile's basic export product. Also, essential to the PDC program were the stabilization policies and the wage policies.[15]

No other political party in the history of Chile had been in a better position to attempt a transformation of the political system than the PDC, which between 1965 and 1969 both controlled the executive and had an absolute majority in Congress. Despite this majority and the executive's commitment to reform, their success was partial at best. Opposition to a constitutional reform bill came from both corners of the political spectrum and deprived the administration of the required two-thirds of the vote. Both the Chileanization of copper and land reform bills were substantially modified by Congress and fulfilled only partially the expectations of the government and Christian Democratic constituents.

Also central to the program were the legislation on peasant syndicalization, which gave the rural workers the right to form unions and to strike, and the incorporation of the marginal into political society through the "Popular Promotion" program. Opposition to these bills also came from the right and the left, and although a peasant unionization law was approved by Congress in 1967, it is clear that most of the progress in these areas was due to actions of the executive branch.[16]

In brief, one has to conclude that the major goals of the administration could not be accomplished in the political environment of the 1960s. The reforms pressed by the administration threatened every conceivable sector of the society because they involved relinquishing rights and prerogatives that had become part of the sociopolitical and economic fabric of the nation. The policies of the communitarian state required at least a minimum degree of consensus on the existence of a national interest and that consensus did not exist in Chile. However, through political compromises either with the Right or the Left, the administration obtained partial reforms that impinged upon society in the years to come. Among those, the reforms in the countryside were essential in transforming the peasants into active political actors. These partial reforms effectively destroyed the bases of the populist state but could not create a new form of state to replace it. The reforms also set in motion a process of massive political incorporation characterized by the development of new intermediate organizations and a process of political mobilization and polarization. The impact of these processes was felt between 1970 and 1973.

During the three years of the Allende administration Chile underwent a number of political changes that had begun long before Allende came to power, but which were accentuated by the policies pursued by the administration. The program of the Popular Unity (UP) combined a number of structural transformations, such as land reform and a complete nationalization of copper, with redistributive measures. Having diagnosed a profound crisis in the entire political and economic organization, the UP argued that the crisis could be solved by transforming the existing system of dependent capitalism into a socialist system. The role of the UP was to initiate the process of transformation of the state and the society. According to Allende, the simultaneous transformation of the economic base and the transformation of the state within the existing institutional framework constituted the Chilean Road to Socialism.[17]

Essential to Allende's strategy was the notion that the existing constitutional structure would mark the beginning of a process of change in the economic role of the state, which, in turn, would transform the basic economic structures of the society. Once the original transformations had taken place, the dialectic process originated by then would produce the transformation of the legal superstructure. In other words, from Allende's standpoint the entire process rested on the success of the economic program and its capacity to change the distribution of economic power in society. In practical terms, given the fact that the administration only controlled the executive branch, it was required to increase the popular base of support. Two policies would spearhead this process: the creation of the social property area and the income redistribution policy.

Although a thorough analysis of the policies and the conflicts that led to the downfall of the Allende regime falls outside the scope of this chapter, a few issues

need to be highlighted. First, although the redistributive policies produced beneficial political results they also produced a large fiscal deficit, which by 1971
amounted to 36 percent of the total budget, generating an unprecedented inflationary spiral. Second, the dependent nature of the economy made the regime vulnerable to external economic and political pressures. Third, the government had
to confront not only a hostile political opposition, but also the divisions within the
UP, which largely undermined the program and its goals.

Moreover, the dual process of polarization and mobilization that had began
during the Frei administration only served to increase the pressures over an already
weakened government. By 1972 the political center, which had served as the arena
for stability and compromise, disappeared, and at the same time a number of new
pressure groups appeared both at the right and the left of the political spectrum.
With the disappearance of the political center the basic fabric that held Chilean
politics together disappeared as well, and the political conditions for the military
coup became clear.[18]

In conclusion, both the state and the regime faced numerous and contradictory pressures, which had begun in the early 1960s and were fostered by the un-
fulfilled promises of reform and change of politicians both in the PDC and the
Left. The continuous expansion of the state functions in a context of limited resources exhausted the state and produced a dramatic deterioration of the economy,
which only augmented the existing political conflict. In the process the political
center disappeared and both the political arena and society at large became polarized, creating the conditions required for military intervention.

Authoritarianism and Neoliberalism:
The Making of a Capitalist, Apolitical Society

From the very beginning the Pinochet regime faced two fundamental tasks:
the disarticulation of the remnants of the previous political order and the reorganization of society along new lines. The former was accomplished through the
massive use of repression while the latter was carried out through a long-term
process, which fundamentally transformed the Chilean political system. The new
organization was shaped through a series of laws and a new constitution enacted
between 1978 and 1980.

From its inception the regime pursued the depoliticization of society and the
creation of a subsidiary authoritarian state. Arguing that the interventionist state of
the past was to a large extent responsible for the economic problems of Chile, the
Pinochet administration declared that "the state should only assume direct responsibility for those functions which the intermediate or minor social groups are
unable to deal with."[19] Statism, according to the ideology of the administration, im-

paired the full development of the society and should be replaced by a market ideology. The new ideology inspired by the ideas of Milton Friedman and Frederick
von Hayek was applied by their Chilean disciples: The Chicago Boys.

Although the Chicago Boys, and particularly their leader, Sergio de Castro,
had had a very close relationship with the military since 1972, it was not until 1977
that they took control of economic policy making and greatly influenced the future political structure of the country.[20] The period between 1978 and 1980 was crucial both for General Pinochet and for the monetarist economists, since they not
only consolidated their power but also set the bases for Chile's new institutionality.
The central political maneuvers were the 1978 plebiscite and the 1980 Constitution and both of them were designed to consolidate power not in the hands of the
armed forces but in the hands of General Pinochet, establishing a unique system
of personal rule.

The central socioeconomic reforms were defined by a set of laws that totally
restructured the economy and the relations between the individual and the state.
From our standpoint what needs to be highlighted is the nature of the new constitution and the impact economic reforms had on the political future of Chile. What
is clear is that the creation of a capitalist society was linked to the continuation of
the authoritarian system; that the process of political opening was linked to the success of the economic model, and that the market economic system was designed
to constitute the foundation of any future democratic system. In the words of De
Castro the country will continue advancing successfully only if, first, "the efficient
political conduction of the present regime continues," and second, "we have the
time to secure the results of our success."[21]

Given Chile's legalist traditions the enactment of the 1980 Constitution had a
major impact not only on the institutionalization and legitimacy of the regime, but
also on the country's political and economic evolution, and although the constitution did not represent the will of the people but simply the will of General
Pinochet and a few advisors, it set the parameters for the evolution of the political
system in the years to come.

The constitution established two different periods. The transitional period,
from 1981 to 1989 (but that could have been extended until 1997), involved the institutionalization of the existing regime, maintaining and even increasing the per-
sonalist, repressive nature of the government.[22] According to former minister
Mónica Madariaga the first eight-year period was to be devoted to the creation of
the new political structures and the consolidation of the economic model, while
the second one would provide the time required to apply the new norms in an already "normalized" society.[23] The second period, from 1989 to 1997, which the
constitution calls "democratic," resembles more an authoritarian regime since it
established a very strong executive, a Congress that had been deprived of very basic

functions, a judiciary dependent on the executive for its nomination, and armed forces the power to supervise the political system. In its initial form the constitution also limited political pluralism and created a very powerful constitutional court dependent on the president.

The constitution also institutionalized the reduction of the functions of the state by transferring many of these functions to the private sector, as well as the atomization of the society by limiting the channels of political participation and enhancing the role of the market as the central regulator of socioeconomic activity. What is important to note is that the neoliberal economic model is now part of the constitutional makeup of the country and that it has set the parameters for the actions of the new regime. As General Pinochet and De Castro argued repeatedly, the economic strategy and the political system "are indivisible parts of the social fabric, and both of them have served as the source that inspires the new institutionality."[24]

Nowhere does the conjunction of the political and economic systems become more evident than in the establishment of the eight-year transitional period. From an economic perspective, according to the projections of De Castro, by 1989 the country would have enjoyed ten years of high rates of economic growth, which would have totally transformed the nature of the Chilean economy. In fact, the market economic model would have not only made of every Chilean a property owner but would have also eliminated poverty from the face of Chile, eliminating forever the threat of marxism. According to De Castro "this, and none other, is the motive behind the 8 year transitional period."[25] The success of the model, the limitations on political activity summed to the atomization of the society produced by both the constitution and the socioeconomic reforms enacted by the regime would, in turn, secure the political success of the regime, guaranteeing the renewal of the mandate to General Pinochet for another eight years. By the end of the sixteen-year period Chile would have been transformed into an apolitical capitalist society.[26]

A full analysis of the economic problems that Chile experienced between 1982 and 1985 falls outside the scope of this chapter. What is clear is that by the end of 1982 the economy was in shambles. GNP had fallen 14.5 percent, the industrial sector decreased 21.69 percent, and the unemployment rate reached 30 percent. The price of labor, which had fallen dramatically during the first years of the regime, fell again below its 1970 level.[27]

Given the connections between the economic and the political models, the economic crisis was followed by the largest political crisis that the administration had experienced since coming to power. General Pinochet managed not only to stay in power but also to strengthen his rule through a set of repressive policies. In the process, political parties and unions reappeared, and although repressed and with very limited power they managed to put the regime on the defensive. In the long run the crisis set the basis for the rebirth of political activity since it opened the door for the formation of political coalitions, the revitalization of the trade union movement, and the development of a grassroots protest movement. An opposition political bloc, the Democratic Alliance, appeared in the otherwise vacant political spectrum, and although it did not achieve the goal of speeding up the process of democratization, it managed to break the immobilism of the administration and to set in motion talks between the government and the opposition, which dealt with the need for legislation regulating the activities of the political parties. At the same time the government began a new period of repression geared to contain the protest movement.[28]

From an economic standpoint the crisis led the government to abandon the orthodox monetary policies, to disband the powerful economic groups, to take over the banks temporarily, and to assume private debt. As Edwards notes, by 1983 "the financial sector was in some way at the same juncture it had been ten years before. It had been nationalized and it was tightly controlled by the state."[29] Most importantly the crisis destroyed the mystique that the market-oriented policies were faultless, and although the model was maintained, government officials had to recognize the need for adjustments. After 1985 the model was refurbished, but by then the organized political opposition had acquired a small space in the political arena and it had forced the regime to initiate a dialogue, and to respond to at least some of the demands made by the opposition.

In charge of the readjustment of the economy was the minister of finance, Hernan Buchi, who maintained the neoliberal model but increased government intervention in the economy in order to promote certain areas or control important economic actors. Central to Buchi's policies was the promotion of exports by increasing government support to this area of the economy and promoting foreign investment in Chile. During the 1985–1988 period the economy grew at about 5 percent per year while the debt was reduced by about $4 billion. Inflation remained stable at about 20 percent, and the process of privatization received a boost thanks to a new set of government policies.[30]

As a result of the political pressure exercised by the organized political opposition and the timetable established in the constitution that called for a plebiscite by 1989 to decide on the future of the regime, the representatives of the administration reluctantly and gradually began to negotiate the laws that would govern both the plebiscite and the elections. Those laws dealt with the legalization of the political parties and the establishment of an electoral registry and, although the laws included important limitations to political freedoms, pluralism, and union rights, they provided the legal framework required to hold the referendum and to launch the transition process. Throughout the process the government maintained the upper hand and managed to impose its views in a number of crucial issues.

The opposition, on the other hand, managed to resolve a number of internal differences, formed the "Concertación de los Partidos por el No," and emphasized the need for social peace, social justice, and a new political regime. Pinochet's defeat in the October 1989 referendum led to a further recognition of the role and importance of the opposition as the administration agreed to begin preparations for the presidential elections and to initiate talks with the "concertación" regarding the need to reform the 1980 Constitution.

In brief, the nature of the transition process in Chile was determined by the nature and ideology of the Pinochet regime. First, the personalistic type of authoritarian rule served General Pinochet well for about fifteen years and, as Karen Remmer argues, "Pinochet's preeminence is at once the source of his regime's durability and unusual policy performance."[31] But at the same time the patrimonial, personalistic style of rule led the regime to attempt the elimination of political activity and deprived General Pinochet of a political organization he could use if the economic model did not produce the expected political results.

Second, the entire political edifice was built on the success of the economic model and its ability to keep people atomized and passive for about one generation. Two issues seem relevant here. One is that the balance of the sixteen years of military rule shows a very mixed record of economic successes and failures,[32] and the second relevant issue is the enormous human rights violations. Most of the success can be attributed to the "revised" application of the model made by Mr. Buchi who managed to increase exports, reduce the debt, increase foreign investment, reprivatize the banks, and obtain high rates of economic growth. The model also generated a process of concentration of capital in the upper income sectors, while increasing poverty. By 1985, 45 percent of the population was living below the poverty level and about 20 percent was in conditions of extreme poverty.[33]

Democratization: Politics and Economics During the First Two Years of the Aylwin Administration

Because General Pinochet left power within the rules for transition he established rather than military defeat or economic chaos, he was able to define parameters to Chilean democracy. The nature of Chile's democratization was thereby determined by the constitutional and legal framework inherited from seventeen years of military rule. The legacy left by the Pinochet regime includes not only a new institutional framework, but also a new economic organization. The regime left also a society that had suffered the impact of years of human rights abuses. This section deals with macropolitical and macroeconomic issues, human rights issues, and the nature of civil-military relations in post-transition Chile. The central argument is that we have seen a limited transition to democracy, and a limited attempt to deal with both the legacy of socioeconomic inequities and human rights abuses.

Chile's current political system was designed, not by a cadre of democratically minded politicians or legal experts, but by a group of individuals handpicked by General Pinochet who held authoritarian political ideas and did their best to legitimize the power of General Pinochet and retain authoritarian powers after the disappearance of military rule. Nonetheless, the process of transition evolved after Pinochet's defeat in the 1989 plebiscite and involved limited negotiations between the regime and the opposition. The opposition had limited power to pressure the regime for substantial political changes. In fact, two parallel processes evolved after the plebiscite: on the one hand there is the imposition by General Pinochet and the hardliners of policies geared to maintain the autonomy and political influence of the military and to retain authoritarian structures in key areas of the economy and the society. This policy resulted in a set of laws, the organic constitutional laws, that determined the structure and autonomy of the Central Bank, television broadcasting, and the armed forces, as well as key appointments in the army, the judiciary, universities, and so on.[34] The impact of these laws and appointments has been the establishment of authoritarian enclaves within the system. In the case of the armed forces, as Garretón argues, they have consolidated the existence "of a state within the state,"[35] given the fact that the commander in chief cannot be removed by the civilian authorities.

On the other hand, there was a process of negotiation between the regime and the opposition. Negotiations turned on a set of constitutional reforms suggested by the opposition and partially accepted by the regime. These reforms included the reduction of the first presidential period from eight to four years, reduction in the power of the National Security Council, measures designed to facilitate the process of constitutional reform, and the elimination of ideological restrictions on political parties. These reforms were approved by a referendum held in July 1989. What is important to highlight is that throughout the process the regime maintained the upper hand and was able to determine the nature and extent of these reforms. Consequently, the role of the armed forces as "protectors" of the political system could not be changed. From the standpoint of the opposition, although the reforms were partial at best, they were accepted as a reflection of a more compromising attitude on the part of the government and they were seen as a first step in what seems to be a long struggle between democratic and authoritarian forces in Chile.

As Pinochet and military elites began to look to the political future, they began to search for mechanisms and organizations that would project their power into the future. The major problem encountered was the lack of a political structure that could operate during the transition period and beyond. Pinochet's determination to create an apolitical system, based on a combination of technocratic and patrimonial concepts (such as his declaration, "I am the state"), precluded the development of a strong political movement capable of capitalizing on the regime's support among the upper class and sectors of the middle class. In other words, the neopatrimonialist approach to politics held by General Pinochet lacked a long-term political project and simply rested on the ability of the patrimonial ruler to stay alive and in power. As Remmer has shown in her study of military rule in Chile, the concentration of power in the hands of General Pinochet was such that even the armed forces became excluded from conducting the government[36] and true to their Prussian inheritance simply obeyed the orders of the commander in chief. Just like in Spain, the *caudillo* held all the reins of power.

In the new political spectrum, the Right became divided into two political forces: the UDI representing the hard-line elements identified with the Pinochet regime, and Renovación Nacional (RN) representing the more democratic sectors of the Right. RN was looking forward to participating in the new regime and, consequently, was willing to support partial reforms to the constitution. The UDI and RN formed a political coalition, and while General Pinochet and the UDI prevailed in terms of the presidential elections by launching Hernan Buchi as a presidential candidate, Renovación Nacional managed to secure advantages in the selection of parliamentary candidates.

The opposition, on the other hand, unified under the banner of the "Concertación," was able to solve its differences and to accomplish two central tasks: to negotiate with the regime as a bloc and to have one candidate in the presidential elections, the Christian Democratic leader Patricio Aylwin. The parties that formed the coalition managed to reach electoral agreements in regard to the parliamentary elections as well.

As one tries to understand the nature of this posttransition process it is important to examine the new electoral system and its impact on the parliamentary elections. The law designed by the Pinochet regime established a system known as "sistema binominal mayoritario," which intended to transform the nature of the political party system from the traditional three-thirds to a biparty system. According to the law each district elects two representatives and each party can present two candidates. Voters choose one candidate and the winners are determined by the total vote received per list. The list with the largest number of votes gets one seat and the second seat is elected from the second list that has at least half of the number of votes. There is little doubt that the system was designed to favor the Right, since, as Valenzuela argues, "if there are two lists presented, the top list presumably the opposition could earn as high as 65% of the vote and still win only one seat, while the second list (presumably pro-Pinochet) needs only 33% to earn another seat."[37] The laws also designed the congressional districts in a way such that rural areas, supportive of the regime, elected more deputies than urban areas, where the opposition was stronger. Thus the "20 smallest districts, with a population of 1.5 million, elect 40 deputies, while the seven largest with a comparable population, can choose only 14."[38]

In the short term the electoral laws gave the Right a sizeable parliamentary representation and forced UDI and RN to form a coalition (the Right obtained 34 percent of the Senate seats and 40 percent in the Chamber of Deputies). In the long run, the system secures not only the continuation of a political farce, but also gives the Right a veto power over constitutional reforms. The attempts on the part of the Aylwin administration to reform the system have so far failed.[39]

The opposition managed to present a unified front in the 1989 elections, obtaining 47.8 percent of the Senate seats and 60 percent of the seats in the Chamber of Deputies. But given the restrictions imposed by the military on the process of constitutional reform, the civilian government of President Alwin lacked the votes required to enact reforms necessary to democratize the system. In fact what we see in posttransition Chile is that although the Right does not control either the executive or the legislative branch, it has the power to maintain the system as it is and it can obstruct reforms dealing with the electoral laws, the structure and power of the Supreme Court, the autonomy of the armed forces, and the power of groups and individuals, such as the appointed senators, who have no popular mandate.

Another central characteristic of posttransition Chile is the absence of a viable Left. Here one has to analyze the combined effect of years of repression and the process of reform launched by Mr. Gorbachev in view of the failure of the Soviet interpretation of Marxist-Leninist ideology. The impact of both processes has been radically different on the Socialist and the Communist parties. The Socialist party responded to the domestic situation by launching a process of ideological renovation, stressing the importance of political democracy, and reducing its commitment to marxism. Some Socialists have even proposed the total elimination of marxism from their ideology. In practical terms the process of renovation facilitated the alliance with the Christian Democratic party and the formation of the Concertación.

The Communist response to both the domestic and international changes has been characterized by isolation and denial. Throughout the 1980s the party proposed armed struggle against the regime, a policy that was not supported by the USSR and that the Chilean Communists had a lot of trouble applying. The Communists were excluded from the transition process by the Pinochet regime and as the electoral process advanced they failed to abandon the policy of popular rebel-

lion and refused to accept the new electoral system, which only increased their isolation. At the same time the leadership had to confront the impact of Gorbachev's
reforms. Throughout 1989 and 1990 perestroika and glasnost were interpreted as a
reinterpretation of the traditional dogma and as the result of the failure of one form
of socialism: bureaucratic socialism. Pressures to apply perestroika were contained
by the leadership and prompted the formation of a dissident movement, which
proposed a process of ideological renovation. Among former Communists one sees
today a three-way division: the orthodox group, those who abandoned the party because they supported Perestroika, and those who were expelled because of disagreements with the leadership.

When President Aylwin took office in 1991 the macroeconomic landscape was
characterized by profound distributive inequities, a high social debt, and the reduction in the social functions of the state. Most importantly, according to a
CEPAL study 5.5 million people, or 44.4 percent of the population, were defined
as poor while the indigent (extremely poor) amounted to 16.8 percent of the population. Nonetheless, the civilian government has shown a strong commitment to
the military regime's economic model and it has reinforced the role of the market
as the central economic agent. The Alwin administration sought to consolidate the
gains of the military in the areas of economic growth, fairly low inflation rates, and
debt reduction, but simultaneously recognized the depth of the socioeconomic
problems. The central issue was to improve the socioeconomic performance of the
model and address questions of social equity and extreme poverty.[40]

Here again one sees the connections between the political and the economic
transformations and the need to make both transformations simultaneously. So far
the Aylwin administration has reduced tariffs, signed a number of free trade agreements, liberalized investment procedures, and controlled inflation, strengthening
the neoliberal approach and achieving a 5 percent GNP growth in 1991 and a remarkable 9.7 percent for 1992, a positive balance of payment of 500 million U.S.
dollars and a growth of international reserves of about US $1,300 million. Inflation
was only 18 percent in 1991 and the unemployment rate decreased to about 6 percent in 1991 and 4.5 percent in 1992.[41]

What remains to be analyzed is the social side of the economic picture. The
Aylwin administration has insisted that social equity could result only from high
rates of economic growth and a strong performance throughout the economic system. At the same time it would like to see an improvement in the distribution of
income via better salaries and wages and high employment rates, as well as a re-
activation of the social function of the state. The crucial question here concerns
the likelihood of achieving these goals given the extent of socioeconomic ine-
quality.

The government of President Aylwin defined its social policy along four fundamental lines: equity, solidarity, efficiency, and an integral approach to social problems. The most important accomplishments have been tax reform and the agreements reached in the area of labor laws to reform the Plan Laboral (the regressive labor legislation designed by José Piñera during the Pinochet regime). The agreements reached by representatives of the government, entrepreneurs, and unions have allowed for substantial wage improvements at least among the workers who participated in the process (the income of the labor sector is estimated to have increased by about 6 percent during 1991 and 5 percent in 1992).[42] Not included in this process were workers in small and medium sized enterprises, the independent workers, and the unemployed.

The passage of tax reform legislation allowed the regime to increase social expenditures by about 2 percent of GDP. Given the magnitude of the social problems there is no question that this 2 percent is insufficient; however, it has allowed the government to at least indicate its intention of reversing the policies of the previous administration. The administration has, also, continued the policy of the military regime of providing very small, and certainly insufficient, subsidies to the lowest income groups. The market approach to pensions and health has also continued and the inequities in those areas continue as well. For instance, in the health area recent data shows that in 1990, while the private sector spent US $228 per person covered, the public sector spent only $75 (the private sector provides services for about 20 percent of the population, while the public sector is responsible for the remaining 80 percent).[43]

In sum, we see also the continuation of the policies designed during the authoritarian regime in the area of social policy, with marginal changes geared to deal with extremely pressing issues. The most important accomplishment here is the reduction in the number of poor people. According to the administration, between 1990 and 1992 the number of people living in poverty was reduced by 700,000.

The third dimension or process of democratization that has been central in Chile, and in other countries as well, is the question of human rights and the power of the armed forces. Here the Aylwin administration took a number of initiatives during the first year that attempted to deal with these issues, including failed attempts to reform the Penal Code, the Anti-Terrorist Law, the Internal Security and Arms Control Laws, the Military Code of Justice, and the Press Law. Again, the central issue here is the veto power that the Right has over major reforms. To the extent that the administration failed to obtain the passage of the electoral reform bill any real reform in this area could take place only if there is a major division in the right-wing coalition.

The Alwin administration appointed the Rettig Commission, or Commission for Truth and Reconciliation, to investigate human rights abuses.[44] The commission produced a detailed report of the human rights abuses carried out by the armed forces and the police between 1973 and 1987 and it criticized both the courts and the military for their behavior. President Aylwin, in turn, endorsed those accusations and responded by suggesting the need for moral and economic reparations and accused the armed forces of human rights violations. In practice, the law authorizing the reparations was not passed by Congress until February 1992 and as it was passed it is going to benefit only a very small proportion of the victims since the Right was able to limit the scope of the law.[45]

In regard to the responsibility of the armed forces, the central issue is the existence of the Amnesty Law of 1978, which protects the military. Solá Sierra, the Chilean human rights leader, has effectively described the feelings of many Chileans as she argues that "the families [of those who disappeared or were detained and tortured] feel emptiness in the area of moral and public revindication of the victims . . . that there is "a veil of impunity" over the human rights abusers and that the amnesty law should be either annulled or reformed." The general secretary of the presidency, Enrique Correa, responded that "the government will not promote any initiatives geared to modify the Amnesty Law because the political conditions are not favorable."[46]

The words of Mr. Correa are quite useful to understand the dilemma of the posttransition government in this area. Clearly the administration and the parties in the coalition would like to see a degree of justice done in this area. But the present political structure simply does not provide for any effective tools to prosecute the members of the military and police involved in human rights violations. General Pinochet has managed not only to maintain control of the armed forces but also exercise a veto power over the elected officials through the "authoritarian enclaves" that exist throughout the system and threats to the civilian authorities.

Conclusion

In the body of this chapter I delineate the major characteristics of the political and economic systems of Chile during three different periods: between 1925 and 1973, during the Pinochet regime, and during the Aylwin administration. During each of these periods the analysis has focused on the characteristics and compatibility of political and economic systems. Between 1925 and 1973 one sees the expansion of the political system and the political arena, as well as the expansion of the economic and social functions of the state and attempts to democratize not only the political system, but also the distribution of wealth. From this perspective, the imbalance between political expansion and improvements in distribution of wealth was central to the crisis in the late sixties. In other words, the deepening of political democracy was not followed by any form of economic democracy given the veto power of the Right over legislation. When economic changes began, the democratic process was halted.

The Pinochet regime was characterized by the concentration of power in the hands of General Pinochet and a small group of advisors, as well as the atomization of the society through a set of economic and social reforms, reinforced by the widespread use of repression. The market policies produced, at the same time, a concentration of capital and economic power that mirrored the concentration of political power. Authoritarianism and neoliberalism were just "las dos caras de la misma moneda."

What we have seen after military rule is a limited transition both in the political and the economic areas. The institutional framework for transition designed by the Pinochet regime has not been substantially changed, given the nature of the electoral laws and the requirements to modify the constitution. Furthermore, there have been only marginal reforms in social policy, while in the human rights area the military and the police officers remain protected by laws passed during the Pinochet regime.

To the extent that both the government and the opposition have recognized and accepted the institutionality inherited from the past, democracy in Chile will remain limited. There is no question that from the standpoint of the political elite a slow transition and the maintenance of this "authoritarian democracy" is not necessarily a problem; on the contrary, it might be a blessing in disguise since it isolates the regime from pressures from below. The dramatic decline of the Left only reinforces this situation since it deprives the lower-income groups from their traditional channels of representation.

Thus, the current political and economic discussion is limited by the structures inherited from the past and the disappearance of the Left. In this context it seems reasonable to suggest that the "deepening" of the democratic system is going to be slow at best and that General Pinochet's policies will continue defining the basic parameters of the process.

The Symbolic Value of Economists in the Democratization of Chilean Politics

VERÓNICA MONTECINOS

Introduction

The present wave of democratization has merged with another recent worldwide trend: the rise of economists to high political office.[1] Often, it is the incompatibility of these two trends that analysts find so striking. The growing power of technocrats is viewed as a serious—and inevitable—threat to the nature and the conduct of democratic politics. In contemporary Latin America, democratic practices appear eroded from within, as technocrats dictate the content of presidential decrees, bypassing parties and other representative institutions.[2] The Chilean case suggests, however, that the relationship between the political ascent of professional economists and the reality of democracy contains some interesting and unexplored complexities.[3]

During the process of transition to democracy, opposition economists became massively incorporated into party life. Some have remained in traditional roles as specialists in technical matters. Others have moved up as party leaders. Many party economists were employed in liaison roles, representing the party in public events, writing for the press, and taking up tasks typically performed by party bureaucrats. From the right to the left, parties now have economists running for office and managing the parties' internal affairs.

In this chapter, I emphasize the political significance of cultural and organizational forms to analyze the apparently singular way in which economist-politicians may have, and have not, contributed to the restoration and deepening of democracy in Chile.

Chilean Economists in Politics

In Chile, the rise of economists to positions of political power has followed a gradual and incremental trajectory.[4] In the 1950s, economists constituted a small and rather marginal professional group. In 1960, President Alessandri, himself a right-wing pragmatic entrepreneur and an outspoken skeptic of the economics profession, appointed for the first time an economist to head the Ministry of Economy. However, the control of economic policy remained in the hands of others, mainly engineers and businessmen. President Frei went further, making economists chief executives at the Central Bank and other economic agencies. Despite these appointments, the power of economists remained limited. Economists did not dominate the key Ministry of Finance, and they often complained that their plans did not receive enough consideration. Under Allende, economists advanced still a bit further, but it was under Pinochet that economists finally achieved hegemonic control.[5] The Chicago Boys dominated various policy areas, displacing lawyers and other professionals. In fact, according to a former justice minister, the "non-economists" in the Pinochet government felt "like insects."[6]

Far from reversing this trend to power, the transition to democracy has reinvigorated it. Economists' growing involvement in party politics in the 1980s contributed to moderate ideological differences and strengthened pragmatism and unity within the opposition. In 1990, President Patricio Aylwin named economists as ministers of finance, economy, public works, education, planning, and labor. Even the highly political post of minister secretary of the presidency was occupied by an economist. The Central Bank, the Budget Bureau, and various undersecretaryships were headed by economists. The economic team, forming the core of what Aylwin liked to call his "supraparty" administration, was remarkably stable and successful in the implementation of a coherent set of policies that emphasized fiscal prudence, economic growth, limited redistribution, and a basic commitment to a market economy.[7] This strategic policy design was maintained after President Frei Ruiz-Tagle took office in 1994. Although the parties strengthened their role, the Frei administration was also defined as supraparty in character, and the number of economists appointed as cabinet members (in finance, economy, public works, education, labor, and health) and in other high posts remained high.

The growing prominence of economists in government has been compounded by the role that economists are playing as leaders of political parties.[8] How can we account for the visibility of economists in party politics? How can we explain the apparent readiness with which the old party elites have entered into a form of cohabitation with economists-turned-politicians?[9] Answers to these questions seem to require an exploration of the organizational nature of political parties.[10]

By thinking of parties as organizations, we discover the relevance of arguments recently advanced by institutionalist theorists in sociology and political science. Institutionalists tell us that one cannot understand changes in the structure and behavior of organizations without paying attention to the context in which they operate. Organizations must display visible signs of conformity to environmental demands in order to receive legitimacy and support.

Proponents of institutionalism urge us to no longer treat culture as if it were a residual variable in the analysis of organizational and political phenomena.[11] In this view, rules, norms, taken-for-granted assumptions, conventions, routines, and symbols support the production and reproduction of social and political arrangements. "Political democracy depends not only on economic and social conditions but also on the design of political institutions. [Institutions] are arenas for contending social forces but they are also collections of standard operating procedures and structures that define and defend values, norms, interests, identities and beliefs. . . . rituals, ceremonies, stories and drama permeate politics."[12]

Following the 1973 military coup, the institutional order that had supported Chilean politics for most of the century collapsed and new forms of legitimation emerged. For more than a decade, political parties looked for refuge and continuity among other civil organizations, struggling to survive in an environment dominated by the logics of repression and technocratism. Women's groups, religious institutions, mother's clubs, soup kitchens, cultural groups, and research institutes kept the parties alive. However, the "demobilization" of society did not lead to its "depoliticization."[13]

By the end of the 1980s, it was clear that parties had successfully reclaimed their legitimacy as central political actors. But in the process, political parties had to accommodate to a new set of institutionalized rules and highly rationalized myths. The origins of these rules and myths must be traced, in part, to two developments: First, the practical and symbolic reinforcements that the professional claims of government economists provided to Pinochet's dictatorial state. Second, the growing worldwide political influence of the economics profession.[14]

Crisis and Change in Institutional Environments

Chileans had come to take for granted that their collective identity, national pride, and sense of social order were embedded in their respect for the rules of constitutional government and democratic politics. The professional code of the military stressed political abstinence and subordination to civilian authority. Politicians carried out the task of compromising over policies, and class and group interests, and were generally respected public figures.

The party system was the most highly structured in the region, with relatively cohesive and disciplined organizations and stable electoral cleavages.[15] Chilean parties played a role in the recruitment of state personnel as well as in the formulation of state strategies for development and social reform. Electoral contests were frequent and deeply rooted in the loyalty to party subcultures. Parties served important instrumental and expressive functions—job opportunities, family life, and even forms of speech were influenced by party affiliation.

In the 1960s, maximalist ideological rhetorics, more acute redistributive conflicts, and new forms of political violence challenged the traditional compromising style of political elites and the incrementalist nature of reforms. The fragility of the party system became exposed as centrifugal tendencies came to dominate in a dynamics of polarized pluralism.[16] Signs of strain also appeared in civil-military relations. At the time of the coup, mounting economic problems added gravity to a generalized sense of uncertainty and crisis. Yet the legitimacy of democratic traditions remained fundamentally unquestioned.

The military takeover developed into a lasting authoritarian regime only with a frontal assault on the taken-for-granted assumptions of Chilean politics. Although armed resistance from Allende's followers was largely irrelevant, the coup leaders promptly redefined the climate of crisis as a situation of war in order to guarantee military compliance and control over the population.[17] In the official rhetoric, the state of internal war was a step in the achievement of progress, harmony, moral renewal, and patriotism in civic affairs. The political traditions of civilian rule were officially scorned as corrupt, inefficient, divisive, and corrosive to the national interest.

Rites of degradation, including assassination, torture, and imprisonment, fell upon new and ever-expanding categories of enemies, subversives, terrorists, traitors, or simple dissenters. Congress was closed. Parties were subject to a recess (in 1973) and were eventually dissolved (in 1977). Party leaders were harassed or persecuted, political meetings were outlawed, party property was confiscated, and party access to the media was impeded. The void left by the elimination of Congress, political parties, unions, and a weak judiciary was gradually filled by the secret police, military courts, ad hoc committees, technocrats, and General Pinochet in his dual role as president and commander in chief of the army.[18]

Seventeen years of control over state powers provided the regime enough time and plenty of resources to attempt the institutionalization of a new structure of power, to erode old conceptions about the appropriateness of values and institutions, and to promote a whole new set of social routines and cultural forms. Pinochet and selective groups of loyalists[19] took their gradual accumulation of extraordinary powers as a unique historical opportunity to bring about a revolution of vast proportions.

The Rationalization of Governance

Great efforts were centered on the foundation of a new normative order. As one of their most central concerns, regime leaders engaged in the design of institutions unpolluted by the vices of politicization. Politicians had no place in the foundation of the new Chile, for their practices and their language were dangerous and irresponsible. The commitment to effectiveness and order was symbolized with the rituals of coercion and the rhetoric of scientific management. The values of discipline and patriotism and the comforts of consumerism and modernization would make people learn to appreciate the virtues of the new system—even if policies resulted in years of sacrifice, bankruptcies, and unemployment.

Initially, it was the imposition of economic policies of stabilization to deal with the immediate crisis of shortages and inflation that produced Pinochet's approval. The most radical group among government economists forcefully argued that short-term solutions had to be linked to a reversal of forty years of "wrong" economic policies, excessive state interventionism, bureaucratic privileges, and political patronage. Counting on Pinochet's support, inspired neoconservative economists began advancing a comprehensive experiment that included the deregulation of financial markets, extensive trade liberalization, and the privatization of state assets and functions. In short, a new system of governance was created.[20]

Economic experts had been consulted before. Frei and Allende had encouraged their economic teams to create new bureaucratic agencies in order to implement plans and extend executive control over regional and sectoral policy. However, the suspension of politics and the systematic use of repression allowed for a qualitative shift in the influence of technocrats.

The Chicago Boys (former graduate students at the University of Chicago were key figures in the economic team) attempted to demystify the state as the embodiment of the common good, attributing inefficiencies to the self-interested behavior of bureaucrats and politicians.[21] They advised that only the most "modern" tools of the economics profession should provide the basis for policy analysis. Economists met little challenge to their rhetoric of neutrality,[22] professional competence, and revolutionary vehemence. Opposition economists were ridiculed as *gásfiters* (plumbers), marginal members of the profession. Politicians and other social activists were silenced, in exile or in prison.[23] Critical entrepreneurs appeared as biased, recriminating the authorities for their own inefficiencies. Lawyers, although useful in providing a semblance of legality in a country so devoted to legalism, could not advance any comprehensive vision of their own.[24]

Under the protection of Pinochet's powers and their own professional authority, neoliberal economists led a vast process of rationalization of government structures. The use of scientific methods and the widespread adoption of rational models of decision making would confirm that rituals of interest representation and the role of political parties in policy making were not only nefarious but irrelevant and obsolete. Economists' methods, language, and myths became institutionalized conventions.[25] The regime's choice of the "right experts" was not dictated by the technical complexity of the problems it confronted. After all, policy decisions always involve conflicts and even when the experts try hard at choosing rationally, ambiguity remains pervasive. It was the legitimacy of their policy-making style that became essential in the Chicago Boys' rise to power.

Econometric models and other bureaucratic rituals attempted to eliminate redundant state employment, fiscal sanity, administrative decentralization, and efficiency and effectiveness in all policy areas. The alleged apoliticism of the Chicago Boys and their ideology of rationality[26] contributed to the introduction of unpopular measures, as well as to the enforced compliance of reluctant bureaucrats,[27] skeptical (statist and nationalist) generals, and unfriendly entrepreneurs. Pinochet himself needed to justify his claim to a major place in history, "and neoliberalism seemed to coincide with his dream of creating a prosperous nation free from ideological conflict."[28]

The economic team appeared as the most cosmopolitan group in the administration, in tune with ideological debates in industrialized countries, where managerial mentalities attacked the incompetence and rigidity of public institutions and promoted privatization, under the assumption that the "government was not the solution to problems, government *was* the problem."[29] Enthusiastic reactions to the economic model among international circles of academics, bankers, and multilateral lenders gave crucial resources and a needed break from criticisms of political repression.[30] In dismantling the state apparatus, Pinochet "wanted to be ahead of both Reagan and Thatcher."

Control over the training and the recruitment of successive generations of economists into the government bureaucracy generated a large pool of individuals who had learned only the free-market catechism.[31] Eager to join the top ranks of what had become the most prestigious profession in the country, young economists faithfully applied the rules transmitted by their mentors and gladly staffed government agencies. Even when these appointments took them to provincial outposts, novel economists perceived the opportunity for professional advancement, especially when, in exchange for their government service, they were offered scholarships and other forms of aid to continue their studies abroad.

The economic team was large, powerful, and driven by ideological fervor, but how much was actually achieved in its attempt to rationalize government? Institutionalists tell us that although administrative reorganizations are often frustrated because of bureaucratic inertia, government reorganizations constitute "symbolic and rhetorical events" in which "outcomes can be less significant than process."[32]

Despite fluctuations in economic performance,[33] the Chicago Boys were able to maintain their influence. Their reforms produced outcomes of enormous consequence. Substantive changes were introduced in the areas of tariffs, finance, and industry. There was a massive privatization of state enterprises; services in education, social security, labor, agriculture, and health were transferred from the state to the private sector. In the early 1990s, Chile was widely regarded as a showcase of successful marketization. I stress here, however, the political consequences were as important as the policy results. Government reforms by economists under Pinochet created and legitimated a new concept of politics-as-administration at considerable odds with the old habits of Chilean party politics.

Organizational Changes and Party Modernization

Faced with fast changes in the country's political economy and with the uncertainties of a protracted process of regime transition, Chilean parties had little choice but to adjust their structures and routines to what had become the prevailing assumptions about the relationship between politics and policy making. Denied access to public resources, and with their existence as political institutions questioned, parties looked for alternative material resources and new principles of legitimation to survive as organizations and reconstitute a viable party system to govern after the transition to democracy.

Institutionalist theorists emphasize that organizations conforming to the technical and institutional demands of their environments maximize their legitimacy and increase their survival capabilities.[34] Under democratic conditions, political parties face competitive pressures for measurable results as well as strong institutional pressures. When elections are banned and ideological discourses are silenced, institutional demands for increased rationalization become paramount.

The type and extent of the adjustments that individual parties made to enhance their chances of organizational survival after the coup were influenced by the way in which the military regime targeted each of them, by their location in the party system, and by their own organizational history. Internal power struggles and shifts in the respective dominant coalitions were also important in determining the direction and the pace of the adjustments. Far from constituting automatic responses to new environmental demands, organizational changes in parties remained partial, tentative, and controversial.

Those closer to the center of the party system tried to demonstrate their seriousness as contenders for government control by signaling their disposition to comply with some of the new rituals of appropriate governance. Pragmatic alliances and the visible deployment of economists were among the variety of strategies that these parties adopted to deal with their organizational vulnerability.[35] Farther to the left in the party system, these professionalizing trends did not find fertile terrain.

Sectors of the Right, identified with neoliberalism, supported the "modernizing" thrust of Pinochet's technocrats and entered the democratic transition with newly founded parties, hoping to capitalize on the regime's economic accomplishments and on their own organizational innovations.[36]

In 1983, when the first hints of a political opening appeared, a group of the most ideologically inclined technocrats of the administration founded UDI (Union Demócrata Independiente), now the second largest party on the right. As several economists occupied leadership positions in UDI, the neutrality of the market and the depoliticization of intermediate organizations were converted into key ideological concepts. Why did economists become party leaders? "Because they came up with new recipes, they broke with the traditional way of doing politics. . . . Many party lawyers feel they are a generation in close affinity with economists. Lawyers and economists in the party are on the same wavelength."[37]

The nontraditional background of UDI leaders (at one point, Julio Dittborn and Joaquín Lavín, two young economists with government experience, were made party president and secretary-general) helped to distance the party from the style of the old political Right.[38] UDI promoted the political mobilization of the business community, afraid that populists could return to govern. Party members formed think tanks to shape the tone and direction of policy debates and tried to adopt new political technologies, including polling and the use of computers for grassroots lobbying.

Renovación Nacional (RN), formed in 1987, became the largest party on the right. Its core came from the traditional political Right and it is a party dominated by lawyers. However, as party leaders hurried to acknowledge that "the lack of an economic team in the party constitutes a weakness," efforts were made to recruit conspicuous members of the economics profession.[39] Some party lawyers were glad to be provided with new kinds of information and arguments that could make the party appear as a "modern" conservative party.[40] More traditional politicians have actively resisted these attempts to "modernize" the party. Internal struggles in RN are often described as intractable. But in the opinion of a former party leader with training in economics, these conflicts constitute only a stage in the evolution to a more professionalized party. He said: "At the beginning, the old politicians had difficulties following the arguments of economists. While they focused on the political power of unions and entrepreneurs, the economists looked at bargaining and economic consequences." Talking about his own experience he said: "I knew I had committed a huge mistake on the second day. I wanted to work with a calendar, I wanted things to be thought out, programmed. The old politicians said, 'don't worry, things must be resolved as they come'. . . . that is, 'al tufo' [a folk expression for intuitive judgment]." In his opinion, although the tensions between the old and the younger party members remain, there has been "like a fusion: Jarpa (the old party leader) becomes more of an economist and Piñera becomes more of a politician. . . . Now the party operates with programs, phases, and meetings with agendas."[41]

In RN, economists are seen as inducing the party to pay higher political costs than necessary, especially among landowners and other traditional constituencies. Economists tend to reject party discipline, are not willing to sacrifice their professional autonomy and reputation, like to work only with other economists, and ignore the authority of party leaders, even when voting on important legislation in Congress. One of Piñera's main advisors, an economics professor who was not affiliated with the party, readily admitted: "Sebastián has trouble with the 'cúpulas' but he does well with the people. The people will vote for the candidate best qualified to solve the country's problems."[42]

On the political Right, the conception that economists have appropriate answers not only to technical problems but also to the concerns of the general public is far from constituting a generalized belief.[43] However, many signs point to the erosion and discredit of the style used by party notables in the past. The place of those who meet at the party headquarters to "talk about politics" is being disputed. Economists are seen as contributing to the emergence of a "modern conception of politics," a more professionalized approach, in which parties can be "managed" like a business. "In economics what counts is the allocation of resources. And that is precisely what political movements aspire to," said an economist of RN. That party's secretary-general, a lawyer, told me: "What would I do without economists! They facilitate relations with entrepreneurs, improve the party's finances and advise legislators."[44]

On the left, economists' entrance to party politics also generated relevant controversies. After the coup, issues of security and revolutionary morale became far more important for the Communist party than the incorporation of economic or technical elements. Members of the Communist party turned inward, toward their own party subculture, as they sought shelter from unrelenting persecution.[45]

The Communist party had traditionally had a relatively small cadre of *técnicos*, although by the mid-1980s, many party members had received professional training while in exile. One such party economist said in 1988: "There is no money to form a technical department in the party . . . [and] creativity is less important than the political work. In the Instituto Lipschutz [where party *técnicos* gathered] the science of economics has been revalued and efforts are being made to incorporate technical elements into the political strategy. But the Lipschutz group is ahead of the party leaders."[46] Outsiders perceived the tensions between groups of professionals and the direction of the party as a schism between the *"PC culto* [illustrated] and *the PC oculto* [clandestine]." Unprecedented dissidence and a series of resignations and expulsions shook the party, but the traditional orthodoxy was kept intact.

When street protests first emerged, ten years after the coup, and opposition parties initiated a more active collaboration, the Communist party had already discontinued its old policy of alliances, opting for a strategy of military confrontation and popular insurrection against the regime. Since then, the Communists remained isolated from concertationist efforts and the mediating role played by party economists in other opposition groups did not develop. Little of the "renovation" experienced among the Socialists ever emerged.

Persecution and exile made the Socialist party break up into several factions that reunited only shortly before the 1989 presidential and congressional elections. In one of the main factions, called "renovated," exile was a learning experience in internationalism. Party intellectuals, many of them economists, lived the conservative revival in North America and Europe, the crises of marxism, eurocommunism, and the *socialismos reales* and, from those experiences, elaborated a new, more pragmatic, political vision. One observer noted that "The *renovación* points not only to a re-foundation of socialism but to a true re-foundation of politics."[47]

By contrast, the PS Almeyda (a group led by Clodomiro Almeyda, a former university professor and minister under Allende) was known as the *históricos* because of its emphasis in maintaining the revolutionary traditions of the Socialist party. The organizational reconstruction of this sector was undertaken by younger militants who favored a confrontational approach to the dictatorship and paid little attention to the party's economic thinking or the formation of an economic team.[48] For them, the more "intellectualized" conception of politics, typical of the "renovated" wing of the party, was an object of disdain. These leaders were proud that they "never got a doctorate degree [in a foreign university]. They remained closer to the reality of the country."[49]

Economists' ascending influence within the opposition was also noticeable among the Christian Democrats. At CIEPLAN and other think tanks, prestigious members of the profession received international support and growing national attention.[50] A process of ideological moderation within the party and the shift from a strategy of hegemonic domination to one of alliances and coalitions were facilitated by the congregational capabilities of these economic teams.[51]

However, as the organization of a united front against Pinochet was delayed for several years,[52] the parties and the party system were deemed partly responsible for the slow pace of the regime transition. Opposition analysts emphasized the need to increase trust and "rationalize the political debate," to prevent a new escalation of confrontational rhetoric and over-ideologization.[53] Politicians, even in those ranks, appeared as "too provincial," having lost initiative and legitimacy.

To the extent that the political class was seen as inept, afflicted by problems of personalism, excessive factionalism, and lack of trust, and trapped in a discourse of recriminations, guilt, and self-doubts, politically talented economists began to capitalize on the structural and perceived weaknesses of politicians. The dispersion and atomization of the political class made it possible for many economists to construct their political identities outside the traditional channels of party machines. Alejandro Foxley reflected on his own involvement in politics: "Politicians lost practice in the exercise of their profession. Their performance is torpid. . . . I get tired of waiting for the moment when I can work as a macroeconomist, so I ask myself, where can I be most effective now? The answer is: in politics."[54]

Groups of "modernizers" or "renovators" among the Christian Democrats and Socialists signaled their commitment to realism and pragmatism, adopting a public language and ceremonial behaviors typical of rationalistic models of decision making. The idea that more accurate information leads to better decisions and more successful policy implementation was behind the campaign for the modernization of politics.

Although many economists did not have credentials as good party members, they possessed a number of other valuable assets, including externally validated roles, their strong professional reputations, and their expertise. In order to strengthen their positions, political parties were compelled to incorporate economists and their contributions. Opposition economists had the academic degrees, the language, and the arguments to dispute the hegemony of the Chicago Boys. With prominent economists in opposition parties, Pinochet and his technocrats could no longer disqualify the opposition on the grounds of insufficient analytic capacity or irresponsible conceptions in the management of public affairs.

The involvement of economists in party life offered the opposition new opportunities to resume the public space. "It was easier to criticize the economic policy (managed by civilians) than to call attention to the violation of human rights," said a Socialist economist. One of his colleagues added, "In order to avoid prison, parties asked economists what to say." Economists could also more easily discuss economic issues in which politicians and even entrepreneurs felt insecure.[55] In Almeyda's critical perspective: "The politicians assume that the *técnicos* are correct because they do not want to think."[56]

Moreover, economists had good contacts with foreign foundations, academic centers, and international organizations.[57] They helped the parties obtain the financing of research projects and improved the parties' capability to generate and process information relevant to policy making. Economists helped to convince the public that the parties were modern, concerned with rational principles of administration, and therefore worthy of increased confidence and credibility.

To be sure, resistance to the penetration of this new type of expert/politician existed.[58] After all, economists are widely known for their critical stance regarding party politics, their intolerance of the irrationalities and ambiguities of political life, their intellectual arrogance, and the many biases that currently typify their professional training, which has become increasingly dependent on formal empiricism and very prone to forgetting the needs of the world outside academia.[59] The party bureaucrats and activists, those who had the resources and knowledge that under normal circumstances made the party exist, resented the change of style and feared a loss of power.

Even though economists and their ideas were not easily assimilated into the parties, they could be displayed as a sign of external legitimation.[60] The creation of research institutes, loosely coupled to party structures and staffed mainly by economists, was an important way of coping with these internal conflicts. While the rest of the party remained heavily atomized, attached to old conventions, and operating in precarious clandestinity, these institutes could respond to the rationalistic conventions of the new institutional order and show technical sophistication and political flexibility in their policy analyses.

Organizational theorists tell us that in times of crisis or exceptional environmental turbulence, task forces and informal structures are created.[61] The dialogue among economists was seen as instrumental in facilitating interparty negotiations. "Economists can influence their peers in other parties," said a politician. A Christian Democratic economist told me: "I attend political negotiations because on the other sides, they have economists. . . . Economists talk to each other in the same language. They have many similarities, they form a confraternity."[62]

In the search for political agreement, the image of moderation, independence, and pragmatism possessed by economists had a particularly high symbolic value. "To move in the direction of political consensus, it is necessary to supersede the party mentality and work out agreements on concrete issues, and on empirical evidence, not on general ideas," said a member of CED, one of the private research institutes where the opposition met.[63] When economist Sergio Molina (a finance minister in the 1960s) convened opposition personalities in the Acuerdo Nacional, in 1985, "he began to be more important than the people he convened," I was told in one of the interviews. Molina explained his mediating role: "I am perceived as the least Christian Democrat. They see me as honest, less sectarian, more flexible."[64]

As more concrete programs were elaborated and discussed within the opposition, it became apparent that even small parties could enhance their political presence with a strong economic team. By contrast, "If politicians go nude, they do not enter the fashion show."[65] Slowly, concerns for factual rigor and technical specificity became more central. The old-style politicians felt less resourceful, although they were still powerful. "There is a fear of making technical errors." Gabriel Valdés talked about the transformation of Chilean politics in these terms: "Politics is becoming less driven by illusions and more by reality. In the past, there was not enough consideration of the costs and benefits of expansive policies. . . . Economists have contributed more precision, but they do not easily win over their respective parties. The opposition has found areas of agreement in the debate over economic problems, but the political leadership is not yet permeated by these agreements. At CED we propose very concrete solutions. They are forced to recognize the realities."[66]

Conclusion

The conspicuous display of economists by parties in posttransition Chile signals a new conformity with new rituals that supposedly grant political legitimacy: the concern for policy effectiveness, macroeconomic stability, and international competitiveness. In this sense, the political visibility of economists showed that parties were committed to make political transition and democracy "work." Political elites have brought economists to the upper levels of party leadership not simply because they needed their technical expertise with increasingly complex and specialized problems.[67] Chilean parties have incorporated economists in response to some of the same pressures that government agencies around the world have been facing in the last few decades. In a world dominated by rapidly changing and unpredictable economic forces, it is the need to cope with the uncertainties that those environmental changes generate that gives economists an advantage over others. As economists are called on to reduce the kind of anxiety that modern politicians fear most, they manage to acquire their own bases of power.

Of course, since policy outcomes are mostly beyond their control, economists cannot guarantee that their policies will not result in economic disaster and political defeat. But at least, the very presence of economists with appropriate credentials at the top of decision-making structures can serve as an indicator that efforts were made to comply with the accepted standards of professional practice and that all necessary measures were taken to secure approval in the inner circles of economic wisdom and international finance, to which economists have privileged access. In this sense, government and party elites, like leaders in many other modern organizations, are more likely to stress the ceremonial dimensions of their performance over the quantification of the actual results of their actions.[68]

The employment of economists as party leaders can also be interpreted as a case of "structural isomorphism," a concept that analysts of organizations have elaborated to describe the manner in which organizations in a given field become increasingly homogeneous, and more similar in their structure and actions.[69] Isomorphism is the result of imitation and compliance with normative or coercive pressures from the environment.

By offering economists a chance to advance from the role of advisors to the role of political leaders, parties are not only simply duplicating a well-established pattern found in state bureaucracies. In order to cope with the uncertainties of the transition and the changes brought about by a long period of authoritarian rule, Chilean political parties have imitated each other in a race to attract the most prestigious economists to their ranks.

Economists are expected to provide parties with the appropriate methods to manage their internal finances, the right kind of guidance in their dialogue with government policy makers, international foundations, banks, and private entrepreneurs. Economists are also expected to facilitate the access of parties to international networks of communications, banks, and foundations. Economists are seen as a safeguard against old forms of populism and traditional practices of clientelism. Above all, economists serve a symbolic function. Their presence indicates a respectful compliance with a new ritual. In a world in which democracy is equated with successful marketization, they have become a basic source of legitimacy.

Conflicts over the degree of autonomy granted to professionals is a common theme in the study of organizations. Since people with specialized training tend to look beyond organizational boundaries for guidance and approval, bureaucratic (or political) controls do not easily adjust to their specific demands and contributions. Party professionals face this dilemma in an acute way. They cannot publicly criticize the party, but, as professionals, they cannot afford to lose face vis-à-vis their peers.[70]

Interviews with party officials indicate the tensions involved in the political activism of economists. Parties have a hard time explaining to their constituencies the arguments that their own economists defend. On the right, economists often introduce ideas that go against the interests of landowners and industrialists. When an economist at RN argued that, "A policy to protect *only sixty* fruit exporters does not make sense," politicians representing agricultural districts wanted to see him expelled from the party. On the left, unions and the less "renovated" leftist leaders question the extent to which socialist economists have gone too far in their "neoliberal" concerns, their emphasis on productivity, and guarantees for private investment and economic liberalization.

Many in Chile have interpreted the political visibility of economists as a transitory phenomenon that responded to a specific phase of the transition process.

Therefore, it would fade away once parties reestablished their identities under truly democratic rules. Some believe that the deideologization of politics has been superficial and that the modernization of party structures is still at an embryonic stage. By focusing not so much the content of the economists' contribution to changes in party life, but rather the symbolic impact of economists in political institutions, this analysis has broadened the question of economists and the character of democracy in posttransition Chile. The historical record indicates that Chilean technocrats are replaced by politicians when the economy gets into real trouble. That was the case under Alessandri in 1961, Frei in 1967, Allende in 1972, and Pinochet in 1982. However, even in the absence of an economic crisis, it may be possible for politicians to supplant technocrats and pursue the (re)construction of democracy in Chile.

Direct Appeals, Political Machines, and Reform

Deepening Democracy in Brazil, 1985–1995

KURT VON METTENHEIM

Introduction

This volume argues that the central task for deepening democracy in Latin America is to link competitive party-electoral politics to open, pluralistic styles of governance. This article reviews Brazil's first ten years of civilian rule from 1985–1995 to suggest that after an initial period of caretaker government under President Jose Sarney from 1985–1989, and a period of plebiscitary adventurism with President Fernando Collor de Mello from 1990–1992, the election of President Fernando Henrique Cardoso in 1994 combines new movements for political reform with traditional mechanisms of competitive mass politics in Brazil. To understand the prospects for deepening democracy through plebiscitarian appeals, alliances with patronage machines, and the implementation of political reform in Brazil, scholars must shift away from concepts and theories derived from European experiences with parliamentary government and civil-society–driven change. In their stead, new comparative perspectives are needed to recognize the different trajectories of democratization through direct popular appeals, fluid alliances with patronage machines, and political reform, which are typical of presidential and federal systems in the Americas.

Shifting the comparative perspective from Europe to the Americas reveals the extent to which presidential institutions shaped Brazilian politics from 1985–1995. Despite the legacies of military rule and the lack of presidential elections until 1989, the separate and direct election of executives and legislatures encouraged popular appeals and permitted the nomination of party professionals directly to executive posts and administrative offices.[1] These mechanisms of mass politics typical of presidential institutions also produced a trajectory of political development also typical within this form of government; a rapid and sweeping reorganization of party-electoral politics through a sequence of alliances between national political elites and diverse regional and local patronage machines. During and after the critical events of transition, the broad popular appeals of campaigns for executive offices defined new issues and created new leaders, often in quite volatile, even plebiscitarian terms. Once elected, executives deftly negotiated electoral alliances and legislative coalitions because they were free to distribute administrative appointments. Regarding economic policy, a creative sequence of economic packages from 1986–1994 permitted Brazilian governments to avert hyperinflation without imposing orthodox measures of severe fiscal and monetary austerity.

However, despite the rapid sequence of changes during the first ten years of civilian rule in Brazil (1985–1995), the mechanisms of precocious political development typical of presidential and federal systems failed to fully materialize.[2] A central reason is that direct presidential elections were not held until 1989. Even then, the traditional mechanisms of Brazilian presidentialism were not fully in place. Since 1932, the Brazilian electoral system has combined direct elections for executive office with legislative elections through proportional representation in an effort to ameliorate the populist and plebiscitarian character of presidentialism.[3] While this traditional combination of legislative and executive elections diffuses power and encourages political alliances, the 1989 presidential election was held in isolation. This contributed to a pattern that is a central concern of this volume; that, after transition from military rule in Latin America, competitive politics may simply be grafted onto exclusive policy-making styles in centralized executives.

This same concern about the deleterious consequences of centralized governance pervades classic analyses of Brazilian politics. Indeed, a retrospective glance through Brazilian history suggests that central elements of Brazilian politics emerged from a process best described as the grafting of liberal and democratic institutions adopted from abroad onto Brazil's patrimonial society. Observers of the Brazilian Empire (1822–1899) argue that rural patriarchs simply reorganized their clientele into voting blocks after Dom Pedro I introduced universal free male suffrage after independence from Portugal in 1824. Writers of Brazil's first republican constitution in 1891 attempted to decentralize imperial power by adopting federal institutions from the United States. However, governors (then called presidents) rapidly asserted their dominance and created single state parties.

After Getulio Vargas's Estado Novo (1937–1945) reversed this devolution of power to regional oligarchs by centralizing state agencies and organizing working class and popular sectors into corporatist institutions, the period of competitive politics that followed (1945–1964) once again reflected the grafting of competitive elections onto centralized policy-making styles. Indeed, a path-breaking analysis in Brazilian political studies is Souza's argument that the irresponsible leadership that led to the breakdown of democracy in 1964 can be traced to the lack of access by party politicians to the key policy decisions of the time. Because core issues of economic policy remained under the exclusive control of presidents and their policy teams, legislators and party politicians were reduced to trafficking patronage and oratorical promises.[4]

The protracted transition from military to civilian rule (1974–1985) also contributed to this problem of grafting competitive elections onto centralized policy making in executive offices. Military leaders in Brazil first liberalized elections for legislative offices in 1974, but the transfer of power to civilians occurred only eleven years later. Juan Linz insightfully described the peculiar coexistence of directly elected governors and military government on the national level, which lasted from 1982–1985, as a somewhat extreme situation of diarchy or dual power.[5] Rather than a means for selecting new civilian political elites, elections during Brazil's "Long Road of Liberalization" served as mechanisms, first for military elites to liberalize their rule, then for negotiations between military leaders and opposition groups.[6] In sum, both military government and the prolonged, ambiguous transition to civilian rule widened the traditional gap between competitive party-electoral politics and centralized policy making in Brazil.

Can competitive party-electoral politics be linked to pluralistic patterns of governance to deepen democracy in Brazil? Although analysis of recent events may be premature, the movements for the moralization of Brazilian public life that produced the impeachment of President Collor in late 1992 and the election of Fernando Henrique Cardoso in 1994 suggest that significant changes may be underway. Indeed, the failure of President Collor's bold policy initiatives arose from his inability to maintain intermediary links between state and society through negotiations with political parties and interest organizations of business, labor, and other groups. Immediately upon inauguration in 1990, President Collor implemented a dramatic and initially successful series of policies designed to reduce inflation and modernize the economy. But the subsequent unraveling of political support in the face of corruption charges suggests that a new era of political reform and public intolerance for centralized policy making may have arrived. President Collor's impeachment suggests that the direct popular appeals that drive Brazilian politics must be linked to not only viable policies of economic adjustment, but also sustained negotiations with the diverse representatives of political and civil society.

The prospects for linking party-electoral politics to pluralist patterns of governance are considerable because, in comparative perspective, Brazilian governments averted severe monetary and fiscal policies of austerity during the 1980s. The Sarney, Collor, Franco, and Cardoso administrations avoided imposing not only traditional anti-inflationary measures of monetary and fiscal austerity but also rapid measures of privatization and trade liberalization characteristic of Chile, Mexico, and Argentina. Instead, civilian governments in Brazil since 1985 have pursued gradual trade liberalization to encourage the modernization of the country's industrial park while avoiding deindustrialization and the dramatic social consequences of orthodox economic policies. Consequently, economic and social forces in Brazil rely on its large internal market and economies of scale to adapt to the competitive internationalized economy of the 1990s without the severe social and economic consequences produced by austerity programs adopted by other Latin American governments.

Furthermore, the success of President Fernando Henrique Cardoso's gradual, inclusive, and transparent approach to policy making suggests that open, pluralistic governance and effective economic policy are compatible.[7] The Cardoso administration was able to reverse the vicious cycle of policy failure and popular exclusion that predominated during the 1980s in Brazil by linking party-electoral politics and social organizations to governmental initiatives. The failure of seven economic packages to reduce inflation, adjust the economy, and provide sustainable growth from 1985 to 1994 suggests that exclusive policy making by technocratic teams of economists in executive offices is no longer viable in Brazil. All seven economic packages were designed in secret and announced unexpectedly to shock inflationary expectations, freeze prices and wages, and halt speculative market forces in financial and currency exchange markets. Although plans and their economic consequences differed, a common and critical weakness was their lack of support among politicians, the business community, labor, and (after the first Plano Cruzado under Jose Sarney) an increasing popular cynicism about dramatic economic initiatives.

This chapter attempts to understand new patterns of change in Brazil from 1985 to 1995 first by reviewing how patronage, populist appeals, and precocious democratization emerged in Brazilian history. This brief historical review is followed by analysis of how these realities of mass politics both shaped the transition from military to civilian rule in Brazil and generated reform movements that led to the impeachment of President Collor and the election of President Cardoso. After clarifying historical patterns, the mechanisms of precocious democratization, and the emergence of recent political reform movements, this analysis compares President Cardoso's gradual style of governance to the failed economic packages that preceded his presidency. The conclusion returns to the broader concerns about deepening democracy in this volume to explore the implications of Brazil's experience of rapid change within presidential and federal systems since the transition to civilian rule in 1985.

Patronage and Popular Appeals in Brazilian History

A few remarks about the origins of party-electoral patronage during the Brazilian Empire (1822–1889), the organization of Brazilian federalism during the Old Republic (1889–1930), and the trajectory of competitive politics in the postwar period (1945–1964) are in order to clarify both the traditional mechanisms of Brazilian politics and the persistent gap between electoral politics and centralized governance. The first element critical for understanding Brazilian politics is party-electoral patronage.[8] Much of the exceptional trajectory of Brazil in nineteenth-century Latin America is due to the manner in which the national political institutions of the empire were built upon a wide net of party-electoral patronage. Instead of the war, division, and discord that wracked other newly independent nations in Latin America, party-electoral patronage provided solid political links between central imperial institutions and the variety of provincial and local institutions throughout the vast Brazilian territory.

Far from a static characteristic of social structure or Ibero-American culture, patronage in nineteenth-century Brazil is of interest because of its changing political content and context. The classic work of Brazilian political analysts Vianna and Beiguelman suggest that three critical moments defined the organization of patronage during the sixty-seven years of parliamentary monarchy.[9] First, a grant of free male suffrage with low-income requirements by Dom Pedro I upon independence in 1822 transformed the *paternal* clans that ruled the large farms (*fazendas*) and vast rural areas of Brazil into *political* clans. Second, once electoral resources were thereby established, the decentralizing Criminal Code of 1832 encouraged these newly empowered leaders of political clans to resolve conflicts with their counterparts and build institutions on the county level. The final moment of political development during the empire occurred in response to the recentralization of power, beginning with the Additional Act of 1836 and culminating in the 1841 Regency. Political alliances for and against centralization emerged on the national level between existing county (*municipio*) and provincial party-electoral machines. These national political alliances became the Liberal and Conservative parties that dominated Imperial politics until 1889. In sum, the development of patronage during the Brazilian Empire can be understood as a sequence of cumulative responses in party-electoral politics to the adoption of new liberal and monarchic rules and procedures from abroad.

The second element critical for understanding democratization in Brazil is federalism.[10] The authors of Brazil's first republican constitution in 1891 sought to reverse the centralization of state power during the empire by establishing states' rights to contract foreign loans, levy export taxes, write constitutional, criminal, and electoral law, and form autonomous military organizations.[11] Unusual gubernatorial powers were grafted onto this constitutional design when President Campos Salles attempted to avert further civil wars between political factions within states by ruling that federal deputies would be seated only if they were approved by their respective state governors. Governors retained this legal prerogative to seat their congressional delegations throughout the old republic. Governors thereby consolidated single parties within their states and dominated negotiations of electoral alliances and legislative coalitions on the federal level.[12]

After World War II and the end of the Vargas dictatorship, the period of competitive politics from 1945–1964 combined for the first time the mechanisms of change typical of presidential and federal systems in the Americas. Direct elections for president, governor, and mayor were held throughout the 1945–1964 period in Brazil. Once elected, executives freely appointed party politicians to administrative posts. Governors, regional party politicians, and new state elites from Getulio Vargas's Estado Novo thereby linked local patronage machines to their party-electoral organizations which, in turn, were linked to the broad popular appeals of presidential elections through electoral alliances, legislative coalitions, and administrative nominations typical of spoils systems.[13]

In an argument that reflects a central concern of this volume about democracy in Latin America today, Souza argues that competitive elections were simply grafted onto centralized patterns of government policy making after 1945. For Souza, late party development[14] produced a precocious period of democratization from 1945–1964 because candidates for executive office broadened popular appeals and negotiated fluid alliances with the diverse patronage machines on the local and regional level throughout the vast electoral territory of Brazil. Souza's analysis of the 1945–1964 period—which ended in political confrontation and military intervention—first described the trajectory of political development through popular appeals and alliances with patronage machines in Brazil. This analysis seeks to extend Souza's analysis by arguing that the Brazilian experience from 1945–1964 is both typical of political change within presidential and federal systems and central for understanding the prospects for deepening democracy today in Brazil.

Popular Appeals and Patronage Machines from 1985–1995

A rapid series of alliances between national party elites and state and local patronage machines were renegotiated during the transition from military to civilian rule in Brazil.[15] After legislation calling for direct presidential elections was defeated in 1984, several *national* leaders of the government party, PDS (Partido Democratico Social), resigned to form the PFL (Party of the Liberal Front) and negotiate the "Democratic Alliance" with the opposition party PMDB (Partido do Movimento Democratico Brasileiro). Then, during 1985 and 1986, *local* and *regional* politicians rapidly realigned from government parties to the PMDB: first in expectation of the estimated 130,000 federal administrative nominations after President Sarney's inauguration on January 15, and later during 1986 in expectation of perhaps fivefold that number of state-level administrative appointments to be distributed by governors after the 1986 elections.[16] By 1986, many of the mayors and municipal representatives of towns across Brazil that had delivered votes under military rule for the government party had negotiated their affiliation with the PMDB. In sum, while the mechanisms of the distribution of administrative appointments to professional politicians and the rapid realignment of party elites explain much of party-electoral politics through 1986, these elite-centric events failed to deepen democracy because they occurred within the Congress and the restricted electoral college designed by the military.

While direct elections for president were finally held in 1989, the contest exacerbated the plebiscitarian character of presidentialism because it was held in isolation from other legislative and gubernatorial contests.[17] Because elections for governor, as well as federal, state, and municipal legislatures, were scheduled for November 1990, party alliances and machine politics mattered little in 1989. The careers of politicians were not directly at stake in the presidential election. Consequently, instead of being forced to negotiate diverse electoral alliances across Brazil, the 1989 presidential campaign occurred almost exclusively on television.[18] A relatively unknown governor from the small northeast state of Alagoas, Fernando Collor de Mello, was thereby able to dominate the first six months of the campaign through television appearances and denunciations of bureaucratic abuse. After Collor reached over 45 percent in preference polls by June, he refused to participate in the live television debates of the first round (accurately reflecting the damaging prospects of sustained attacks from adversaries).[19] Collor won over 28 percent in first-round voting, with Inacio da Silva (Lula), the candidate for Partido dos Trabalhadores (Worker's Party, PT) entering the runoff election with 16 percent. While Lula dominated the first television debate of the second round and surged in the polls to tie Collor only ten days before the December 15 vote, the Worker's Party candidate failed to dominate the second debate as he did the first and was unable to counter the damaging effect of negative advertising in the final days of the campaign. Collor convinced voters that a victory of Luiz Inacio da Silva and the PT would destabilize society and turn Brazil away from a liberalizing world by mounting a series of personal and political attacks seven days before the final election. On December 15, Collor received 35,089,998 votes (42.7 percent), defeating Lula with 31,076,364 votes (37.8 percent).

Collor's style of policy making and governance confirms that a mix between presidential initiative, popular appeals, and a fluid process of negotiation with legislators are still critical in Brazil. Brazil's first directly elected president after military rule took office in March 1990 as hyperinflation loomed and the country ended its first decade of negative per-capita growth since 1945. Nine months later, few doubted the ability of presidents to initiate and implement policy in Brazil. President Collor reasserted executive authority and shocked investors on 16 March 1990 (the day after inauguration) with a comprehensive plan to reduce inflation, lower the federal deficit, liberalize trade, and modernize the economy. And despite his party's controlling only 5 percent of the Federal Chamber upon inauguration, President Collor confiscated an estimated 80 percent of Brazil's liquid financial assets by decree and unveiled a dramatic package of economic reforms. The Collor administration quickly achieved its short-term economic policy goals, producing government surpluses, reducing interest rates, extending the terms for government paper, and stabilizing the exchange rate.

Throughout 1990, the new administration received strong support from the media and the public (confiscated savings were returned), faced virtually no congressional and little social opposition, and overrode governors who were more concerned with consolidating the support of state and local machines for the 1990 elections than organizing national opposition at the end of their term. But President Collor's policy achievements were only temporary. A central cause of returning inflation was the inability of Collor administration officials to secure a national agreement on wage and price guidelines with business and labor in September 1990.[20] Indeed, once the recession deepened, business support for the Collor administration's neoliberal program rapidly dissipated—a development that confirms the argument presented in the introduction to this volume about splits between business groups and economists in neoliberal coalitions. While the representative organizations of Brazilian business maintained formal support for the market-oriented policies of the government, they increasingly objected to restrictive monetary policies that had forced real interest rates to 65 percent per year (triple the norm) and produced a record number of bankruptcies during 1990. Verbal sparring between Mario Amato, head of the powerful Federação de Industrias do Estado de São Paulo (São Paulo State Federation of Industries, FIESP) and presidential staff increasingly dominated headlines.

In sum, the problems of governance during the Collor administration were not economic or technical, but political. The inability of the Collor Plan to keep inflation low had less to do with policy mistakes than deeply entrenched inflationary expectations and the lack of negotiations between the Collor administration and political and social actors in Brazil. From the international side as well, the unwillingness of the international financial community to reduce Brazilian debt obligations was also political. The lack of debt reduction under Brady Plan initiatives had less to do with the extent of economic adjustment achieved by the new administration than with Brazil's place on the list of political priorities in a new world context of emerging East European economies and post–Persian Gulf geopolitical concerns. For Brazil, this meant returning inflation and recession from 1990 through 1992, a period during which the poor and unorganized fell further behind, while business and other organized sectors of Brazilian society were able to survive because they operate largely unscathed with financial instruments indexed against inflation to function as de facto currencies.

Political Reform: The Impeachment of Collor
and the Election of Cardoso

On 29 September 1992 the Brazilian Chamber of Deputies voted 441 to 38 to suspend President Fernando Collor de Mello from office and initiate a formal trial in the Senate, 76 of 81 of whom subsequently voted on December 29–30 for impeachment.[21] This unprecedented removal of a Brazilian president began in May 1992, when Collor's brother accused the president of extensive involvement in corruption, use of campaign funds for private ends, and participation in the extensive influence peddling organized by his 1989 campaign finance manager. The impeachment of Collor in late December 1992 effectively neutralized campaigns for the adoption of parliamentary government in the plebiscite to be held on 21 April 1993. Instead, 55.4 percent of voters chose to maintain the presidential form of government, while 66 percent chose to maintain a republic.

Soon after the referendum in which Brazilians chose to retain presidential institutions, Foreign Minister Cardoso was called on by then President Itamar Franco (Collor's vice president) to accept the key economic ministry, the Ministerio da Fazenda, on 21 May 1993, a post he retained until assuming campaign duties full-time in May 1994. Far from proposing dramatic initiatives or unveiling economic packages, Cardoso sought to assure business leaders and the public that their lives and investments would no longer be submitted to a sequence of government plans, which tend to radically alter prices, incomes, savings, currency exchange rates, and investment returns. Indeed, by 1993 Brazilians appear to have tired of dramatic initiatives. Since transition to civilian rule in 1985, seven major policy packages and innumerable intermediate adjustments were unexpectedly imposed by the federal government.

Instead, Cardoso adopted a gradualist approach focusing on fiscal reform, monetary restraint, and the need for a more transparent public view of the economic policy process. Repeated ministerial appearances in the media assured Brazilians that inflation was high but stable, that the government was not going to freeze wages and prices or confiscate savings, that draconian adjustment policies would be averted, and that interventions into financial or currency exchange markets would also be minimized. Indeed, the achievements of Cardoso as economic minister were piecemeal, even minor if compared to the dramatic sequence of economic packages preceding his tenure. For example, progress on the fiscal front was secured by negotiating legislative support for a 15 percent reduction of constitutionally mandated transfers from the federal government to states and municipalities in late February. Cardoso subsequently sought to unify the profusion of financial instruments used as de facto currencies because they index against inflation. The Unidade de Valor Real (Real Value Unit, UVR) was designed to become a single measure of inflation that could be readjusted daily by the government.

Focusing the attention of investors and the public on a single government index permitted Cardoso and his economic team to gradually ratchet down inflationary expectations by setting and subsequently meeting realistic fiscal and monetary performance targets. By May 9, Cardoso was able to accompany the announcement that a new currency would be launched on July 1 (made by his successor at the Ministry of Fazenda). This demonstrated once again that Cardoso and the Franco administration were determined to publicize policy measures well ahead of time rather than attempt to shock inflation out of the economy by unexpectedly unveiling secret economic packages. The stabilization of the new currency, the *real*, quickly began to symbolize the success of this gradualist approach in reducing inflation and projected Cardoso into the presidential race.

The popular appeal of Cardoso's tenure as economic minister was based on the significant redistribution of wealth to poor Brazilians which the Real Plan produced. Not only did inflation fall, but real wages increased an estimated 20 percent during the first six months after the plan (June 1994–January 1995). Furthermore, the real income of poor Brazilians increased an estimated 50 percent during this period, because of government efforts to secure the prices of subsistence goods.[22] Indeed, at an international conference on poverty in Amsterdam, Cardoso's Minister of Education Renato de Souza claimed that over 15 billion USD had been transferred from the financial sector to poor Brazilians since the introduction of the Real Plan and the reduction of inflation. This redistributive impact of economic policy reflects the direct, transparent, and plebiscitarian character of politics in Brazil; Economic policy generates widespread public support because of its substantive impact.

Understanding how the Franco and Cardoso administrations reduced inflation without imposing severe measures of fiscal and monetary austerity requires recognition of the specific context and content of inflation in Brazil. Recent economic theories of inertial inflation, largely based on the persistently high inflation in major Latin American countries during the 1980s, are partially correct to the extent that they emphasize the indexation of prices, wages, and financial instruments as a critical dimension that keeps inflation high and relatively stable.[23] Since the mid-1980s in Brazil, business, finance, and virtually all asset-holders had shifted assets to savings and investments indexed against inflation. In other words, de facto currencies pervaded the Brazilian economy in the 1980s. Consequently, inflation no longer affected business, finance, and asset holders in ways expected by traditional economic theory. Indeed, the persistent reduction of real wages in the face of high inflation throughout the 1980s and early 1990s was functional for the market economy in the short term because it transferred wealth away from wage and salary earners and toward businesses. While this new generation of economists in Brazil who argued that indexation was the primary cause of inflation in Brazil were essentially correct, their policies once implemented failed to keep inflation down because of an exclusive policy-making style and the lack of political negotiations to buttress broad plans of fiscal and monetary reform.

In sum, after five years of policy drift, failed packages, and record inflation under the caretaker presidency of Jose Sarney from 1985–1990 and the false heroics of Fernando Collor de Mello from 1990–1992, the more open, gradual style of governance adopted by Fernando Henrique Cardoso not only to set the stage for reducing inflation without orthodox austerity but also for Cardoso to step from economic minister to president. The traditional mechanisms of party-electoral politics in presidential and federal institutions—direct popular appeals and alliances with patronage machines—describe central aspects of Cardoso's ability to win the presidency in first-round voting on November 15.[24] Both the electoral alliance and governing coalition between Cardoso's Social Democratic PSDB (Partido da Social Democracia Brasileira, Party of Brazilian Social Democracy) and the conservative PFL have received significant criticism from partisans, journalists, and Brazilian intellectuals. Even Cardoso's campaign manager feared during the presidential race that, because of the traditional conservative character of the PFL, core supporters from southeast urban areas would shift to the Worker's Party if the campaign went into a second round. However, these concerns in late June soon gave way, due to the successful reduction of inflation, the immense popularity of the new stabilized currency (*real*), and the significant redistribution of wealth secured by government policies.

The sheer velocity and range of fluctuations among voter's intentions during the 1989 and 1994 presidential campaigns also suggest that the plebiscitarian character of direct popular appeals continues to drive political events in Brazil. During the 1989 contest, Fernando Collor de Mello's ratings in the polls rose rapidly to 45 percent, then fell to 28 percent in the first round. In 1994, Worker's Party candidate

Luiz Inacio da Silva fell from a high point of 42 percent in polls taken on 1 May to 22 percent in a poll on 30 September, accurately reflecting his final share of the vote. Fernando Henrique Cardoso's trajectory in opinion polls from 16 percent of voters' preferences on 3 May to 48 percent on 30 September is even greater. This velocity and range of change among voters' intentions in Brazil is considerably greater than the glacially slow shifts that traditionally characterized well-educated, ideological voters and well-organized party systems in Europe.[25]

This volume emphasizes the importance of political leadership for building democratic institutions and deepening democratic practices in Latin America. In this respect, it must be noted that the 1994 presidential campaign brought to the fore two of the most important new independent political leaders who emerged in opposition to military rule in Brazil. After first confronting the military regime in 1979 by leading metalworker strikes in São Paulo's industrial suburbs, Luiz Inacio da Silva organized not only Brazil's first independent labor unions, he also founded and helped form the Worker's Party (Partido dos Trabalhadores, PT) which became the principal force on the left in Brazilian politics during the 1980s.[26] Fernando Henrique Cardoso's trajectory is no less innovative for a Brazilian politician. An internationally recognized intellectual, Cardoso first stepped from sociology to the Senate in 1982 and became a central figure advocating political reform during the events of transition from military rule (1985) and the writing of the constitution (1988). After machine politicians led by Orestes Quercia (São Paulo governor 1986–1990) asserted control over the national directorship of the PMDB in 1988 (in expectation of dominating the 1989 presidential race), Cardoso split to found the Party of Brazilian Social Democracy (PSDB) along with other PMDB center-left dissidents. In comparative and historical perspective, the emergence of a social-democratic reform president and an independent-left worker's party in opposition as the two central political forces in Brazil after transition from military rule are indeed remarkable political developments.[27] The choice between Lula and Cardoso in the 1994 election suggests that the traditional mechanisms of party-electoral politics in Brazil may provide the setting for the emergence of new leaders, the implementation of significant reforms, and the deepening of democracy.

Once in office, President Cardoso soon realized the importance of international constraints on domestic reform. Cardoso took office with high hopes and far-reaching reform proposals, in part based on the confidence of an estimated 36 billion USD in foreign reserves at the beginning of 1995. Then, the Mexican currency and stock exchange crisis led foreign investors to stampede away from both the Brazilian stock market and the newly stabilized currency, the *real*. In one week, the Brazilian Central Bank was forced to spend an estimated 10 billion USD and issue a further 12 billion in government paper to sustain the value of the *real* in local currency markets, first at 0.90 to 1.0 dollar, then at 0.93 to the dollar.[28]

Once the currency crisis passed, President Cardoso shifted his attention to domestic problems requiring urgent attention. The central goals are to reform the Social Security System,[29] to privatize state firms while avoiding speculative bonanzas, to redesign the Tax Code, to renegotiate federal, state, and municipal transfers, and to end state monopolies in critical sectors for economic development such as telecommunications, banking, petroleum, transportation, and health care. The tasks are complex and their institutional and political setting different. Some measures, defined in the 1988 Constitution, will require a three-fifths vote of Senate and federal deputies. Other measures can simply be decreed through "provisional measure" prerogatives of the presidency. Still others will require significant negotiations with private sector or regional interests and institutions. For example, the Cardoso administration appears to have abandoned plans to liberalize Article 52 of the 1988 Constitution, which prohibits foreign investment in the lucrative domestic commercial banking sector (44 billion USD or 8 percent of GNP), suggesting that domestic lobbies and national interests remain critical actors.

Conclusion

Events moved rapidly in Brazil during the first ten years of civilian rule after 1985. Six direct elections for federal, state, and municipal legislatures and executives were held during this period. A new constitution written during 1988 that extended social rights, clarified traditional Brazilian institutional arrangements, and called for a national plebiscite in April 1993 for voters to choose between parliamentary and presidential government (55 percent voted to retain presidentialism). The first directly elected president in Brazil since 1960, Fernando Collor de Mello, was impeached in late 1992 after two years in office. Civil society organizations that helped delegitimize military rule and secure the transition to civilian rule continued to deepen citizenship and impact politics.

Although these developments from 1985 to 1995 will require further analysis beyond the scope of this chapter, the content of democratic politics in Brazil appears to differ considerably from existing interpretations and expectations. Scholars of democratic politics in Brazil and Latin America have tended to focus on either the dynamic role of new independent social organizations, or the institutions (parliamentarism) most suitable for the consolidation or stabilization of democratic politics.[30] Both perspectives failed to perceive patterns of change during and after the transition from military rule that are typical of presidential and federal systems. That the rapid realignments of patronage machines and the impact of plebiscitarian appeals were not appreciated by scholars is unusual because, since classic works in party sociology by Bryce, Ostrogorski, and Weber, the short-term advantages of presidential and federalist systems for the rapid development of mass

electoral-party politics has been widely recognized.[31] Indeed, the similarities between the U.S. experience before civil service reform and Brazilian electoral-party
politics after the transition from military rule are striking. From 1985 to 1995, the
Brazilian institutional framework of presidentialism and federalism permitted executives to directly nominate party professionals to executive posts. Executives
were thereby able to rapidly organize and reorganize party-electoral alliances on
the federal, state, and local levels.

The movements for political reform that impeached President Collor in late
1992 and permitted Fernando Henrique Cardoso to win the presidency in 1994 suggest that political comparisons between the United States and Brazil must be pursued beyond the scope of this chapter. The progressive-era reforms that reacted to
the brazen corruption and political monopoly of parties in early-twentieth-century
America may provide further points of reference for understanding political reform
and democratization in Brazil.

Ten years separate the transition from military to civilian rule in 1985 and the
inauguration of Fernando Henrique Cardoso on 1 January 1995. During this time,
Brazilians witnessed a parade of political elites apparently destined to control party
organizations and dominate elections. A new generation of opposition intellectuals like Cardoso seemed to determine the future of Brazil during the symbolic void
left by a crumbling regime and an uncertain transition. However, once electoral
politics became routine, most intellectuals failed to sustain their presence in party
committees, convention floors, and other day-to-day tasks of party-electoral organization. The first elections under civilian rule thereby appeared to confirm the most
dire predictions of party sociology, with career politicians and their party-electoral
machines apparently prevailing over intellectual elites, business leaders, and other
amateur politicians from civil society.[32] However, precisely when the cynicism of
party sociology had appeared to prevail, widespread corruption generated unexpected social movements for the moralization of Brazilian public life, culminating
in the impeachment of President Collor in late 1992 and the election of Fernando
Henrique Cardoso in 1994. Only time will tell if these realities of direct popular appeals, alliances with patronage machines, and political reform will continue to
deepen democracy in Brazil.

Between Restructuring and Impasse

Liberal Democracy, Exclusionary Policy Making, and
Neoliberal Programs in Argentina and Uruguay

ALDO C. VACS

The consolidation of liberal forms of democratic rule in Argentina and Uruguay raises a number of questions concerning the patterns of political representation and features of the policy-making processes in both countries. It is particularly important to examine the extent of popular representation afforded by the existing electoral systems as well as the degree of participation of different groups in the policy-making processes while assessing the prospects for deepening democracy. In practice, both issues are correlated: in a liberal democracy, electoral representation is the device that allows citizens to exercise, as voters, or acquire, as elected officials, the right to influence or formulate public policies. The following analysis—without overlooking the importance of the national electoral settings—is mostly focused on the processes of formulation and implementation of the Argentine and Uruguayan public policies and on their respective outcomes since the transition to democracy. The goal of this examination is not only to assess to what extent specific political and socioeconomic factors have affected the viability of liberal policy making in each country but also to evaluate, in the light of these developments, the chances for the emergence of deeper (or shallower) forms of democratic participation, representation, and governance.

This chapter argues that domestic differences help explain why Argentina's posttransition administrations were relatively successful in completing the neoliberal political economic restructuring while their Uruguayan counterparts failed to attain this goal. Argentina's state corporatist tradition, in which the state played a central role as a socioeconomic and political actor, nurtured the conditions for the destruction of organized opposition to the neoliberal project through the atomization and subordination of civil society and the concentration of power in the executive branch. In contrast, the milder Uruguayan form of societal corporatism allowed the survival of strong political parties and socioeconomic organizations that remained relatively autonomous in relation to the state and were able to thwart the implementation of the neoliberal program by isolating and effectively challenging the executive's bid to compel the acceptance of neoliberal policies on unwilling sectors of the population.

To assess the validity of this interpretation, this chapter examines the rise, evolution, and outcomes of the neoliberal programs implemented in Argentina and Uruguay since the 1970s. The first section analyzes the emergence and fate of these policies under the authoritarian regimes and during the transitions to liberal democracy. The second and third sections study in more detail the succession of neoliberal policies advocated, formulated, and implemented by the civilian democratic administrations in both countries, attempting to clarify the political and socioeconomic reasons why the restructuring attempt succeeded in Argentina and failed in Uruguay. The concluding section discusses from a more general perspective the links between liberal democracy, economic liberalism, and styles of policy making in the two countries, pointing out the dilemmas that arise when trying to formulate and implement liberal economic policies in a democratic environment while underscoring the importance of some of these political and socioeconomic factors in generating dissimilar outcomes in the two countries.

The Political Economy of Decline in Argentina and Uruguay: Import Substitution Exhaustion, Authoritarian Neoliberal Projects, and Transition to Democracy

The emergence and consolidation of liberal democracy and economic neoliberalism in Argentina and Uruguay represent the latest stages of a process that ensured the exhaustion of the import substitution industrialization model and the simultaneous decline of the populist-oriented political regimes prevalent in both countries since the Great Depression. There are obvious differences between the Argentine cycle of political instability initiated in the 1930s, that resulted in a succession of populist and developmentalist civilian administrations followed by antipopulist military governments, and the relative democratic stability with economic redistribution enjoyed by Uruguay in the same period, which until the late

1960s was punctuated only by the *dictablanda*—soft dictatorship—of Terra in the early 1930s and the Baldomir "constitutional coup" of 1942.[1] However, it is possible to argue that beneath their divergent political evolutions both countries experienced similar political-economic and social tensions associated with the decline of the industrializing and redistributionist experiences that ultimately led, in the 1970s, to the rise of authoritarian military regimes committed to implement similar neoliberal restructuring programs. In retrospect, the Uruguayan and Argentine military coups of 1973 and 1976 and the ensuing authoritarian regimes represented the temporary culmination of a protracted process of political and economic decay symptomatic of the exhaustion of the prevailing model of development. In both cases, the domestic and international factors that brought about the decline of the import substitution industrialization model fostered the demise of the existing political regimes—disregarding their more pluralistic or authoritarian features—which had been associated with a set of public policies, in their populist, Keynesian, or mixed variants, that were no longer considered suitable to secure economic growth, social peace, and political governability.

The Argentine Case

In Argentina the decline of the classic import substitution industrialization model became observable in the 1950s, when economic stagnation and the saturation of the domestic market by locally produced light manufactures indicated the need to promote the production of consumer durable, intermediate, and capital goods. The required changes in economic strategies resulting from this situation—which included adjustment programs aimed to reduce the growing balance-of-payments deficits, incentives for foreign investment in order to attract new capital and technology, and stabilization plans aimed at reducing inflation—affected the nationalistic and redistributionist premises of populism and led first to the weakening and collapse of the Peronist regime, and afterward, throughout the late 1950s and continuing into the early 1970s, to a succession of failed attempts by developmentalist military and civilian governments to restructure the Argentine political economy.[2] Notwithstanding their different origins and ruling styles—partially pluralistic under the elected Frondizi, Illia, and Perón administrations, more authoritarian under the 1955–58, 1962–63, and 1966–1973 military governments—the political regimes established during this period practiced to different degrees exclusionary or repressive policies toward important sectors of the population, particularly against the supporters of Peronism and leftist groups. At the same time, these governments maintained the state's position in the economy while trying to shift the country's industrialization strategy in a new direction that combined relative protection and support for local producers with incentives for foreign investment and financial capital in an attempt to promote exports (especially of manufactures), foster international competitiveness, and modernize the most dynamic sectors of the economy.

These attempts failed, in part as a result of adverse international and domestic economic trends and situations such as the relative scarcity of foreign investment, global recessions, unfavorable trade and financial environments, infrastructural deficiencies, inflationary pressures, hard currency shortages, and state mismanagement. However, to a large extent, the failure of these developmentalist attempts was also related to the continuous presence in the Argentine scene of the social and political actors and behaviors that had fostered the rise of populism and had been able to outlast its decline. As has been pointed out by J. C. Portantiero, the populist phase had left as its legacy a "high organizational density" that even during authoritarian periods "allowed the formation of 'distributive coalitions' . . . able to block, through multiple vetoes, the organizational capacity of a new social regime of accumulation" while reinforcing the conditions for economic decline and political ungovernability.[3] In this context the struggle among well-organized socioeconomic sectors for preserving or augmenting their respective shares of the dwindling economic pie was focused on the state, trying to use it as an instrument for the attainment of these sectoral goals, and ultimately leading to inflation, social conflict, and a progressive state paralysis that intensified the economic crisis and heightened political instability.

The 1976–1983 military regime was inaugurated after the abortive attempts made by the military governments of the "Argentine Revolution" and the Peronist administrations had clearly shown the impossibility of trying to break the impasse as long as most of these corporatist forces continued to operate without restraints. Determined to attack the causes of this stalemate in a radical manner, the new authoritarian government believed that the loosening of free market forces—up to then fettered by the existence of an interventionist state and a semi-closed economy typical of the import-substitution industrialization strategy—would not only create the conditions for renewed economic growth but also discipline social actors, destroying the socioeconomic and political basis for the emergence of populist and corporatist experiments.[4] In these new circumstances, the existing distributive coalitions would perceive the futility of trying to influence public policies in their favor because the market, and not the state, would assume the role of allocating resources and distributing income eliminating, as a result, one of the main causes of the high levels of social and political mobilization that affected governability. Once these conditions were met, the military and their civilian allies envisioned the establishment of a more stable and less participatory political regime in which some form of restricted electoral competition would be authorized.

For a number of reasons, including the restrictions imposed by the armed forces on the economic team's ability to reduce military budgets and privatize state enterprises, the application of misguided economic policies (especially the strategy of "foreign exchange rate lag" that led to the overvaluation of the peso), the persistent refusal of the economic agents to modify their expectations and behavior in the expected direction, and adverse international conditions after 1979, the authoritarian regime failed to attain its ultimate political-economic goals and collapsed amid growing domestic economic problems, a foreign debt crisis, political opposition, and military defeat.[5] However, between 1976 and 1982 it succeeded, through brutal repression and the application of regressive economic policies, in changing Argentina's socioeconomic structure. The regime was successful in reducing the power of organized labor, atomizing the middle sectors, creating conditions for the growth of leading capital sectors (made up of large horizontally diversified and vertically integrated domestic economic groups and foreign corporations linked to the local and export markets) and the elimination of declining ones (which specialized in distinctive activity and particular production for a specific market), and reducing the state commitment to social and economic policies aimed to protect low-income groups and small and medium producers linked to the domestic market.[6] As a result, the Argentine society that emerged from military rule was much more heterogeneous and fragmented than the organizationally dense one that had facilitated the development of the distributive coalitions typical of the pre–1976 period, while the economic and political conditions reinforced the trend toward the acceptance of liberal prescriptions to promote growth and stability.

The Uruguayan Case

In Uruguay the first signs of the exhaustion of the import-substitution model of development were also perceived in the late 1950s.[7] The economic surplus generated by the beef and wool export sectors (which had enabled the interventionist welfare state to promote, through its fiscal, monetary, trade, and exchange wage policies, a process of import-substitution industrialization accompanied by a progressive redistribution of income and the establishment of a wide social security net) began to plummet as a result of negative domestic and international trends. At the same time, the protected light industrial sector based on imported raw materials and driven by domestic demand reached the limits of its expansive capacity. These negative trends that affected the two crucial components of the Uruguayan economic model led to stagnation that was rapidly translated into fierce redistributionist struggles among socioeconomic sectors anxious to preserve their economic shares in a shrinking economy. This resulted in inflationary pressures, social strife, and a growing realization by powerful groups that the broad social coalition that had supported Uruguay's interventionist and redistributionist "compromise state" and facilitated democratic stability had become an obstacle for the transformation of the economic model.

Since the late 1950s, successive attempts to overhaul the Uruguayan political economy without introducing radical alterations in the political, social, and economic systems failed to generate the expected results.[8] The antistatist and antiprotectionist program promoted by the conservative faction of the Partido Nacional (Blanco) and the "Ruralista" group that came into power in 1959 was thwarted by its own inconsistencies and the determined resistance of organized labor, industrial groups, urban middle sectors (particularly state employees), and important political groups. The stabilization and adjustment plans formulated by technocrats and supported by the right-wing faction of the Partido Colorado during the Pacheco Areco government (1968–71) and the early phase of the Bordaberry administration (1971–73) were more radical in their neoliberal monetarist content and enjoyed more solid support from the agricultural, industrial, and commercial elites but were hindered by persistent opposition from organized labor and sectors of the middle class, the growing factionalization of the traditional Nacional and Colorado parties that eroded the basis of political support for the neoliberal strategy, the rise of the leftist Frente Amplio that obstructed its implementation, and the escalation of armed actions on the part of the Tupamaro urban guerrilla movement that sharpened their confrontation with the armed forces.

In this critical context, conservative civilian governments, with the open support of the economic elites and the military, gradually limited the political participation of different sectors and weakened the democratic features of the regime. The constitutional reform of 1966 had facilitated a greater concentration of power in the reconstituted unipersonal presidency and created a number of autonomous technocratic agencies aimed to isolate public policy making from social and political influences.[9] However, by themselves, these institutional mechanisms proved inadequate to overcome the opposition to the neoliberal project. Beginning in 1968, with the inauguration of Pacheco Areco and intensified under Bordaberry, authoritarian measures became habitual means to implement the neoliberal economic policies such as the banning of leftist groups and publications, the use of the state of emergency to restrict civil liberties and labor rights, the appointment of technocrats instead of politicians to public office, increasing illegal repression, and the growing military participation in public affairs (that culminated in the creation of a military-dominated National Security Council with broad powers). The June 1973 coup led by Bordaberry at the behest of the military represented only the culmination of this long process of democratic decay with its closing of Parliament, the elimination of all constitutional safeguards, and the ensuing dictatorship.

The 1973–1985 authoritarian regime, which some authors have described as close to having a "totalitarian" configuration,[10] formulated and implemented a neoliberal program of restructuring of the Uruguayan political economy that anticipated many of the features of the post–1976 Argentine experience. The import-substitution development model was declared exhausted and blamed for most of Uruguay's economic problems, and the pluralistic, state-centered political system was indicted as one of the main obstacles to the necessary changes. The economic program designed by the minister of economy and finance, Alejandro Vegh Villegas, and his group of technocratic advisors called for the liberalization of the productive, trade, exchange, and financial sectors; the end of "statism"—lifting of protectionist policies and price controls, deregulation, deep cuts in the public budget and employment, and privatization of public enterprises—and the elimination of inflation through stringent monetary policies and reductions in real wages and social expenditures.[11] It was expected that the creation of a free market environment would increase competition and productivity, lead to the elimination of inefficient economic sectors, and facilitate the reinsertion of Uruguay into the international economy through an export-led strategy based on specialization and comparative advantages. In social and political terms, it was expected that the shrinking of the state and the unleashing of market forces together with the severe military repression would destroy the foundations of the traditional social and political game, facilitate the elimination of the Left and the "renewal" of the historic parties, and lead to the emergence of a limited democracy—*democradura*—in which the military and civilian technocrats would maintain control over the political system and public policy making.[12]

The Uruguayan neoliberal restructuring project ultimately failed to attain these goals. In part, this failure was due to factors similar to those that upset the Argentine authoritarian experiment: the armed forces' reluctance to reduce military budgets, privatize public enterprises, and cut down the size of the state; the implementation of exchange rate policies that led to overvaluation of the local currency; unfavorable international economic developments after 1979; and the resistance of domestic socioeconomic sectors to modify their behavior. In part, this failure can be attributed to specific Uruguayan circumstances: the military refusal to completely dismantle the traditional two-party system and give full support to the deepening of the neoliberal program (which led to the dismissal of Bordaberry and Vegh Villegas in 1976); the existence of a relatively strong political culture with democratic underpinnings that favored the restoration of the traditional system; the survival of relatively autonomous socioeconomic organizations, including labor; and the resilience of the two major parties (and of, as well, the components of the leftist front—to some extent) that due to their historical tradition, "catch-all" appeal, and moderate features were able to preserve their constituents' loyalty.[13]

In 1980, amid growing evidence of an impending economic crisis, the government organized a plebiscite to ratify a constitution drafted to replace the 1967 charter. The new constitution would have institutionalized a semiauthoritarian regime, legitimizing the exclusion of leftist political groups and perpetuating the military's overseer role in the system. Despite military warnings and the support of the conservative Colorado factions, the Uruguayan voters rejected the proposal by a 57 percent to 43 percent margin.[14] Following this unprecedented defeat in an authoritarian referendum, the military fluctuated between hard-line and moderate responses while engaging in a series of negotiations with representatives of the traditional parties on the terms of democratic transition. These negotiations between a weakening military and a strengthened political elite culminated in the so-called Navy Club Pact that cleared the way for the restoration of Uruguay's liberal democratic political system and the reassertion of civilian supremacy after elections.

The 1984 general elections took place under the traditional system of *lemas* and relatively few candidates were excluded as a result of military vetoes.[15] To a large extent these elections resulted in the restoration of the political status quo that prevailed before 1973 although with a higher degree of intraparty factionalization and growing ideological polarization among the electorate and candidates: the two traditional parties gathered 76 percent of the vote (Partido Colorado: 41 percent; Partido Nacional: 34.9 percent) while the Frente Amplio obtained 21.7 percent, mostly concentrated in the capital city, Montevideo. One of the Colorado candidates, Julio M. Sanguinetti, who led a center-right faction (Batllismo Unido), was elected president with 31 percent of the vote.[16]

The military attempt to restructure the political system had failed; however, the legacy of the authoritarian regime in social, economic, and political terms was not eradicated by the restoration of liberal democracy. As enumerated by Gerónimo de Sierra, these enduring transformations included a smaller and more fragmented industrial working class, net emigration of economically active population, a regressive distribution of income, a growing informal sector, crisis of the small and medium enterprises linked to the domestic market, concentration and centralization of capital, oligopolization and strengthening of large economic groups, decisive role of the private—mainly foreign-controlled—financial sector in the economy and in creating an off-shore sector, and a huge foreign debt.[17] In these conditions, the particular characteristics of Uruguay's restored liberal democratic regime and the existence of important political actors who supported or opposed the implementation of policies aimed to complete the neoliberal restructuring created a conflicting set of opportunities and constraints for the postauthoritarian civilian administrations.

The Argentine Restructuring:
Emergent Liberal Democracy, Executive Dominance,
and the Consolidation of Neoliberalism

In Argentina, the development of a liberal democracy with strong exclusionary elements, which restricted participation in the decision-making process and in which the elected authorities exhibited a growing commitment to continue the neoliberal restructuring launched by the authoritarian regime, was a gradual and often wavering development that unfolded under two different administrations, the Radical one of Raul Alfonsín (1983–1989), and the Peronist government of Carlos Menem (since mid-1989). In both cases electoral promises to shift course, abandoning the economic model favored by the authoritarian regime, fostering political participation and implementing alternative economic policies, were abandoned after some initial hesitation and replaced by the growing use of executive power to foster implementation of free-market policies. By the mid-1990s, the exclusionary neoliberal model was firmly in place and the likelihood of any fundamental alteration seemed remote.

The Radicals' Wavering Path

The Alfonsín years represented a transitional stage in which the clash between the remnants of the old corporatist structures and practices and the emerging liberal ones was still intense, although the capacity of the former to persist ebbed as the strength of the latter increased swiftly. After their unexpected victory, the Radicals initially tried to fulfill their electoral promises, implementing an economic program with Keynesian components.[18] This program was expected to facilitate economic growth and stability as well as a moderate redistribution of income through a general agreement on wages and prices accompanied by state intervention to promote investment and exports and a reduction of payments on the foreign debt. The attempt collapsed after a few months amid growing inflation, capital flight, stagnation, and socioeconomic conflict fostered by the refusal of domestic labor and capital sectors as well as foreign banks and international institutions (such as the IMF) to support it. It became clear that the weakened state inherited from the military lacked capacity to control key economic variables and to impose or promote a political pact among the socioeconomic sectors that dominated the market (institutions of financial speculation and large economic groups) or those who preferred to fight for their economic shares in a traditional way (labor, middle sectors, small and medium farmers, and industrialists). As a result, the original Keynesian economic program was discarded and replaced in June 1985 by the "heterodox" Austral Plan, which combined liberal stabilization measures (increases in public tariffs and taxes, decrease in public expenditures, privatization, monetary stringency, and a new devalued currency pegged to the dollar) with unorthodox ones (wage and price freeze, gradual deindexation, fixed real interest rates). Initially, the Austral plan succeeded in stabilizing the economy and improving the government's popularity but, after a year, the distributive struggle and the pressures on the administration coming from different sectors intensified, while governmental attempts to satisfy some of these demands led to contradictory policies including wage raises and the lifting of price controls.

Finally, facing a new inflationary upsurge and an intensification of the distributive struggle, by mid-1987 the Radical government was forced to acknowledge that both the Keynesian and "heterodox" economic formulae had failed to generate conditions for stabilization or economic recovery and moved in a more orthodox, neoliberal direction. The minister of economy, Juan V. Sourrouille, denounced the "populist and facile model . . . closed . . . centralized and statist" and announced successive economic packages aimed to open and deregulate the economy, privatize public enterprises, reduce the size of the state, and cut public expenditures. Despite their increasingly orthodox contents, these packages fell short of satisfying the demands made by business groups, who considered them insufficiently liberal and no longer trusted the ability of the government to implement any program. They were also, as expected, rejected by working- and middle-class sectors that had experienced an abrupt drop in their real wages and salaries.[19] The voluntary agreements between the government and the industrial and commercial associations to temporarily freeze prices in exchange for a governmental promise to reduce fiscal expenditures and money supply, freeze public tariffs, and maintain the exchange rates collapsed in early 1989. This collapse was a result of several factors, including the open opposition of the agricultural sector that refused to sell foreign exchange and organized lockouts; a speculative run on the dollar in the financial sector; labor mobilization and strikes demanding wage raises; the growing reluctance of the IMF, World Bank, and foreign banks to disburse new funds; the industrial and commercial sectors' price increases; and the government's inability to control the fiscal deficit.

In the political arena, developments such as the growing electoral strength of the Peronist party and the emergence of its unpredictable presidential candidate for the 1989 elections, Carlos Menem; the military rebellion led by Colonel Seineldín in December 1988; and the ill-fated guerrilla assault on the Tablada garrison in January 1989 compounded the uncertainty and generated further distrust of the government among powerful economic groups and the population at large. In early 1989, a frantic run on the dollar—the so-called "February market coup"—depleted the Central Bank reserves and led to a hyperinflationary explosion that facilitated Menem's victory in the May presidential elections, generated shortages, riots, and looting in May and June, and forced the early transfer of power from Alfonsín to Menem in July instead of December 1989.[20]

The Alfonsín administration had ultimately failed to meet the crucial challenges of governance: adequately managing the economy, guaranteeing social peace, and maintaining political stability. This failure to solve the problem of democratic governance can be attributed, in part, to the inability of the Radical administration to steadfastly follow a policy course aimed to complete the transformation of the Argentine model of social accumulation. By attempting to pursue a middle course between Keynesian and neoliberal strategies, between state intervention and free market policies, between social concertation and technocratic fiat, and between inclusionary and exclusionary policy making, the Alfonsín administration ended up alienating domestic and foreign economic, political, and social actors, fostering the worst hyperinflationary surge in Argentina's history, and facilitating the formation of the broadest possible hostile coalition.

This wavering approach that hesitatingly progressed toward more exclusionary policy-making practices, while never completing this course, was clearly perceived in a number of policy-making areas, including economic, labor, military, foreign, and social policies. In economic terms, policies were designed inside the executive by a small group of experts isolated from civil society and Congress as well as from the other departments and agencies of the administration. During the first phase of the administration, the economic team had roots in the Radical party and was more politically oriented; during the 1985–early 1989 period, the economic cabinet became much more technocratic in its origins and composition; and finally, in a desperate attempt to negotiate with the opposition during the chaotic last months, a more politically oriented group was again appointed. However, in all these cases, actual decision-making power was concentrated in the hands of the economic teams, and the consultations—mostly about implementation—took place only after the most important initiatives had been sanctioned and announced by the executive. This exclusionary approach was justified by the arguments that the economic crisis required swift and decisive action that could be hindered by advance consultation while the democratic legitimacy and popular support for the administration empowered it to make autonomous decisions. Thus, the successive economic packages were designed in secrecy, disclosed suddenly to the population, and often enacted by decree, ignoring constitutionally defined congressional mechanisms.[21] At the same time, however, once the policies had been announced, the Radical government tried to encourage socioeconomic concertation between industrialists, business, agricultural producers, and labor through the creation of institutional mechanisms, such as the "Concertation Table" (1984), the "Economic-Social Conference" (1985), and the "Emergency

Agricultural Council" (1986), or through state-led negotiations with different sectors, such as the ones established with labor groups in 1987 to moderate their demands and control prices with industrial and commercial associations during 1988–89.

A similar style—characterized by its isolation and concentration of decision power in the executive—distinguished the attempt made in 1984 to change the labor laws in order to democratize and reduce the weight of the trade unions. This ultimately failed to pass Congress and led to disappointing attempts to break the unity of the Peronist confederation by granting control over the ministry of labor to a particular group before replacing it with members of the administration when the strategy of co-optation failed to stem the workers' antagonism. Alfonsin administration military policies also fluctuated between the poles of responding to popular demands to bring human rights violators to trial and carrying out unilateral decisions to pardon most of them. In response to military uprising, the government first called for popular support to defeat uprisings, then made concessions to the military rebels without in the end maintaining popular support or satisfying all the military demands. In sum, in this as in most other areas, the Alfonsín administration reduced the participation of the legislative branch and civil society in the policy-making process but fell short of attaining the degree of concentration of power and exclusion necessary to impose policies.

Menem's Neoliberal Remodeling

After his inauguration Menem surprised many of his followers and adversaries alike by maintaining and deepening the neoliberal course favored by his predecessors. The promises of huge wage raises (*salariazo*) and of a "productive revolution" based on the revival of the domestic market during the electoral campaign were forgotten even before inauguration and replaced by a neoliberal economic program to be executed by some of the most representative figures of Argentina's conservative elites. Top executives of the holding Bunge and Born were appointed ministers of economy—initially, Miguel Roig; and, after Roig's sudden death, Néstor Rapanelli—in a complete reversal of the traditional Peronist hostility toward this diversified transnational economic group.[22] The turn was completed with the appointment to important economic posts of conservative members of the traditionally anti-Peronist UCD—Unión del Centro Democrático, union of the democratic center—and well-known representatives of orthodox economic thinking such as Javier González Fraga (president of the Central Bank) and Domingo Cavallo (minister of foreign relations).

The Menem administration's initial measures included a severe program for economic stabilization and structural adjustment, aiming primarily to contain hyperinflation, which involved a devaluation and the elimination of subsidies; the lifting of restrictions on foreign investment; reduction of public expenditures to attain a balanced fiscal budget; privatization of state enterprises including the phone, airline, and railroad companies; and tax reform.[23] However, they also included an unorthodox freeze on wages and salaries and a freeze on prices negotiated with 350 companies in exchange for a state commitment to maintain stable public tariffs and interest and exchange rates.

Meanwhile, in a context of hyperinflationary fear and under presidential pressure, the congressional sanction of the laws of state reform and economic emergency facilitated the implementation by the executive of structural changes aimed to consolidate a free-market economic system.[24] The state reform law, enacted in August 1989, authorized the administration to privatize, partially or totally, a large number of state enterprises and services including the phone, airline, railroad, shipping, coal mining, and highway companies, the postal and insurance services, the public television and radio stations, and several petrochemical companies. The economic emergency law, passed in September 1989, reduced the industrial and mining promotion subsidies and the preferential purchase regime for local manufactures, suspended hirings and authorized dismissals in the public sector, and canceled some special salary systems for state employees.

Organized labor, often defined as the "backbone" of Peronism, received tremendous blows after Menem's inauguration, which culminated in the split of the General Confederation of Labor (CGT) and an unprecedented weakening of the labor movement. Peronist labor organizations had participated in the electoral campaign, projecting a responsible image that lessened the fears of the middle and upper sectors while enhancing Menem's reputation as a leader able to prevent the repetition of the labor strife that had affected the country under the Alfonsín administration. However, some labor leaders—like Saul Ubaldini, the secretary general of the CGT—had refused to forego the possibility of strikes under a Peronist administration and were severely criticized by Menem loyalists in different unions. After the inauguration, several loyalists were appointed to important positions in the administration and formed a coalition—the Mesa de Enlace, union coordination table—whose main purpose was to unconditionally back the administration policies.[25] This group demanded a meeting of the CGT congress and, in a tumultuous meeting, elected a new direction integrated exclusively by pro-Menem union leaders. The CGT split into two rival organizations, weakening its traditional ability to influence policies: the pro-Menem CGT stated its complete loyalty to the administration and support for the economic plan, including the adjustment and privatization policies; the opposition CGT declared its support for

Menem but made it clear that this support was not extended to the economic policies and that it would continue to fight for higher wages and against dismissals in
the private and public sector.

Nevertheless, the weakening of organized labor, the bewilderment of the opposition, and the backing of conservative political and business sectors to the neoliberal aspects of the economic plan did not suffice to secure its success. The ex-
porter's opposition to the exchange policies resulted in growing reluctance to
exchange their export earnings in the Central Bank, forcing the administration to
announce substantial reductions in the export taxes applied to agricultural and industrial products.[26] Some labor organizations, especially in the public sector and
those led by populist and leftist groups in the private sector, rejected the economic
policies and demanded a reconsideration of the privatization process and substantial wage raises. After a brief truce, business groups started to raise prices once
again. In turn, the inability of the administration to reduce the fiscal deficit and
growth of the money supply, and to accelerate the pace of the privatization process,
resulted in lack of external support (from the IMF, World Bank, and developed
countries' governments) and continuous attacks from local business and financial
groups.

This broad opposition sealed the fate of the minister of the economy, and in
December 1989, Rapanelli was replaced by Antonio Erman González. The new
minister exhibited the traits necessary to perform the role of neoliberal pacesetter.
González had belonged to Menem's group of closest advisors since the early 1970s
and his loyalty to him was unquestioned. He was neither a member of the ruling
party (Gonzalez belonged to a conservative faction of the small Christian Democratic party) nor of any important socioeconomic organization and thus was able,
with the president's support, to isolate himself from political and sectoral pressures
aimed to check or halt the liberalization program.

Gonzalez's first announcements reflected the presidential decision of quick-
ening the pace of economic liberalization: the establishment of a completely free
exchange market, removal of all price controls, elimination of the increase on export taxes, the conversion of public debt obligations into dollar denominated
bonds, and a small wage raise.[27] Subsequently, when faced with an inflationary
surge, González announced a set of emergency policies, the Plan Bonex, that
eliminated the commercial bank short-time deposits and forced their conversion
into ten-year dollar-denominated bonds (Bonex 1989), froze public utility rates,
and emphasized the government's determination to halt the expansion of the
money supply by reducing the fiscal deficit.[28] In early March 1990 another emergency package increased export, value-added, and capital gains taxes; eliminated
state secretariats, undersecretariats, and state banks; ended the Treasury financing
of public deficits; and suspended the collective bargaining contracts for public em-

ployees.[29] These stringent monetary and fiscal policies contributed to stabilize the exchange rate. The cuts in public spending generated operational surpluses for the Treasury, reducing the quasifiscal deficit and contributing to curb the expansion of the monetary base. However, these cuts affected the quality and availability of essential public services, including health, education, and justice. The application of the adjustment program also had a regressive impact on the distribution of income, increasing poverty and reinforcing the growing concentration of income and wealth noticed during the Alfonsín years.[30]

The privatization program began also to be implemented at a firmer pace.[31] The national phone company, ENTEL, the national airline, Aerolíneas Argentinas, the railroad services in the main grain-producing areas, sections of the federal highway system, and the exploration and production activities of the national petroleum company, Yacimientos Petrolíferos Fiscales, were put on the auction block. The haste with which the plan was devised and the lack of adequate regulatory provisions resulted in improvisations, allegations of improprieties and corruption, and inadequate valuations of the assets owned by the state companies. In order to deal with these problems, the minister of economics was put in charge of all the state enterprises with a presidential mandate to control spending, reduce the number of employees, and speed up the process of privatization.

The implementation of the neoliberal program revealed some cleavages among business groups. The largest financial, industrial, and agricultural interests strongly supported these policies, although expressing some reservations concerning the pace of the privatization, the government's inability to balance the budget, and the persistence of the exchange rate lag. The smaller financial institutions, agricultural producers, and industrialists supported the free market ideology and orientation but opposed its practical consequences: decline in private domestic demand, lack of government contracts, and inability to benefit from the privatization process. In the political sphere, the strongest backing came from the small conservative parties that had been soundly defeated in the elections but whose programs advocated radical free market and free trade policies.

In early 1991, a number of situations that included charges of widespread corruption (particularly the accusations of bribery against high officials made by the U.S. ambassador), persistent inflation, less than expected fiscal revenues, and the rise of the dollar indicated to Menem the convenience of reshuffling the cabinet while deepening the application of the neoliberal program. González was appointed minister of defense and replaced by the up-to-then minister of foreign relations, Domingo Cavallo—a Harvard-trained economist, former president of the Central Bank during the last military government, and former Peronist representative elected in 1987–89. Cavallo had long believed that Argentina's economic problems were institutional, the result of the existence of a "socialism without plan and capitalism without market," advocating, among other alternative policies, market liberalization and an outwardly oriented strategy of growth instead of the traditional Peronist approach based on state intervention and the expansion of the domestic market.[32]

Cavallo's economic package—the so-called "Convertibility Plan"—completed the neoliberal turn. A new currency was created, the *peso*, freely convertible in dollars at a parity rate of one for one; the more rapid privatization of public enterprises and a debt for equity plan were announced, as well as massive dismissals in the public sector; the Brady Plan was accepted as the means to reduce foreign debt; and taxation reform and further opening of the economy were promised.[33] Later in 1991, a comprehensive executive decree deregulated most of the economy and established a free-market environment lifting regulations concerning transportation, professional and commercial activities, import and export trade, financial transactions, collective bargaining, and social security arrangements, while most official regulatory agencies were abolished.[34] The use of an executive decree to modify or eliminate more than forty different laws was justified by the government for reasons of need and urgency, but this explanation was rejected by the opposition, which denounced the method as unconstitutional and argued that the administration refused to request congressional approval due to the controversial nature of many of the measures. Interestingly, Radical opposition focused on the method used to implement these measures and not on their contents. Nevertheless, judicial challenges to the validity of the decree were turned down by the courts and the measures were swiftly implemented.

Cavallo's neoliberal economic policies succeeded in accomplishing some impressive results in 1991–92: inflation was contained, the GDP grew at a significant rate, privatizations moved forward, the rate of exchange remained unchanged, and capital inflows increased. At the same time, the program reinforced the trends toward regressive income distribution, concentration of wealth, and oligopolization of the economy, facilitated imports and hindered exports leading to a growing trade deficit, and failed to reduce unemployment. Although during this period some political reversals hit the government (loss of some senatorial and provincial races), support for the stabilization features of the program remained significant as the congressional elections of 1991 illustrated and, more important yet, the neoliberal policies of the Menem administration generated a number of structural, market-oriented transformations that appear to be irreversible: the interventionist state and distributive socioeconomic coalitions that were the basis of the populist and developmentalist experiences of the past are no longer viable.

Perceiving divisions and weakness in the labor movement, the Menem administration reacted forcefully against its opponents, dismissing state workers, imposing obligatory conciliation in conflicts in the private sector, and recognizing the pro-government branch of the CGT as the only one with legal entity.[35] A bill limiting the right to strike of public and private workers employed in health services, public utilities, telecommunications, public transportation, education, and justice administration was sent to Congress and, after Peronist and opposition representatives refused to pass it, the measure was enacted by presidential decree in October 1990.[36] Afterward, new executive measures were enacted to further weaken labor's capacity to challenge the neoliberal policies. These included new rules for collective bargaining that decentralized the negotiation process and eliminated state intervention; labor contract laws were modified making it possible for employers to change the conditions of work, fringe benefits, and wages; wage and salary raises were tied to increases in productivity; and new legislation limited the capacity of the trade unions to control the social coverage institutions (*obras sociales*) that provide health and recreation services for workers, which had traditionally been the main source of funds for organized labor.[37]

The hesitation of the Peronist party to champion the shift toward neoliberalism also resulted in successful governmental attempts to gain control over its structures. Although calling for unity and stating their solidarity with Menem, the president of the party and governor of Buenos Aires, Antonio Cafiero, and his "renovating" sector, had suggested the convenience of a more gradual economic transformation, the preservation of some traditional social policies, and had failed to ensure congressional support for some governmental initiatives. Menem's political operatives repeatedly accused Cafiero and the party leadership of opposing the administration and demanded their resignation. The opportunity to remove Cafiero and his group from their party offices came in mid-1990 when, due to the opposition of pro-Menem factions associated with non-Peronist parties, a provincial constitutional reform supported by Cafiero and the Radical party was overwhelmingly defeated by the Buenos Aires electorate. As a result, Cafiero and his supporters resigned their party positions and Carlos Menem was elected the new president of the party. Menem, in turn, asked for a leave of absence and appointed his brother, Senator Eduardo Menem, as acting president of Peronism.[38] Afterward, the party machine remained under the tight control of the administration and supported without exception all the executive's policy initiatives. In turn, the economic stability generated by the neoliberal plan allowed the candidates of this dependent Peronist party to obtain a victory in the congressional elections of late 1991, facilitating the continuation of its subordinated status in relation to the executive.

The government actions shattered the chances of labor and party opposition but, at the same time, disarticulated and weakened two pillars of its popular support: the organized labor movement and the Peronist movement. The problem of gaining support for the administration's program was compounded by the fact that the state's shrinking affected the possibility of obtaining such support through traditional clientelistic practices, such as offering jobs or services to the low- and middle-income sectors of the population. Faced with this decline in support and mobilization capacity and the rejection of a coalition by the right-wing faction of the Radical party, the Menem administration began to search for a new constituency among the middle- and upper-class groups that approved Menem's turn toward neoliberal policies. In April 1990, a rally to support the privatization and orthodox adjustment program was organized by conservative journalists, businessmen, and politicians.[39] The support for economic neoliberalism expressed in this demonstration confirmed the revival of the conservative ideology upheld by rightist parties and reinforced Menem's inclination to cement alliances with political groups representative of upper- and middle-income sectors and interests.[40]

This conservative shift was also encouraged by the collapse of several Peronist provincial administrations and the emergence of local center-right and right-wing parties. During 1990 the economic crisis, the mismanagement and, in some cases, the corruption affecting the Peronist provincial administrations had resulted in the impeachment or resignation of the governors of Tucumán, Tierra del Fuego, Jujuy, and Chubut, and growing popular discontent in Santa Fe, Catamarca, and Buenos Aires.[41] At the same time, there was the emergence of new conservative parties led in some cases by former members of the 1976–1983 military government, such as Fuerza Republicana (FR—republican force) created by General Domingo Bussi, or the revival of traditional provincial parties, such as those in Salta, Jujuy, Corrientes, and Mendoza. Faced with the possibility that these parties would be able in 1991 to win some governorships and elect an important number of representatives to Congress, Menem took distance from the bankrupt Peronist administrations and emphasized the support offered by the provincial parties to his economic program. In different occasions, he also preferred to support extra-party candidates favorable to the neoliberal program instead of traditional Peronist politicians who were less trustworthy, placing himself in an autonomous position and playing the role of great elector independent from his own party. By 1993, as he tried to gather support for a constitutional reform that would authorize his re-election, Menem relied on a submissive Peronist party, labor confederation, and congressional delegation to facilitate the passage of the reform bill through Congress while looking toward the small conservative and neoliberal parties to secure the necessary two-thirds majority.

The concentration of decision-making power in the hands of the executive was apparent also in its human rights and military policies.[42] Early on, the Menem administration explored the possibility of obtaining congressional approval for an amnesty bill that would benefit the military as well as members of the Peronist guerrilla organization, Montoneros, who were imprisoned or indicted. But when the vocal opposition of human rights groups and political sectors convinced him of the impossibility of gaining congressional approval for this measure, Menem issued presidential pardons to those military and civilians sentenced or indicted for human rights violations and politically motivated crimes while lifting the sanctions applied to those involved in failed military rebellions during the previous administration. At the same time, while reducing the military's budget and privatizing their enterprises, the administration tried to cement good relations with the high command by authorizing—against explicit legal dispositions—the armed forces' participation in the planning and execution of operations aimed to prevent and repress activities that could undermine domestic order and stability, granting them moderate salary raises, and earmarking the proceedings of the sale of military properties for the modernization of the armed forces.

Regarding the judicial system, the administration aimed to prevent any intervention of the judiciary in the policy-making process and to limit the court's ability to perform their overseeing role.[43] The nomination and appointment of judges sympathetic to the administration eliminated many of the potential obstacles to the use of executive power to implement controversial economic, labor, social, and foreign policy initiatives. This process culminated with the successful passing through Congress of a law that increased from five to nine the number of Supreme Court justices. The packing of the court with Menem loyalists prevented any judicial opposition to the administration's policies and perfected the process of concentration of power in the executive that had been completed in other areas.

After completing half of its tenure, the Menem administration considered that the unrelenting pursuit of neoliberal restructuring and the growing concentration of power in the executive branch had clearly paid off in political and economic terms as the political landscape was clearly dominated by the president and the economy remained stable and showed signs of recovery. In fact, the only difficulty that the model appeared to face at the time was related to Menem's promotion of a constitutional reform that would permit his reelection. Supporters of the model feared that in order to gain support for this reform the president would be tempted to bend the neoliberal course in a less orthodox direction. This danger was manifested in Menem's contradictory statements about the need to stay the neoliberal course while, at the same time, building a more "humane capitalist system, with deep social and ethical contents," and it was manifested as well in the establishment of conversations with labor representatives to discuss wage policies.[44] The reaction of the supporters of the neoliberal program to this threat was swift and effective: they initially opposed the constitutional reform and Menem's reelection aspirations because, as one influential champion of neoliberalism stated, "I love the economic model. I would like to see Menem reelected. But I am opposed to the timing of the reform proposal. I do not like the price Menem will have to pay to obtain it. I do not want him to give in to the unions or to the governors. I do not want politics to endanger the model."[45]

Faced with this opposition and the lack of enthusiasm of different political groups for the reform, Menem relented and reaffirmed a neoliberal stance. Negotiations with labor groups were discontinued and wage policies remained unchanged. In November 1992, a general strike organized by some leaders of the CGT—but disowned by the pro-Menem labor groups—to demand higher wages was met with governmental scorn. Asked to comment on the strike, Menem denounced it as an attempt by labor leaders who lived in the past "to play some role in the leadership of the state," adding that "they can hold one or 20,000 strikes, but they can alter neither our path, nor the economic model, nor the proposals we are submitting to the parliament to make the labor legislation more modern and flexible."[46]

Afterward, Menem asked for several cabinet resignations—including the replacement of the ministers of labor, education, interior, and defense—and presented these changes as a clear reaffirmation of the administration's willingness to deepen the application of neoliberal measures in these areas. By December 1992, foreign support to the government's policies was reflected in the final agreement reached with the creditor banks to reschedule the foreign debt and that resulted in the incorporation of Argentina to the Brady Plan.

Meanwhile, the main opposition party, the UCR, remained in disarray, unable to block Menem's initiatives or to elaborate alternative programs. The preeminence of Peronism was confirmed in the congressional elections of September 1993 in which it obtained 43 percent of the votes (against 30 percent of the Radicals) and was able to win nine extra seats in the lower chamber. Interpreting these results as a confirmation of his popularity, Menem renewed his campaign to amend the constitution that, at the time, did not allow presidential reelection. The December 1993 negotiations between Menem and the president of the UCR, Alfonsín, resulted in an agreement in which, in exchange for supporting the reform, the UCR obtained the president's promise to replace three pro-Menem Supreme Court justices for less partisan personalities and a commitment to support constitutional provisions aimed to limit executive power, create the post of chief of cabinet responsible to Congress, shorten mandates, reform the judiciary, and reinforce controls on the administration. This pact cleared the way for Congress to call for a constitutional reform.

Although both Peronist and Radical shares of the vote declined in the April 1994 constitutional assembly elections they still gained a substantial majority in the convention. The constitutional reform was completed and approved in August 1994.[47] It included among the new provisions the possibility of presidential reelection and thus cleared the way for Menem's candidacy to a four-year term in the

May 1995 elections. In these elections, held on May 14, 1995, half of the electorate showed a clear preference for political and economic stability while a substantial minority rejected the Radical party as an alternative for its incapacity to perform an adequate opposition role.[48] Menem obtained close to 50 percent of the vote, followed by the candidate of a center-left coalition, FrePaSo, with 29 percent, while the UCR, in its worst election ever, finished a distant third with less than 17 percent. At the same time, the Peronists gained an absolute majority in the lower house and preserved their control over the Senate and most provinces.

As Menem started his second presidential period in July 1995 it was clear that the 1994 constitutional amendments designed to reduce the presidential concentration of power—such as the creation of a chief of cabinet and some supervisory agencies responsible to Congress—might not be very effective. In practice, by retaining control over the ruling party, its congressional delegation, most governors, and the judiciary, Menem would be able to continue to pursue the same elitist and exclusionary policies that characterized his first term. Moreover, the decline of the main opposition party, the relative fragility of the center-left coalition, and the weakness of the socioeconomic organizations reinforce this impression, making it difficult to foresee in the near future an increase in popular participation and the development of more representative institutions.

The Uruguayan Impasse: Liberal Democratic Restoration, Policy-Making Discord, and the Trials of Neoliberalism

In Uruguay the civilian government that emerged from the democratic transition intended to preserve and, if possible, to deepen some of the neoliberal features inherited from the authoritarian regime. However, unlike Argentina, the efforts in this direction made by the Colorado administration headed by Julio M. Sanguinetti (1985–89), by its successor, the Blanco government of Luis Alberto Lacalle (1990–94), and by the second Sanguinetti administration (inaugurated in 1994) have met effective resistance that frustrated the completion of the neoliberal restructuring project.

The reasons that explain the tenacity of this successful resistance and the relative inability of the executive to overcome it seem to be related to the features of the restored Uruguayan political system as well as to the endurance in civil society of solid socioeconomic organizations capable of withstanding executive pressures. The incomplete neoliberal restructuring attempted by the military government had left in place most of Uruguay's traditional political features and, in some cases, had even contributed to revitalize them as a reaction against the discredited authoritarian practices limiting the chances for posttransition executives to prevail over congressional, party, and socioeconomic opposition. Uruguay's transition thus

resulted in the restoration of its liberal democratic political system, the renewal of
its political culture, and the re-emergence of a civil society characterized by the existence of lively political parties and Parliament, institutionalized checks and balances, entrenched rules governing political interactions, participatory values,
widely shared perceptions of a social welfare contract between state and society,
and autonomous socioeconomic groups.[49]

Democratic Restoration and Neoliberal Misadventures

In the economic sphere, the first Sanguinetti administration was faced with a
difficult situation whose manifestations included a declining GDP (negative rates
of growth of -9.4 percent, -5.0 percent, and -3.3 percent in 1982, 1983, and 1984, respectively), falling investment, growing unemployment and declining real wages,
high inflation (55 percent in 1984), fiscal deficits, decreasing export earnings, a
huge foreign debt, and a staggering accumulation of arrears in the debt owed to
the local banks by domestic borrowers.[50] Sanguinetti's economic program was relatively orthodox and focused on efforts to reduce inflation and the fiscal deficit, increase exports, renegotiate foreign debt payments, and solve the domestic private
indebtedness crisis.

After his inauguration, Sanguinetti's economic policies were formulated by
the executive without previous consultation or concertation although, as in Argentina, there were attempts to facilitate its implementation by negotiating ex post
facto support from different groups as long as the essential contents of the policies
were not altered. In this context, the economic initiatives taken by the administration included negotiations with the IMF and the creditor banks that resulted in an
orthodox stabilization program (stringent monetary policies, public expenditure
cuts, public rate and price raises, and tax increases, particularly of indirect taxes);
authorization for agricultural and industrial firms to refinance their debts, and a
bailout of the banks and financial institutions most affected by the crisis; and the
maintenance of the market-based export-led growth model as well as the financial
and commercial opening of the economy promoted by the military government.
The implementation of these economic policies during the Sanguinetti period resulted in some modest gains: the decline of the GDP was reversed, although the
rates of growth fluctuated between 7.5 percent in 1986 and 0.5 percent in 1989; the
fiscal deficit decreased but was not eliminated; balance-of-payments surpluses were
obtained in some years; and real salaries grew at a declining rate (14 percent increase in 1985 but only 1.5 percent in 1988) though remaining below their 1981 levels. At the same time, other economic indicators worsened: inflation remained
high (over 63 percent each year between 1985 and 1988 and up to 90 percent in
1989); net investment remained close to zero; unemployment stayed high; and the

foreign debt grew (from close to 3 billion dollars in 1984 to more than 4 billion in 1989).

These results were interpreted by the government not as an indication of the shortcomings of the neoliberal economic program but as evidence that the free market policies should be deepened and strictly enforced in order to promote economic stabilization and growth. In this regard, the administration tried to open a debate on the necessary modernization of the Uruguayan economy and state that could lead to the emergence of a social market economy—*economía social de mercado*—characterized by the existence of a free market environment, adequate social conditions, and a leaner and more efficient (technocratic) state. The importance of debating issues such as the need for a new model of accumulation, the role of the state, and the relationship between state and society was accepted by the most important political and socioeconomic actors. However, many of them—including organized labor, small producers, leftist parties, and important sectors of the traditional parties, including the ruling Colorado party—rejected the narrow teleological confines that the government tried to impose on the debate and preferred to engage in a broader discussion that challenged the neoliberal assumptions and goals embraced by the administration.[51] Faced with a denunciation of its modernization model as one that facilitated foreign domination, uncontrolled privatization, and the establishment of a vulnerable service economy while requiring the depoliticization of civil society and a technobureaucratic concentration of decision-making power in the executive, the Sanguinetti administration opted for abandoning this attempt to develop a broader political ideological basis for the neoliberal deepening. Subsequently, the debate was framed in terms of governability; that is, it was focused on how to ensure the necessary support for the administration's policies while making minimal, if any, concessions—especially in terms of economic policies—to the opposition. In practice this was translated into seeking pragmatic agreements with political actors (and occasionally, with socioeconomic groups) whose support was considered necessary to secure the approval and implementation of particular policies.[52]

The neoliberal policies of the authoritarian regime had altered the economic and social landscape of Uruguay, but the fragmentary development of this more concentrated, inegalitarian, and dependent accumulation model had failed to completely wipe out some basic elements of the country's traditional political system. The same political "families" that existed in 1973 had come back to the fore, under identical electoral regulations, although in a rather more fractionalized and polarized form. The same constitutional rules of 1967 concerning the role of the executive and Congress and the mechanisms of checks and balances were in place. The same widespread belief in the existence of a social contract that defined social security, health, educational, and public employment rights and opportunities pervaded society. The traditionally autonomous labor, business, and other socioeconomic associations were recreated or remained in place. Finally, the authoritarian experience had generated a positive reassessment among all sectors of the political spectrum of the role played by parties, politicians, and Congress, the importance of political participation, the dangers associated with a wholesale acceptance of technobureaucratic "efficiency," and the importance of operating according to the rules of the liberal democratic system. Thus, although some of the features of the restored Uruguayan political system and culture generated a trend toward moderation and compromise, others clashed with the central tenets of the neoliberal model and hindered the ability of the administration to implement its policies through congressional cooperation or executive dictum.

The executive-congressional clashes started early in the Sanguinetti administration and very soon a policy-making pattern was established that would persist later under the Lacalle administration. Neoliberal proposals advanced by the executive were rejected or modified by Congress or Congress passed bills that eroded the neoliberal agenda; an impasse unfolded with the president insisting on his original proposals, threatening to call for early congressional elections, and using his veto power (or the threat of a veto) to force congressional approval or to block congressional initiatives. Finally, in most cases, some sort of compromise was reached that neither satisfied the executive's neoliberal aspirations nor the congressional majorities' desire to implement Keynesian or populist measures.

In these circumstances, one trend that clearly resembled the Argentine style of policy making was the attempt to concentrate power in the executive. The repeated use of presidential vetoes, the enactment by decree of measures that arguably should have been approved by Congress (for instance, concerning the authority and decisions of autonomous agencies, the imposition of veiled taxes as in the case of gasoline, and the fixation of wages and salaries), and the efforts to secure a docile Colorado bloc in Congress indicate that the Uruguayan executive had the same design as its counterpart in Argentina. However, unlike the Argentine case, its capacity to attain its goals was effectively limited by the strong resistance of the opposition parties, the insubordination of members of its own party (whose loyalty to their respective *sub-lemas* prevailed upon their allegiance to the president), the presence of important socioeconomic organizations able to preserve their independence vis-à-vis the state, and the commitment of substantial portions of the population to the preservation of crucial components of the traditional Uruguayan welfare state.

Faced with these obstacles and aware of the constraints imposed by the domestic circumstances, the executive tried to mobilize international resources in its favor. In part, this manipulation of international forces to reinforce the neoliberal trend and overcome domestic resistances was reflected in the quest for agreements with the IMF, the World Bank, and the creditor banks that included orthodox economic stabilization and adjustment conditions that, once accepted by the executive, could be presented as the only possible program to other political and social actors. This was the case with the agreements reached with the IMF and the foreign banks in 1985 and 1988 for the refinancing of the debt that fit the neoliberal strategy by demanding public deficit reductions, stringent monetary policies, wage restraints, trade and financial opening, and privatizations.

Another international factor in Uruguay emerged from the economic agreements signed with its neighboring countries—Convenio Argentino-Uruguayo de Cooperación Económica (CAUCE) with Argentina and Protocolo de Expansión Comercial (PEC) with Brazil—that culminated in the incorporation in 1991 of Uruguay to the MERCOSUR, the regional economic integration agreement sponsored by Argentina and Brazil.[53] In economic terms, the closer association of a small economy like the Uruguayan with its larger neighbors helped to reinforce some aspects of the process of economic liberalization such as trade and financial opening and the demands to reform the labor, social security, and taxation systems as well as the trend toward an export-oriented model that the government presented as the only viable alternative to stagnation. From a political viewpoint, removal of economic barriers, the international coordination of macroeconomic policies, and the declining role of the national state takes away the decision-making power from civil society and its elected representatives and transfers larger portions of it to domestic or international bureaucrats. The decisions concerning the increasingly complex monetary, investment, productive, and financial issues affecting the country no longer fell under the jurisdiction of the local politicians but tend to be gradually concentrated into the hands of the technobureaucrats promoting the integration process. Thus, new layers of decision making are added to the already existing ones and the gap between the national electorates, their representatives, and the agents that make the decisions widens to such an extent that the notion of democratic participation or consultation in economic policy making becomes meaningless.

Nevertheless, the governmental attempts to use its executive power and appeal to international factors to accelerate and deepen the neoliberal structural reforms failed to overcome the resistance of entrenched sectors. The Uruguayan economic and social structures remained essentially as they emerged from the authoritarian period, revealing the same precarious balance between economic liberalism, in areas such as the financial and external sectors, and redistributionist welfare policies, in areas such as social security, taxation, and public expenditures and enterprises. A similar inability to promote transformations through executive action was also apparent in the labor, social, human rights, military, and judicial spheres of policy making. In most cases the executive was unable to attain control over important actors and to manage developments in such a way as to secure, without paying high political costs, the implementation of its preferred policies.

The Colorado administration failed to eliminate or significantly erode the traditional organizational autonomy and leftist political affiliation of the workers' movement. Although weakened by the repressive actions of the authoritarian regime and by the decline in the numbers of industrial workers, national organizations of the Uruguayan labor movement that were recreated in 1984 under the name of PIT-CNT as the result of the fusion between the newly organized Plenario Intersindical de Trabajadores (PIT, workers interunion plenary) and the traditional Confederación Nacional de Trabajadores (CNT, workers national confederation) subsequently demonstrated its capacity to successfully challenge the government on issues such as wages, social security reform, labor laws, and other policies associated with the neoliberal model.54

Unlike the Alfonsín administration that was able to co-opt part of the labor leadership or the Menem administration that was able to disarticulate the organized labor movement, the Uruguayan government failed to gain political control over the unions, destroy their unity, or modify the labor laws in ways that could weaken the PIT-CNT or the individual trade unions. As a consequence, the Sanguinetti administration faced numerous strikes and was occasionally forced to make concessions concerning its wage policies as well as to discontinue its attempt to introduce labor regulations aimed to replace what the president called the "unionism of anger and resentment" with a "new syndicalism which defends the worker through better productivity and thus gives stability to employees and the enterprise."55

Concerning its military and human rights policies, the Sanguinetti administration was more successful than in the labor sphere in imposing a solution, but this victory was obtained at a high political cost.56 After a number of vacillations concerning the necessity and opportunity of an amnesty for the military who had committed human rights abuses—a measure that the military command first rejected as unwarranted and then demanded as indispensable—and after considerable hesitation concerning the breadth of this kind of legislation, Sanguinetti supported a general amnesty that was stalled in Congress until December 1986. At that time, under considerable pressure from the military to approve the amnesty before several officers were brought to trial, Congress approved and Sanguinetti endorsed sweeping legislation declaring the end of the state's intention and faculty to punish crimes and human rights violations committed by the military during the authoritarian period. The negative reaction of a substantial portion of the population to this general amnesty resulted in a successful campaign led by the Frente Amplio and labor groups to gather signatures for a referendum on this measure. Finally, after considerable delay, the referendum took place in April 1989 with the pro-amnesty vote winning by a margin of 57 percent against 43 percent, although in Montevideo those who rejected the amnesty gathered 55 percent of the ballots. The government had succeeded in passing the measure but at the cost of showing an alarming weakness vis-à-vis the military and fostering a significant degree of opposition among the population.

The Political Economic Deadlock

The presidential elections of 1989 sealed the fate of the Colorados and confirmed their precipitous loss of popular support while reaffirming some of the trends observable throughout the first democratic term.[57] The Blanco party obtained 39 percent of the vote while the Colorados gathered only 30 percent. The Left—which split into two different coalitions, the Frente Amplio and the Nuevo Espacio—gathered 31 percent of the ballots. With these results the candidate of the most voted *sub-lema* in the Blanco party, Luis Alberto Lacalle, who obtained 32 percent of the votes—most of them concentrated in the interior of the country— was elected president for the period 1990–1994. At the same time, the Frente Amplio won the Montevideo municipal government with 48 percent of the votes. Congress remained hopelessly divided into numerous factions with none of them able to attain an operational majority. The 1989 elections showed also the continuation of the erosion of the popular appeal of the traditional parties—more dramatic in the case of the Colorados—and a growth of the popularity of the leftist forces, although this leftward turn was partially neutralized by the split of the Left into more radical (Frente Amplio) and more moderate (Nuevo Espaci) coalitions. As a last slight to Sanguinetti's neoliberal program, in a referendum celebrated together with the presidential election, the voters supported by an overwhelming majority a constitutional amendment that guaranteed the maintenance of the traditional social security system, rejecting the government's attempt to cut benefits and reduce state intervention in the management of the system.

The new Lacalle administration represented one of the traditional conservative factions of the Blanco party, the Herrerista *sub-lema*,[58] and was clearly committed to the implementation of neoliberal economic and social policies that did not differ substantially from those favored by the previous administration. However, Lacalle appeared to have learned one lesson from the experience of his predecessor: in the confrontational liberal democratic landscape of Uruguay, no single political faction could secure by itself the means to enforce a neoliberal program against the will of disparate but powerful political and socioeconomic actors. Thus, in order to try to break the stalemate, the new president invited sectors of the Colorado party to join a coalition cabinet—the so-called "national coincidence"—aimed to secure congressional majorities for his program. Several factions of the Colorado party, including the Unión Batllista and the Radical Batllista groups, accepted the invitation and their representatives were appointed to ministerial positions. Initially, this coalition gave the administration the congressional votes necessary to maintain a liberal economic program.[59] However, the Lacalle administration was unable to overcome congressional and popular opposition to a number of proposals oriented to deepen the neoliberal structural reforms. By early 1992, this opposition was manifested not only in the growing labor unrest and the unrelenting antagonism of the Frente Amplio but also in the calls made by leaders of different factions of the ruling Blanco party who worried about their declining popularity and asked to slow down the pace of the deregulation, taxation, and fiscal reforms and replace the economic team.

Meanwhile, as the unions and leftist groups called for new strikes, an important faction of the Colorado party that had joined the coalition cabinet—the Radical Batllista sub-lema, led by Jorge Batlle—withdrew its support to the administration in Congress, arguing that governmental indecision had stalled the application of the neoliberal program. Different Blanco groups— including the vice president's Movimiento de Renovación y Victoria, the Movimiento Nacional de Rocha, led by Senator Carlos J. Pereyra, and even some members of the president's own Herrerista faction—also declared their opposition to the government economic policies.[60]

A few days after this revolt of the political class, President Lacalle addressed the nation to announce that he had requested the resignation of his cabinet because "the composition of our cabinet is clearly not resulting in votes in congress" and he added that "there is no more room for pretending; we cannot simply administrate the crisis . . . it is necessary to govern and transform our reality."[61] The new cabinet appointed by Lacalle announced a number of measures that attempted to reinforce the neoliberal course including drastic cuts in public expenditures, social security reforms, reductions in public salaries and employment, new taxes, and privatizations. The attempt to concentrate economic decision-making power in the executive and stay the neoliberal course was evident but the outcome in terms of effectiveness was uncertain.

As expected, the response to these announcements by large sectors of the population was extremely negative: by May 1992 the president's performance was approved by only 13 percent of the population and disapproved by 63 percent.[62] Soon, it also became clear that the chances of gaining majoritarian congressional support for the deepening of the neoliberal program were nil. Different factions of the Blanco party stated their opposition to the administration's neoliberal stance and called on the government to "end the suffering of the people" by moderating its policies.[63] The Frente Amplio and the PIT-CNT announced their intention to block the application of these measures and began to collect signatures for a referendum aimed to abrogate the privatization law. A thirty-six-hour general strike called by the PIT-CNT in mid-May paralyzed the country. The Chamber of Deputies defeated the draft bill on social security reform sent by the executive and reaffirmed the preservation of the traditional system.[64] Repeated interpellations of ministers before Congress led to several censorship votes that weakened the executive's ability to obtain agreement for its policies.

Faced with this situation, Lacalle and Economic Minister Ignacio de Posadas began to call on the entrepreneurial associations and business groups to support the neoliberal measures and exert pressure on Parliament to approve them while threatening with the dissolution of both congressional houses and early elections.[65] Thus, when the social security reform bill foundered, Lacalle asked for "the cooperation of entrepreneurs whose costs are at risk and whose competitiveness will be greatly compromised if this issue is not resolved."[66] Concerning the refusal of Congress to accept further budget cuts, the economy minister called on business organizations to put pressure on the representatives, declaring that "we do want to emphasize the responsibility of business organizations on this issue. . . . I call on them to exercise their rights before those who represent them directly. . . . Ask to be heard in congress because the spending reduction the country needs will not be achieved through the effort of the executive branch alone."[67] The business groups stated their critical support for some of the neoliberal policies but did not abandon their traditionally cautious approach to political involvement, preferring to maintain collaborative relations with the political parties and congressional factions avoiding any open confrontation with them or open alliance with the executive.[68]

Meanwhile, in a number of occasions the president emphasized that, without the neoliberal transformations advocated by the executive, Uruguay would be unable to join the MERCOSUR and obtain the expected economic benefits. According to Lacalle, "the MERCOSUR represents the largest qualitative change for our country since our independence. . . . However, we will not be able to join this great opportunity . . . if we do not implement immediately and quickly—today— the transformations that are needed and that are not the patrimony of just one political party."[69]

The response to the administration's desperate calls for support was disappointing and failed to reverse the trend toward growing executive isolation and to remedy the inefficacy of its policy approach. By mid-December a critical component of the neoliberal program, the privatization law, was rejected by a substantial majority in the referendum propitiated by the Left and the labor organizations.[70] Lacalle promised to respect the results but, after criticizing his adversaries for "opposing the modernization of the country," he reaffirmed his decision to follow the same economic course and not to change his social policy nor replace the cabinet. The political-economic impasse in Uruguay was by then complete: the application of the neoliberal program had been halted but the opposition did not have the capacity to formulate and implement an alternative program.

The general elections of 27 November 1994 marked the end of the Blanco administration and resulted in the presidential election of Sanguinetti for a new period (1994–1998).[71] However, the vote was split into practically identical fractions with the Colorado party obtaining 32.3 percent of the vote, the Blanco party 31.1 percent, and the Frente Amplio 30.8 percent (with Nuevo Espacio coming a distant fourth with 5.2 percent of the vote). Thus, Sanguinetti's narrow victory was obtained only as a result of the application of the peculiar *lema* electoral system that allowed him to add the votes of other Colorado candidates although he gathered 20 percent less of the popular vote than the single candidate of the Frente Amplio, the mayor of Montevideo, Tabaré Vázquez. Once again congressional seats were divided among three main groups with similar strength, which, in turn, exhibited numerous internal factions making it impossible for the Sanguinetti administration to secure any viable majority. Once again, Sanguinetti would be forced to negotiate temporary agreements to pass bills that he favors or use the presidential veto to block those that he opposes.

It is difficult to predict with certainty what will be the most likely outcome in Uruguay of the renewed conflict between an executive determined to impose a neoliberal restructuring program and the dissenting forces that challenge its ascendancy. It seems, however, that the chances of permanent institutionalization of a liberal democracy with strong concentration of power in the executive and able to successfully pursue free market policies are limited. If the experience of the last few years is a valid indicator of future trends the stalemate will continue and the pressures for the modification of the neoliberal program and even for a reversal of this course will not disappear. Thus, the future may bring in Uruguay renewed calls for the transformation of the current political economic configurations especially in terms of promoting broader and more effective citizens' participation in the decision-making processes and for restraining and controlling the impact of free market forces on different sectors of civil society. These calls for non-neoliberal restructuring may assume the form of demands for transitions from liberal democracy to democratic liberalism, the creation or resurgence of forms of consociational democracy, and even the possibility of new longings for workable forms of democratic socialism.

Conclusions: On Liberal Democracy, Economic Liberalism, and Policy Making in Argentina and Uruguay

In Argentina and Uruguay the exhaustion of the import substitution industrialization model and the parallel decline of the populist and redistributionist experiences marked the beginning of a series of political economic experiments aimed to reestablish conditions for economic growth, social peace, and political stability. Subsequent attempts made by democratic or authoritarian governments to modify the political economic model in a state-led developmentalist direction by eliminating some of its redistributionist and nationalistic features failed due to adverse international trends and the effective opposition mounted by the socioeconomic and political actors whose fortunes were linked to the subsistence of the populist and welfare states. The bureaucratic-authoritarian regimes of the 1970s and 1980s attempted to solve the problem by combining the use of military repression with the implementation of neoliberal programs designed to atomize and weaken these socioeconomic and political groups while uprooting the foundations of their power and the sources of their behavior. The use of coercion and free markets as weapons to disarticulate the distributionist coalitions and generate the conditions for the establishment of a liberal export-oriented economy as well as a stable semiauthoritarian regime succeeded in changing some of the socioeconomic structures and processes but failed to attain the ultimate goals of neoliberalism. It became apparent that the authoritarian regimes could implement with relative success some neoliberal policies but that they could not complete the application of the program nor guarantee the maintenance in the long run of these neoliberal strategies. The continuity and deepening of the neoliberal restructuring appears to require the establishment of political structures and procedures able to legitimize the economic model and facilitate its survival during periods of economic and social strain. The Argentine and Uruguayan authoritarian regimes failed to attain this political goal and this failure led to growing political instability as the economic crises escalated, not only forcing them to transfer power to civilian elected governments but jeopardizing the continuation of the neoliberal program of structural transformation.

The groups that emerged or flourished in Argentina and Uruguay in the 1970s and 1980s as a result of the neoliberal innovations recognized by the end of the authoritarian periods the need to develop these political underpinnings to ensure the maintenance and strengthening of the model. At the same time, these groups rejected as dangerous or unrealistic the demands for nonliberal economic policies and broad political participation raised by some subordinated socioeconomic groups and the populist and leftist sectors of the political spectrum. The former were identified as supporters of the economic models and forms of state intervention that led to the economic, social, and political crises of the 1960s and 1970s. The latter were denounced as advocating approaches that in practice could only lead to growing ungovernability and democratic breakdown.

In these circumstances liberal democracy appeared as the best option to create favorable conditions for the accomplishment of neoliberal goals. The basic features of liberal democracy—a government whose legitimacy rests on a claim to

represent the citizenry; individual consent; equality before the law; separation between the private and public domains; majority rule with constitutional limitations; competitive periodical elections; possibility of citizens' participation as voters and candidates; and guarantees for the freedoms of expression, assembly, and
organization[72]—were acceptable as long as they provided the necessary legitimacy
to the political economic model and were not used to restrict property rights, in-
terfere in the market, or recreate populist and redistributionist experiences. Moreover, liberal democratic governments may be more inclined or better prepared
than their authoritarian predecessors to effectively apply neoliberal policies aimed
to reduce public expenditures (particularly the military budget), promote trade liberalization favoring generic consumers over specific groups of producers, obtain
support for privatization and deregulation decisions, and reduce uncertainty concerning the respect for property rights by eliminating the element of arbitrariness
present in authoritarian regimes and underscoring the rule of law.

At the international level other factors reinforced this trend toward liberal
democracy and neoliberal economics and exerted enormous influence on Argentina and Uruguay. In both countries, this mix of political and economic liberalism was presented as the only viable strategy to ensure economic, social, and political development considering not only the collapse of the earlier democratic
distributionist and semiauthoritarian populist models of import-substitution industrialization and of the recent bureaucratic-authoritarian experiences but the simultaneous crumbling of socialist and populist experiences in other parts of the
world. At the same time, the trend toward economic liberalism was reinforced by
the global surge of transnationalization and interdependence in the 1970s and
1980s, which prompted the development of a global capitalist political economy in
which the role of the states has been severely limited by their growing incapacity
to control or modify the nature and the outcomes of free market interactions that
affect economic, social, and political developments within and across national
boundaries.[73] Finally, in Latin America, the pressure for the application of neoliberal programs was reinforced by the emergence of the so-called "Washington Consensus" that advocated fiscal discipline, elimination of subsidies, broad and moderate taxation, market-determined interest and exchange rates, trade and foreign
investment liberalization, privatization of state enterprises, deregulation, and respect for private property rights.[74]

This created a problematic situation because, in the absence of adequate state
intervention, self-regulating market economies tend to allocate the cost of economic transformation unequally among different socioeconomic groups and generate hardship for substantial segments of the population. Thus, to guarantee a
longer-lasting stability of the free market system it is necessary to introduce a value-
rational element of belief in its validity (legitimacy) that is normally obtained from

its association with liberal democracy.[75] This political regime is legitimized by upholding values such as freedom, individual progress, popular representation, and equality before the law that appeal to significant portions of the population. At the same time, liberal democracy prescribes the protection of private property, the separation between the public and private spheres, and the existence of a minimal state confined to the maintenance and reproduction of a liberal capitalist order characterized by the preservation of civil liberties and economic freedom.

Ultimately, it was this notion of liberal democracy that dominated the Argentine and Uruguayan transitions and was shared, at least initially, by substantial sectors of the population—including upper-, middle-, and even low-income groups—who began to link liberal political and economic structures and processes with an underlying notion of efficient allocation of resources, power, and wealth, respectively. Elections were seen as the mechanism through which citizens convey their political choices by selecting their authorities while the market was regarded as the mechanism through which consumers express their economic preferences by exchanging goods and services. From this perspective, free markets and liberal democracy become mutually reinforcing mechanisms that create adequate conditions to preserve and foster political freedom and economic prosperity.[76] In this context, the prevalence of market forces and the trend toward less participative political regimes appears to be reflected in the features of the political leaders who emerge during the period of liberal democratization. These leaders are skillful political operators and tacticians who do not have or rapidly discard after election their ideological ascriptions and campaign platforms to embrace neoliberal strategies.

Notwithstanding these circumstances favorable to the consolidation of elected governments with neoliberal programs, in Argentina and Uruguay the concern over the stability of these emergent liberal democracies becomes an issue when considering the strength and durability of the commitment to this regime by different domestic groups. Obviously, domestic support for liberal democracy depends on a number of political variables such as the degree of devastation brought about by the authoritarian regimes and the intensity of the population's revulsion against these regimes, the depth of the popular belief in the legitimacy of democracy, the ability of democratic governments to establish effective institutional arrangements and to preserve peace and order, the existence of representative political parties, and other political conditions. But there is another crucial element that must be present to guarantee the stability of these liberal democracies: continuous support for the socioeconomic features of the system, namely private property, free markets, consumer sovereignty, and minimal state intervention in the economy.

The critical problem is that if this support is mostly based on the expectation of material benefits—that is, on the belief that a market economy would generate prosperity and that, in the long run, most of the population would partake in the benefits resulting from economic growth—it can ebb if these hopes are lost. If the expectations of economic and social progress held by low and middle sectors are dashed by a continuous incapacity of the market system to generate adequate rates of economic growth and more satisfactory income distribution patterns there will be growing pressures to abandon some of the basic tenets of liberalism and to implement more interventionist state policies to redistribute income, promote employment, and improve social services.

On the other hand, if these attempts to introduce structural changes appear imminent or get underway, powerful domestic socioeconomic groups and foreign actors might revert to their old fears of democracy as conducive to state intervention and restrictions on private profits and property rights. If a situation arises in which the political and economic sides of the liberal democratic equation no longer complement each other—for instance if parties opposed to the neoliberal policies come to power and maintain their electoral promises or are able from the opposition to hinder the application of these policies—the commitment to liberal capitalism might take precedence over the allegiance to political democracy for powerful international and domestic forces. In such a case, the conflict might result in antidemocratic moves and, depending on the correlation of forces, in the breakdown of democracy or in a serious deterioration of the regime's capacity to maintain control over the economic and political circumstances.

The Argentine and Uruguayan liberal democratic governments, when confronted with the rise of these tensions between market and democracy, turned to solutions that, without completely eliminating the liberal democratic features of their respective regimes, represented a consistent effort to reduce political participation, concentrate political power in the executive branch, and intensify the use of legal repressive methods. Some basic elements of a liberal democracy, such as periodic elections, party competition, and majority rule with constitutional limitations were preserved. But, at the same time, there were a number of initiatives designed to further limit the participation or influence of political and socioeconomic groups in the decisions. With different degrees of success, the Argentine and Uruguayan civilian administrations tried to concentrate the decision-making power in the executive branch, especially to facilitate the application of economic policies aimed to strengthen the free market system (privatizations; liberalization of the financial, monetary, exchange, and foreign trade sectors; rationalization of the public sector). At the same time, conscious attempts were made to exclude Congress from meaningful participation in these decisions and to prevent the judiciary from exercising control over them. There were also successful attempts, especially in Argentina, to curtail certain rights and freedoms (strike; collective bargaining; unionization; access to mass media; publicity of state actions) while opposing any expansion of the remaining ones. The use of legal repressive measures to deal with challenges from the opposition forces has intensified, while the role of the military and the security forces in domestic affairs—that at the beginning of the democratic periods was expected to be reduced to a minimal expression—was enhanced. In sum, there were clear attempts in both countries to restrict as much as possible the participatory elements of democracy and to reduce the possibility of any socioeconomic development adverse to free markets, while the merging of liberal democracy and economic liberalism was stressed to the exclusion of any other political-economic alternatives.

The question that remains, however, is why this political strategy was relatively successful in securing the neoliberal restructuring of Argentina while it failed in Uruguay. Paradoxically, Argentina's tradition of corporatism seems to have created the conditions for the destruction of organized opposition to the neoliberal project and facilitated the effective implementation of policies aimed to reduce the degree of state intervention in the economy as well as its capacity to implement redistributionist economic and social policies. In contrast, the Uruguayan tradition of political pluralism hampered the implementation of the neoliberal program. In Argentina it was possible for the Alfonsín administration to partially manipulate and co-opt some political and socioeconomic actors and then for the Menem administration to shatter and subdue political parties and socioeconomic organizations that had been established and nourished by the state and that remained dependent and subordinate to it. In Uruguay, in contrast, neither Sanguinetti nor Lacalle were able to accomplish the atomization and subjugation of these actors to the neoliberal project. This was so because political parties (though linked by clientelistic relations to the state) and socioeconomic organizations (although state-oriented in their actions) preserved their autonomy and were able to effectively block the governmental restructuring initiatives.

In both cases, there was a trend toward concentration of power in the executive branch. In Argentina this shift was bolstered by the existence of political economic circumstances that offered the executive branch the opportunity and resources necessary to impose its will on Congress, political parties, and socioeconomic organizations. In Uruguay this trend toward executive predominance met the resistance of autonomous political and socioeconomic actors and led to growing presidential isolation and impotence. Other specific economic and political circumstances that unfolded in Argentina during the period of consolidation of liberal democracy strengthened the unilateral decision-making capacity of the executive and eased the implementation of the neoliberal program. Among these particular circumstances, the Peronist tradition of personalistic leadership contributed to facilitate the concentration of power in the hands of a charismatic president as well as the exclusion of other actors from the decision-making process. At the same time, the hyperinflationary explosion of 1989 generated a strong longing for economic stability among a substantial portion of the population that superseded any propensity to demand the implementation of policies that could unleash, according to the administration, a new inflationary surge. These particular circumstances were not present in the Uruguayan case, where a political tradition of consensus and compromise curtailed the chances of presidential supremacy while the milder inflation, although prompting demands for stabilization, did not override the proclivity to press for redistributionist policies.

In conclusion, while the Argentine neoliberal restructuring seems to have reached the point of no return, narrowing the range of options that any new administration would face, the Uruguayan impasse retains the potential for diverse scenarios ranging from a neoliberal deepening to a social democratic undertaking. The structural transformations already completed in Argentina with the consequent atomization of civil society and the strengthening of executive capacity to enforce neoliberal policies indicate a high probability that in the future the current style of exclusionary policy making would remain unaltered, although there may be variations in the intensity of the neoliberal drive or even of some of its contents. In contrast, the incomplete character of Uruguay's structural changes and the permanence of relatively solid and autonomous political and social actors that countervailed the executive suggest that there are significant prospects for the emergence of more participatory forms of policy making as well as for a shift away from neoliberal orthodoxy.

CONCLUSION

KURT VON METTENHEIM and

JAMES MALLOY

This conclusion reviews the major contributions of the authors and returns to the common themes presented at the outset of this volume. Looking back at the diverse national experiences examined in preceding chapters, it is clear that several goals have been achieved. The analyses in this volume surpass both dated concerns about transitions from military rule and the ethno- or Eurocentrism implied in theories of democratic consolidation. Furthermore, by focusing on new trends in the region, authors also surpass the forced dichotomy between competitive and participatory democratic theory that has dominated political analysis for over three decades. Contributors instead stress the rich variety and rapid pace of political change in the region and attempt to portray the new risks and opportunities presented by national and regional experiences with the design of posttransition democracy. Deepening democracy is not a theory to be imposed on these experiences. Rather, it is a concept that seeks to capture recent political achievements in Latin America. By emphasizing both new patterns of competitive party-electoral politics and new styles of inclusive policy making and governance, authors have reached beyond existing ideas and academic divisions of labor to clarify promising new developments and face new risks in Latin America.

Again, this emphasis on both party-electoral politics and pluralistic means of governance challenges prevailing positions in democratic theory. Neither the false realism that attempts to restrict definitions of democracy to competitive elections nor the difficult idealism of participatory theories provides sufficient conceptual guides for understanding recent trajectories of change in Latin America. For the self-declared mainstream tradition that dates itself from Schumpeter, democracy in mass society can be no more than a means for selecting leaders through competitive elections.[1] This minimal definition guts core values and ideas from the concept of democracy that must be placed on the agendas of both politicians and social scientists. While more recent advocates of participatory theories of democracy challenge scholars to conceptualize change, the imposing gap between existing politics and participatory ideals often leaves one unsure how to proceed from one to the other.[2] And neither competitive nor participatory theories fully develop strategies for improving access and increasing the influence of organized groups from civil society during the bureaucratic politics of policy formulation and implementation.

Another central theme that runs throughout this volume is that broad claims about causal relations between market capitalism and democratic government are overstated. A major achievement of Latin American social science in the 1970s was to suggest that dependent development in the region countered the expectations of both liberals and marxists who, despite their differences, shared causal claims that insisted on linking political outcomes to economic developments.[3] Until new ideas of dependency emerged from Latin America, liberal scholarship expected that, like their understanding of Europe and North America, economic development would produce social modernization that, in turn, would provide the conditions for political democracy.[4] Marxist debate also turned on the inexorable trends of economic crisis, impoverishment, and underdevelopment, trends that would produce conditions making political revolutions necessary and possible.[5] While these expectations may now seem dated, analysts of the region should avoid repeating their erroneous assumptions. Democracy is not caused by underlying structures or developments in economy and society. Instead, it is built in specific national contexts and remains open to human failure and achievement.

In this respect, Sylvia Borzutzky also counters neoliberal claims about Chile by comparing politics before and after the military dictatorship of General Pinochet. Her comparison suggests that the state has not decreased but instead shifted from a social role to an economic one. Before 1973, the liberal, pluralist, and social tradition of Chilean politics depended on a balance between legislature and executive, a multiparty system, and government policies of education, social security, health, and other social services that were envied by other Latin American nations. Borzutzky argues that Pinochet's military dictatorship changed the substance of democratic politics in Chile, even after the return to civilian rule. Military rule defeated leftist and labor groups, atomized society, and severed the executive from political life. However, contrary to neoliberal ideology, Pinochet and military rulers did not reduce the role and presence of government in society: they redefined it from its traditional social role to exclusively economic concerns.

The analyses presented in this volume also confirm the need for observers of Latin America to move on from debates that attempt to cut complex political trajectories into moments of transition and consolidation.[6] The concept of transition implies two polar regime types of authoritarianism and democracy that often fail to capture the complex and shifting character of Latin American politics. The concept of democratic consolidation is even more problematic because it implies defining limits to political processes in the region. Rather than defining what is and what is not democratic, this volume sought to emphasize new realities in Latin American party-electoral politics, and new attempts at governing the dense mix of public expectations, private interests, bureaucrats, and economic constraints. By focusing on the two dimensions of party-electoral politics and the policy process, authors were able to identify new trends in Latin America during the 1990s.

Indeed, the critical content and attention to context that are central to the idea of deepening democracy may be relevant to analysts of other world regions as they rush to assimilate the dramatic changes in the wake of the cold war. Complex and often incomplete transitions from authoritarian rule have produced reassessment of politics not only in Latin America, but also in Asia, Africa, Eastern Europe, and the new nations of the former Soviet Union. While theories and concepts from Latin America such as state-led development, dependency, bureaucratic authoritarianism, and inertial inflation were quickly adopted by scholars in other regions, a note of caution is in order for those who would export definitions of democracy from Latin America. The concept of deepening democracy may travel only to the extent that it stresses the importance of recognizing regional and national differences. Indeed, perhaps the central conclusion that can be extracted from this volume is that the content of competitive party-electoral politics and open, pluralistic governance depends on particular national and regional contexts.

A central concern at the end of this volume remains the legacies of institutional changes introduced by military governments, ranging from new constitutions to autonomous central banks and electoral laws that split popular forces or underrepresent certain groups, to formal guardian roles for the military. In this respect, one reason for military elites choosing liberalization and transition strategies was that populist and leftist challenges had apparently been defeated and that new institutions had been designed to limit participation and popular influence over policy making. In this respect, Latin American military governments supervised reforms similar to the progressive era in the United States. The United States Federal Reserve was also designed to be insulated from Congress, the president, and voters. Chilean and other Latin American military elites designed similar institutions so that monetary policy could no longer be directly influenced by popular pressures. Because it was thought that popular pressures caused inflation, it followed that making monetary policy a technocratic enclave would avert both hyperinflation and the instability associated with civilian government.

Unfortunately, the concerns about hybrid regimes in Latin America expressed by James Malloy at the end of the volume entitled *Authoritarians and Democrats in Latin America,* which he and Mitchell Seligson edited in 1987, are still valid. The risk remains that isolated executives may continue to conduct exclusive patterns of policy formulation and implementation while democratic politics is restricted to more or less competitive elections. After transitions to civilian rule, newly elected executives often continued to pursue exclusive styles of policy making. But the sequence of failed economic packages, social impoverishment, and political disappointment left by executives and their technocratic teams suggests that the centralization of policy making and governance not only counters core values of the liberal and democratic tradition; centralization in and of itself tends not to produce effective policies and programs. However, the need to deepen democracy by linking party-electoral politics to open, pluralistic governance is more than an empirical claim about post-transition Latin American politics.

Latin America now confronts universal issues of liberal-democratic governance. The liberal-democratic tradition suggests that an essential tension exists between the initial selection of representatives through competitive elections and subsequent pluralistic transactions between representatives and social interests. It is precisely this essential tension between electoral politics and open policy making that provides the central meaning of deepening democracy and distinguishes it from existing approaches in comparative politics. Civilian political elites in post-transition Latin America must simultaneously rebuild state capacities weakened by military rule, implement effective policies of economic adjustment, and set clear precedents and institutional parameters for democratic politics in the future. Perhaps the central argument that runs throughout the analyses of this volume is that deepening democracy may not only meet these tasks, but that in doing so political leaders may also surpass long-standing problems of governance in the region. Deepening democracy is possible in posttransition Latin America because widespread consensus exists that authoritarian solutions failed. The centralization of power by military rulers placed executives above electoral review and cut social groups out of the policy process. Far from freeing military elites to impose rational policies above the traffic of politics, centralization failed to address the substantive problems of Latin America. Military leaders lacked the necessary feedback that produces information, the fora that permit negotiation, the debate that could test their ideas, and the bargaining that could have placed politicians and the public behind their initiatives.

The widespread recognition of populist errors in preceding periods of competitive politics also increases the opportunities for deepening democracy today in Latin America. Few returning civilian elites have advocated the populist solutions of the past. The collective memory of contemporary civilian political elites appears to recognize that the irresponsible escalation of populist demands contributed to the radicalization and polarization that produced military intervention throughout the region in the 1960s and 1970s. In sum, deepening democracy may resolve long-standing problems of governance and instability in the region because it is widely recognized that both the centralization of power by military rulers and the demagogic appeals of populist politicians are no longer viable.

Deepening Electoral Representation

The analyses in this volume suggest that observers of the region need to reassess three influential theories and concepts about party-electoral politics and electoral representation. First, formal models of party organization based on the rigid party systems that emerged within European parliamentary systems fail to provide adequate conceptual guides for understanding Latin American political parties. This error is not new. Indeed, scholars suggested that party systems could solve the political development problems of Latin America some thirty years ago, before the last round of military intervention.[7] Observers of Latin American politics need to develop theories of party organizations and party-electoral politics that avert a new generation of misplaced reformist liberalism that clings to idealized models of rigid party systems and party government in Europe.[8]

Roderic Camp's analysis of Mexico and Enrique Baloyra's work on Venezuela go a long way toward tempering overoptimistic generalizations about political parties and democracy in the region. For Camp, the tenacious party monopoly of the PRI has channeled liberalization to the local and state level and secured neoliberal austerity throughout the 1980s and 1990s through corporatist organization. Camp thereby agrees with Vacs that austere neoliberal policies have been imposed by centralized state agencies and corporatist labor and business organizations rather than open, liberal, and pluralistic politics. Corporatism, that is to say the monopoly of representation through functionally defined groups recognized by the state,[9] is antithetic to the dispersion of power through a variety of independent social groups. The reality that labor, business, and peasants remain subject to functionally defined organizations within the umbrella state-party of the PRI rigidly controlled by state elites suggests that difficult barriers to deepening democracy remain in Mexico. In this respect, Mexico remains a powerful example of a hybrid regime, one in which executives retain power at the center while more or less competitive elections on the local and state level serve as a type of escape valve for social and political pressures.

Although the formal structure of competitive elections and the rotation of parties in Venezuela differs from Mexico, Enrique Baloyra also emphasizes the importance of a de facto party monopoly. Indeed, while oil revenues eased social tensions through the 1980s, urban revolts and military coups during the 1990s suggest that traditional perceptions of stability in Venezuela are amiss. Instead, Baloyra's analysis of the corporatism and corruption suggests that party systems tend to freeze politics and isolate political elites from new social pressures and policy needs. And while the events of military coups and spontaneous popular demonstrations since 1989 in Venezuelan politics may be dramatic, Baloyra argues that party elites will most likely outlive these challenges by granting concessions and minimal reform. Although this volume criticizes competitive democratic theory, the process of populist challenge and political concession by party elites in Venezuela confirms an important insight of elite democratic theories. Even under restricted conditions, competitive elections can communicate demands for change and force political elites to adapt.[10]

The second problem with accepted theories and concepts about party-electoral politics in the region is the misplaced character of liberal-reformist critiques of presidentialism. During and after transitions from military rule, the presidential and federal systems of the region produced not the gridlock, polarization, corruption, and demagogic populism that critics feared but a remarkable variety of political change through direct popular appeals, complex alliances with patronage machines, and movements for political reform. Indeed, critics of presidentialism in Latin America underestimated the political opportunities presented by this form of government. Far from the trajectory of polarization, legislative paralysis, and democratic breakdown that Valenzuela, Linz, Mainwaring, and others fear, presidents succeeded in crafting new political alliances and pursuing new agendas of reform to redefine what was possible during and after recent transitions from military rule throughout the region.[11]

The contributions of Carrion, Gamarra, and von Mettenheim clarify the risks and opportunities for deepening democracy through presidential initiative. Carrion makes clear the risks of authoritarian presidentialism in Peru. The rapid emergence of Alberto Fujimori demonstrates both the risks of direct popular appeals and the ability of executives to use short-term economic achievements to insulate their economic policy teams from other social and political actors. Indeed, the ability of President Fujimori to close Congress, suspend the constitution, violate civil liberties, and ground his rule in a national plebiscite echoes methods used by popular dictators since Napoleon Bonaparte's 1851 coup that ended the French Second Republic.

Gamarra argues that Bolivian president Paz Estenssoro's pact for democracy spanned parties and sustained economic reform in terms that defied the negative scenarios sketched by the critics of presidentialism. And contrary to the notion that only parliaments can remove executives, Brazil's first directly elected president after the transition from military rule was impeached on charges of corruption in late 1992. The analysis of Brazilian politics by von Mettenheim suggests that scholars need to shift away from models derived from European experiences and develop new concepts that capture trajectories of change within the presidential and federal systems typical of the Americas. Since the transition from military rule in 1985 in Brazil, two features of presidential and federal government have rapidly shaped both popular expectations and a series of alliances among party organizations: the separate and direct election of executive and legislature and the prerogative of executives to appoint professional politicians directly to administrative posts.

Furthermore, the impeachment of Fernando Collor de Mello in 1992, the election of Fernando Henrique Cardoso in 1994, and the reduction of inflation in 1994 while redistributing wealth to the poor, taken together, provide strong evidence that effective governance and political reform are possible in Latin American presidential systems. Contrary to neo-liberal, parliamentary, and Eurocentric models alike, it is precisely the fluidity of party alliances and the politicization of public administration and economic policy that produced change. Indeed, the Cardoso administration appears to have reversed the vicious cycle of policy failure and popular exclusion that predominated during the 1980s in Brazil by linking party-electoral politics and social groups to the development and implementation of economic policy.

Scholars should not overstate causal claims about presidential institutions in Latin America. While institutions matter, there are no easy solutions for the imposing structural problems of Latin American politics. Deeply entrenched social hierarchy remains. Citizenship is denuded by patronage and corruption, and social groups continue to bypass electoral politics to extract benefits directly from state agencies. Indeed, the lofty debate among observers of Latin American politics about the formal attributes of parliamentary and presidential government often seems particularly unsuited to both the pace of political change and the continued existence of informal influence in the region. The central realities of the region such as largely unexpected transitions from military to civilian rule, rapidly shifting pacts and alliances, high and hyperinflation, dramatic neoliberal reforms and economic adjustment policies, volatile financial markets, increasingly internationalized economies, and a rapidly shifting new world order in the wake of the cold war suggest that analysts should temper claims about the formal attributes of institutional architecture. While institutions matter, they are deeply embedded in national and regional contexts and the subtexts of informal influence.

The third body of scholarship on electoral representation that will require more care is that of public opinion analysis through surveys. New concepts, theories, and methods are needed to tap the complexity and diversity of Latin American public opinion. Empirical accounts of public opinion and voter behavior in Latin American politics must reflect not only the rich diversity across the region's electorates, but also the complex methodological skills developed by scholars of European and North American electorates. Simple analyses of class, party affinity, or other characteristics of voters easily extracted from standard questionnaires simply cannot provide the basis for adequate theories of public opinion and voter alignment in Latin America. The volatility, transparency, and complexity of change in Latin American public opinion requires comparative analysis that is more sensitive to national and regional differences.[12]

In sum, social scientists need to reassess central assumptions about public opinion, voter rationality, party organization, electoral representation, and other cognate subfields used to analyze democracy in Latin America. Concepts and theories based on Europe and the United States cannot be reflexively applied to the region. And when Latin American developments differ from previous experiences, they should not be disregarded as dysfunctional. Perhaps the central problem with the comparative analysis of democracy is the underlying liberal reformism that seeks to impose ideal patterns of party government, idealized conceptions of voter rationality, and formal models of electoral representation. Indeed, the reformist bent of scholars that tends to set these ideals and models of democratic politics against the perceived imperfections of Latin America is deeply troubling. The essence of the liberal and positivist tradition is doubt and the constant reassessment of theory with evidence—not calls for reform of political realities in the image of formal models. Scholars may indeed find voters that think differently, parties that are organized differently, and different institutions of electoral representation in Latin America. However, when reality differs from theory, theory should be revised. Advocating draconian reform of political institutions is a puzzling departure from the liberal and positivist tradition.

Deepening Democracy Through Open, Pluralistic, and Inclusive Governance

This volume ends with the tempered hope that Latin American political elites can indeed confront the tasks of building democratic institutions while imple-

menting viable economic policies of adjustment, restructuring, and modernization. The legacy of failed packages and imposed solutions throughout the region
leaves little room for doubt: Insulated technocrats and economists in executive
agencies not only truncate democracy, they often fail to effectively implement policies. Economic policy can no longer be developed in isolation from elected representatives and the diverse organizations that seek to represent social groups. Indeed, the analyses presented in this volume suggest that the stuff of
politics—bargaining, negotiation, and compromise—is often critical for the successful implementation of economic policies. Far from the zero-sum images that
seek to counterpose economics and politics (and worse, democracy and effective
economic policy), the analyses of national experiences in this volume suggest that
inclusive pluralist policy making is compatible with sound economic policy.

The contributions by Gamarra, Montecinos, Vacs, and von Mettenheim confirm the importance of two arguments presented in the introduction. First, a basic
tension exists between neoliberal economic theories and the liberal-pluralist tradition. Second, the political coalitions that seek to sustain neoliberal economic policies tend to split. Montecinos argues that all major political parties in Chile have
adopted the language and policy positions of fairly orthodox economic policies.
However, contributors suggest that in Brazil, Argentina, Uruguay, and Bolivia national industrial groups have opposed the austerity of neoliberal policy measures.
This tension appears to emerge, in part because of the divergent interests of specific firms and their representative associations on the one hand and the abstract
performance targets set by economists on the other hand. The coalitions that underpin neoliberal economic programs also split because the exclusive policy-making style adopted by economists in the key economic ministries tends to cut business groups out of the process. Business elites fear policy packages and
unannounced adjustments because they unpredictably and often radically change
interest, currency, inflation, price, and wage rates.

Recognizing the importance of leadership does not imply endorsement of executives who run roughshod over existing political forces. Indeed, another critical
conclusion to be drawn from the analyses presented in this volume is that the leaders who succeeded in recasting democratic politics in their country have done so
by negotiating coalitions among existing political forces. Dramatic economic reforms or broad political designs have fortunately failed to mobilize groups or popular sectors along the lines of past ideologies such as national populism, commu-
nism, or fascism. Instead, successful presidents in Latin America have taken
existing practices and social forces and put them together in new and creative
ways. Specific discussions about specific problems through open, inclusive negotiations with existing political representatives are the stuff of democratic politics. It
follows that social scientists should avoid proposing solutions for democratic poli-

tics with concepts such as social pacts, parliamentarianism, or models for economic adjustment (whether neoliberal or heterodox packages). Instead, analysts of the region should temper their claims and analyze the day-to-day political work needed to maintain the participation of diverse social groups in the sober boring of hard boards that Max Weber regarded as the essence of democratic politics.

The analyses of specific national experiences with governance in this volume provide arguments that cross both national borders and the boundaries of academic disciplines. Montecinos argues that deepening democratic governance requires understanding the exceptional degree of influence that economists have developed in Latin American governments during the period of transition from military rule. Her arguments span the disciplines of political economy and organization theory by suggesting that a new policy consensus has emerged in Chile among a new generation of economists who occupy not only critical posts in economic ministries but also control party politics and define the limits of what is possible. Electoral competition and organizational emulation drove Chilean parties to place economists at the center of party organizations.

Vacs presents a compelling comparison of how Argentina and Uruguay searched for economic policy alternatives during the 1980s and 1990s. While Vacs recognizes both the international economic context and the collapse of policy consensus around import substitution industrialization in these countries, his central argument is that domestic politics determined the character of new policies. Contrary to the widespread perception that elites in the Southern Cone have embraced a new "Washington Consensus" centered around privatization and trade liberalization, Vacs argues that whether and how neoliberal policies are adopted depends on the domestic political setting. Specifically, the legacies of corporatism in Argentina and pluralism in Uruguay explain their different experiences with neoliberal policies during the 1980s and early 1990s.

For Vacs, the Argentine corporatist tradition permitted the Menem government to impose costs of restructuring by destroying political opposition. Radical party leader President Alfonsin (1983–1989) attempted to reduce inflation and stabilize the economy through a series of heterodox and orthodox economic packages that were designed in secret and negotiated only after being unveiled. The descent into hyperinflation during 1989 set the stage for a new conservative coalition unexpectedly led by Peronist party leader President Menem (1989–). President Menem used the populist tradition, the crisis of hyperinflation, and the decree powers of the presidency to implement Economic Minister Cavallo's monetary and fiscal plans to stabilize the peso at one dollar. Further measures of privatization, trade liberalization, and debt reduction through Brady Plan mechanisms completed the policy achievements that secured President Menem's new conservative coalition. Meanwhile, traditional allies in labor remained weakened, split, and forced to conduct collective bargaining during a deep recession.

The experience of Uruguay provides a compelling counterpoint. In Uruguay, the separation of legislative and executive powers, the autonomy of social organizations (and party factions), and the holding of a national referendum on privatization produced steadfast resistance to draconian measures of neoliberalism. Presidents Sanguinetti and Lacalle had no recourse to decree powers and was forced to negotiate policies in the legislature. Furthermore, the complex party list method used in Uruguayan elections encourages opposition. Because unions are independent from state and corporatist control, labor also mobilized against neoliberal policies. In sum, the diversity and complexity of liberal, pluralist, and democratic politics encouraged opposition to presidential attempts to impose the severe costs of economic adjustment through fiscal and monetary austerity and a rushed program of privatization.

The importance of leadership and statecraft for deepening democracy in the region is another central theme that emerges from the analyses of specific national experiences. We have attempted to describe the unique opportunities for democratic governance today in the region by adopting Pocock's idea that, although they are rare, history presents a series of what he calls Machiavellian Moments during which leadership and creativity are critical in shaping institutions.[13] This concept draws attention to the rare opportunity in post-transition Latin America for not only creativity and choice but also the type of open, pluralist, and inclusive governance that can deepen democracy in the region. Given that democratic developments will remain complex, fluid, and unpredictable, the ability of leaders to negotiate, include, bargain, and respect the sequence of actors that tend to suddenly appear on the political stage will continue to matter in Latin American politics.

Unfortunately, our analytic tools fail at this point. We need a more concrete understanding of how the examples and legacies of leadership can be transformed into widely shared principles. We need more secure theoretical foundations for a theory of democracy and governance that surpasses the pessimism of zero-sum visions, obsessions with economic constraints, and lists of barriers to collective action. Precedents abound in Latin America suggesting that statecraft can resolve apparent impasses, muddle through economic constraints, and introduce sets of formal and informal rules or practices that can become a common framework for liberal and democratic political contestation. Creative political leadership and spontaneous popular demands ended military rule, empowered citizens and civil society along new lines of gender, race, ethnicity, and identity, and overcame seemingly intractable problems such as high foreign debt, hyperinflation, and economic adjustment. Although not blind to policy failures and facile appeals to authoritarianism, the series of policy successes through open, pluralistic governance by new civilian leaders in Latin America analyzed in this volume suggests that deepening democracy is possible. The hope at the end of this volume, and this century, is that the traditions and practices of inclusive liberal-democratic politics may become embedded in the political customs, traditions, practices, and institutions of the region.

NOTES

"Introduction," by Kurt von Mettenheim and James Malloy

1. On elite and participatory theories of democracy, see Giovanni Sartori, *Democratic Theory Revisited* (Chatham, N.J.: Chatham House, 1987); and Carol Pateman, *Participation and Democratic Theory* (Cambridge: Cambridge University Press, 1970).

2. For a more balanced view of markets and democratization, see Joan Nelson, ed., *Intricate Links: Democratization and Market Reforms in Latin America and Eastern Europe* (New Brunswick, N.J.: Transaction, 1994); and William Smith, Carlos Acuña, and Eduardo Gamarra, eds., *Democracy, Markets, and Structural Reform in Latin America* (New Brunswick, N.J.: Transaction, 1994).

3. See Jeffrey Sachs, ed., *Developing Country Debt and Economic Performance* (Chicago: University of Chicago Press, 1989), and Rudiger Dornbusch and Sebastian Edwards, eds., *The Macroeconomics of Populism in Latin America* (Chicago: University of Chicago Press, 1991).

4. On late development and state intervention, see Albert Hirshman, *The Strategy of Economic Development* (New Haven, Conn.: Yale University Press, 1958).

5. On the end of the easy phase of import substitution industrialization, see Guillermo O'Donnell, *Modernization and Bureaucratic Authoritarianism* (Berkeley: University of California Institute of International Studies, 1973), and Maria C. Tavares, "The Rise and Decline of Import Substitution in Latin America," *Economic Bulletin from Latin America* 4 (1964): 1–65.

6. On the idea of hybrid regimes as legacies of transitions from military to civilian rule in Latin America, see James M. Malloy, "The Politics of Transition in Latin America," in Malloy and Seligson, eds., *Authoritarians and Democrats: Regime Transition in Latin America* (Pittsburgh: University of Pittsburgh Press, 1987).

7. While pursuing problems of deepening democracy, clarity about the differences between the concepts of state, regime, and government must be maintained. State, in the minimal Weberian sense, refers to the national bureaucratic apparatus of administration, which seeks to retain a monopoly on the legitimate use of force. Political regime refers to enduring forms of governance and ordered access to the power capacities of the state as well as the rules to form and operate governments. Specific governments mediate the relationship between state and regime and give these two abstract political dimensions concrete form and life.

8. On the sequence of democratic breakdown in Latin America, see Juan Linz and Alfred Stepan, *The Breakdown of Democratic Regimes: Latin America* (Baltimore: Johns Hopkins University Press, 1978).

9. For a review of democratic theory from a self-declared mainstream perspective, see Sartori, *Democratic Theory Revisited*.

10. Classic analyses from this perspective remain: Carol Pateman, *Participation and Democratic Theory*, and Peter Bachrach, *The Theory of Democratic Elitism* (Washington, D.C.: University Press of America, 1967).

11. Note the similarity of concerns about delegative democracy in the work of Guillermo O'Donnell: "The combination of institutionalized elections, particularism as a dominant political institution, and a big gap between the formal rules and the way most political institutions actually work makes for a strong affinity with delegative, not representative, notions of political authority. By this I mean a caesaristic, plebiscitarian executive that once elected sees itself as empowered to govern the country as it deems fit." Guillermo O'Donnell, "Illusions About Consolidation, *Journal of Democracy* 7, no. 2 (1996): 44.

12. On the importance of direct plebiscitarian appeals in European history, see Charles Maier, "On the Theory and Practice of the Representation of Interests," in Suzanne Berger, ed., *Organizing Interests in Western Europe* (Cambridge: Cambridge University Press, 1983).

13. Raymond Aron provides an insightful comparison of Tocqueville's and Marx's analyses of Louis Bonaparte's 1851 coup, which ended the French Second Republic, in "The Sociologists and the Revolution of 1848," *Main Currents in Sociological Thought* (New York: Doubleday, 1963), 1:303–40.

14. Public opinion research seeks to combine complex statistical techniques with a more complex view of voters. For a review of research see Benjamin I. Page and Robert Y. Shapiro, *The Rational Public* (Chicago: University of Chicago Press, 1992).

15. On populism in Latin America, see Michael Conniff, ed., *Latin American Populism in Comparative Perspective* (Albuquerque: University of New Mexico Press, 1982). On the importance of populism in understanding Latin American public opinion, see Kurt von Mettenheim, *The Brazilian Voter* (Pittsburgh: University of Pittsburgh Press, 1995).

16. Caveats are in order. First, far from a single pattern throughout Latin America, differences matter. Educated publics in Argentina and Chile may be closer to European voters. More established party systems such as Colombia and Venezuela may have produced strong party identification among voters. Electoral politics in Central America appears to depend less on media images and other patterns typical of mass society. Nonetheless, direct popular appeals appear increasingly to influence voters in the region.

17. See Hanna Pitkin, *The Concept of Representation* (Berkeley: University of California Press, 1968); and Giovanni Sartori, "Representation," *International Encyclopedia of the Social Sciences*, vol. 13, (New York: Macmillan, 1968).

18. On change and transparency in public opinion, see Ronald Inglehart, "Aggregate Stability and Individual Level Flux in Mass Belief Systems: The Level of Analysis Paradox," *American Political Science Review* 79 (1985): 97–116.

19. On party systems, see Giovanni Sartori, *Parties and Party Systems* (Cambridge: Cambridge University Press, 1976).

20. Theodore Adorno et al., *The Authoritarian Personality* (New York: Harper and Row, 1950); Robert Lane, *Political Ideology* (New York: Free Press, 1962); Elizabeth Noelle-Neumann, *The Spiral of Silence* (Chicago: University of Chicago Press, 1984).

21. For example: Michael Margolis and Gary Mauser, *Manipulating Public Opinion: Essays*

on *Public Opinion as a Dependent Variable* (Pacific Grove, Calif.: Brooks/Cole, 1989); Benjamin Ginsberg, *The Captive Public: How Mass Opinion Promotes State Power* (New York: Basic Books, 1986).

22. For recent criticism of presidential institutions in Latin America, see Juan Linz and Arturo Valenzuela, eds., *The Failure of Presidential Democracy: The Case of Latin America* (Baltimore: Johns Hopkins University Press, 1994). The classic statement of the responsible party system model is "Toward a More Responsible Two Party System," Supplement, *American Political Science Review* 44 (1950).

23. See the debate between Burnham and Converse: Walter D. Burnham, *The Current Crisis in American Politics* (New York: Oxford University Press, 1982); and Philip E. Converse, "Change in the American Universe," in Angus Campbell and Phillip E. Converse, eds., *The Human Meaning of Social Change* (New York: Russell Sage Foundation, 1973).

24. Weber makes this argument in both "Politics as a Vocation" in H. H. Gerth and C. Wright Mills, eds., *From Max Weber* (New York: Oxford University Press, 1946), and "Parliament and Government in a Reconstructed Germany," in *Economy and Society* (Berkeley-Los Angeles-London: University of California Press, 1978), 2:1381–1462. Also see M. I. Ostrogorski, *Democracy and the Organization of Political Parties in the United States and Great Britain* (Garden City, N.J.: Doubleday, 1964 [abridged]). James Bryce, *The American Commonwealth* (New York: Macmillan, 1907).

25. See the contribution of Baloyra to this volume.

26. On Machiavelli and the liberal tradition, see Gisela Bock, Quentin Skinner, and Maurizio Viroli, eds., *Machiavelli and Republicanism* (Cambridge: Cambridge University Press, 1990).

27. It is moreover a construction that de facto redefines the usually posited role of political parties in a pluralist democracy.

28. On corporatism in the region, see James Malloy, ed., *Authoritarianism and Corporatism in Latin America* (Pittsburgh: University of Pittsburgh Press, 1977).

29. On the broader problem of economic policy and democracy, see Joan Nelson, ed., *Intricate Links: Democratic Politics and Market Reform in Latin America and Eastern Europe* (New Brunswick, N.J.: Transaction, 1994).

1. "Battling for the Voter," by Roderic Camp

1. See, for example, Terry Lynn Karl, "Dilemmas of Democratization in Latin America," *Comparative Politics* 23 (October 1990): 2–3.

2. See Peter Hakim and Abraham Lowenthal, *Latin American Democracy in the 1990s: The Challenges Ahead* (Aspen, Colo.: Aspen Institute, Inter-American Dialogue, 1991), for a list of sources on democracy.

3. See, for example, Daniel Levy, "Mexico: Sustained Civilian Rule Without Democracy," in Larry Diamond, Juan J. Linz, and Seymour Martin Lipset, eds., *Democracy in Developing Countries*, volume 4, *Latin America* (Boulder: Lynne Rienner, 1989), 4:459–97.

4. For a European and Latin American perspective, see Georges Couffignal, ed., *Réinventer la démocrati, le défi latino-américain* (Paris: Presses de la Fondation Nationale des Sciences Politiques, 1992).

5. For the history of this party see Luis Javier Garrido, *El partido de la revolución institucionalizada, la formación del nuevo estado en México (1928–1945)* (Mexico City: Siglo XXI, 1982);

and Dale Story, for the statement that President Plutarco Calles wanted to "create an electoral instrument that would allow him to continue to dominate the political scene," *The Mexican Ruling Party, Stability and Authority* (New York: Praeger, 1986), 20.

6. Roderic A. Camp, *Generals in the Palacio: The Military in Modern Mexico* (New York: Oxford University Press, 1992), 21–22.

7. Wayne A. Cornelius, "Nation-building, Participation and Distribution: The Politics of Social Reform Under Lázaro Cárdenas," in Gabriel Almond et al., eds., *Crisis, Choice and Change: Historical Studies of Political Development* (Boston: Little, Brown, 1973), 392–498; and Charles H. Weston, Jr., "The Political Legacy of Lázaro Cárdenas and Mexican Politics Since 1940," unpublished paper, 1980.

8. An important contribution of both the National Action Party and the Democratic Revolutionary Party was to promote individual membership. See Soledad Loaeza's comment about PAN, that it "has always favored the individual vote as the ultimate form of political participation, as well as the only valid instrument of change. The party has never believed in social mobilizations distinct from electoral mobilization." "Political Change in Mexico, 1982–1988," in Douglas A. Chalmers et al., eds., *The Right and Democracy in Latin America* (New York: Praeger, 1992), 136. For background on the actual statutes and proposed reforms, *El partido en el poder, seis ensayos* (Mexico: PRI, 1990).

9. See my *Modernization and Political Recruitment: The Case of Mexico*, chapter 7 (1994).

10. The primary sources of initial political recruitment in Mexico are the universities, more recently the private universities.

11. For evidence of this see my *Modernization and Political Recruitment: The Case of Mexico*.

12. Both major parties in 1993 were founded by former officeholders in the government leadership, including Manuel Gómez Moran of PAN and Cuauhtémoc Cárdenas of PRD.

13. This was true of the Popular Socialist Party (PPS), and the Authentic Party of the Mexican Revolution (PARM), which operated for many years.

14. For empirical evidence of this from the 1988 presidential elections, when PAN received its broadest support nationally, see my "Mexico's 1988 Elections: A Turning Point for Its Political Development and Foreign Relations?" in Edgar W. Butler and Jorge A. Bustamante, eds., *Sucesion Presidencial: The 1988 Mexican Presidential Election* (Boulder: Westview Press, 1991), 99–100.

15. For trends during this period, see Wayne A. Cornelius, "Political Liberalization in an Authoritarian Regime: Mexico, 1976–1985," in Judith Gentleman, ed., *Mexican Politics in Transition* (Boulder: Westview Press, 1987), 22.

16. For background on the succession, see Peter H. Smith, "The 1988 Presidential Succession in Historical Perspective," in Wayne A. Cornelius et al., eds., *Mexico's Alternative Political Futures* (La Jolla: Center for U.S.-Mexican Studies, UCSD, 1989), 391–416.

17. Allegations of fraud are widespread. One of the few scholars who has documented electoral fraud in any meaningful, comprehensive manner is Silvia Gomez Tagle, "Democracy and Power in Mexico: The Meaning of Conflict in the 1979, 1982, and 1985 Federal Elections," in Judith Gentleman, ed., *Mexican Politics in Transition* (Boulder: Westview Press, 1987), 166ff.

18. Donaldo Luis Colosio, "Why We Won the 1991 Elections," in Riordan Roett, ed., *Political and Economic Liberalization in Mexico: At a Critical Juncture* (Boulder: Lynne Rienner, 1993), 5.

19. For a revealing analysis of the electoral system in recent years, see Juan Molinar's excellent "The Future of the Electoral System," in Wayne A. Cornelius et al., eds., *Mexico's Alternative Political Futures* (La Jolla: Center for U.S.-Mexican Studies, UCSD, 1989), 265–90.

20. For evidence of these historical roots, see Lorenzo Meyer's insightful comparisons between the Porfiriato and the contemporary regime, in his "The Origins of Mexico's Authoritarian State, Political Control in the Old and New Regimes," in Luis Reyna and Richard Weinert, eds., *Authoritarianism in Mexico* (Philadelphia: Institute for the Study of Human Issues, 1977).

21. For background, see Francois X. Guerra, "Pueblo moderno y sociedad tradicional," in his *México: del antiguo régimen a la revolución* (Mexico: Fondo de Cultura Económica, 1988), 1:182ff.

22. For a superb analysis and insight into recent presidents, and a prognosis for the future of the presidency, see George Philip, who sees a real potential for democratic opening in Mexico, because, "while the system has maintained its control over despotic power, it has been unable to control or entirely cope with the fact that the amount of 'infrastructural' power in the hands of civil society has been increasing." *The Presidency in Mexican Politics* (New York: St. Martin's Press, 1992), 172.

23. For background on the actual functions of the legislative branch, see Rudy de la Garza, "The Mexican Chamber of Deputies and the Mexican Political System" (Ph.D. dissertation, University of Arizona, 1972).

24. For how this is accomplished by the private sector, see my *Entrepreneurs and the State in Twentieth Century Mexico* (New York: Oxford University Press, 1989).

25. For many revealing comments by leading entrepreneurs, as to why they continue to support PRI leadership instead of opposition candidates, see Yemile Mizrahi, "Rebels Without a Cause? The Politics of Entrepreneurs in Chihuahua," paper presented at the Latin American Studies Association meeting, Los Angeles, September 1992), 18ff.

26. For a broad survey of legal norms, democracy, and party competition, see Fernando Potes González, "Democracia Intra-Partidista en México, Consideraciones Juridicas," law thesis, University of Nuevo León, Monterrey, 1991.

27. For these regional and national demands, see their official program in *El Despertador Mexicano* 1 (December 1993): 1–20.

28. For some background to this, see Lorenzo Meyer, "Democratization of the PRI: Mission Impossible?" in Wayne Cornelius et al., eds., *Mexico's Alternative Political Futures* (La Jolla: Center for U.S.-Mexican Studies, UCSD, 1989), 325–50.

29. Another influence, in spite of Mexico's refusal to invite or validate their presence in Mexico, is that of foreign election observers. This has been institutionalized recently through the Organization of American States, which has sent teams to other Latin American countries. See Francisco Villagran de León, *The OAS and Democratic Development* (Washington, D.C.: United States of Peace, 1992). In the case of Mexico, former president Carter's group, through the Carter Center, has been most actively involved in election watching.

30. For evidence of this, see Edward J. Williams, "The Resurgent North and Contemporary Mexican Regionalism," *Mexican Studies* 6, no. 2 (summer 1990): 299–323.

31. Enrique Alduncin Abitia, *Los Valores de los mexicanos*, vol. 2, *México en tiempos de cambio* (Mexico: Fomento Cultural Banamex, 1991), 216.

32. Alberto Hernández Hernández, "Political Attitudes Among Border Youth," in Arturo Al-

varado Mendoza, *Electoral Patterns and Perspectives in Mexico* (La Jolla: Center for U.S.-Mexican Studies, 1987), 214ff.

33. Alan Angell, Maria D'Alva Kinzo, and Diego Urbaneja, "Latin America," in David Butler and Austin Ranney, *Electioneering: A Comparative Study of Continuity and Change* (Oxford: Clarendon Press, 1992), 65. See their statement that "The Americanization of electioneering is one aspect of the general Americanization of consumer standards in Latin America, even if for many poor Latin Americans such standards represent a dream rather than a reality. But the dream is constantly reinforced by TV, which is now almost as widespread in Latin America as in Europe, at least in terms of viewers."

34. For the broader context of this relationship, see my chapter on the media in *Intellectuals and the State in Twentieth Century Mexico* (Austin: University of Texas Press, 1985).

35. See Joseph Klesner, "Realignment or Dealignment?" for the statement that "given the lack of political information and interest observed in the Mexican voter, [these conditions] will likely inflate the role of the media and put a premium on the art of campaigning. In both of the latter realms, the PRI is currently far ahead of its challengers and showed it in 1991" (20).

36. In the *Los Angeles Times* poll, August 1989, 32 percent of all Mexican respondents had traveled to the United States, and 43 percent had relatives in the United States.

37. See Lorenzo Meyer for background on United States democratic influences in Mexico historically. Meyer argues correctly that "U.S. pressure to broaden Mexican pluralism abated suddenly as it had arisen" after 1988, claiming that the possibility of the centrist left-wing forces, and not PAN benefiting from the opening, put an end to U.S. efforts. Meyer should have qualified this statement by confining "U.S. pressure" to the executive branch, not the media, academia, or the legislative branch. See his "Mexico: The Exception and the Rule," in Abraham Lowenthal, ed., *Exporting Democracy: The United States and Latin America* (Baltimore: Johns Hopkins University Press, 1991), 227.

38. See Marjorie Miller, "The Times Poll, Mexico Likes Salinas But Is Split Over PRI," *Los Angeles Times*, August 20, 1989.

39. For example, see Miguel Basáñez, "Lecciones de elecciones: encuestas en Chihuahua y Michoacán," *Este Pais*, September 1992, 33–34, which discusses these partisan problems for polls taken in the important gubernatorial elections in Chihuahua and Michoacán.

40. For the first comprehensive analysis of public opinion polling in Mexico, focusing on these and many other issues, see Roderic A. Camp, ed., *Polling for Democracy: Public Opinion and Political Liberalization in Mexico* (Wilmington: Scholarly Resources, 1996).

41. See the chapter "Election-Related Conflicts," in Americas Watch, *Human Rights in Mexico, June 1990* (New York: Human Rights Watch, 1990), 41–52.

42. Joseph L. Klesner, "Realignment or Dealignment? Consequences of Economic Crisis and Economic Restructuring for the Mexican Party System," paper prepared for "Las Dimensiones Politicas de Ajuste Estructural en México," Mexico City, June 1992, 18. It is somewhat ironic that free trade agreement negotiations, and the agreement itself, have the potential to influence democratization in Mexico, when "For two years the Mexican Government has refused to listen to the opinions of diverse Mexican political organizations, among them the Party of the Democratic Revolution, regarding changes in the agenda, pace and length of negotiations: and furthermore, the Government has turned a deaf ear to the proposals on the subject formulated by independent organizations." Jorge Alfonso Calderón Salazar, "Mexico 1992: Reflections About

Free Trade Agreement, Democracy and National Sovereignty," paper presented at the national Latin American Studies Association meeting, Los Angeles, September, 1992, 14.

43. For an excellent summary of the potential scenarios free trade might engender, see Peter H. Smith, "The Political Impact of Free Trade on Mexico," *Journal of Inter-American Studies and World Affairs* 34, no. 1 (spring 1992): 1–25. The most comprehensive work on the topic is that by Riordan Roett, ed., *Political and Economic Liberalization in Mexico: At a Critical Juncture?* (Boulder: Lynne Rienner, 1993).

44. For some assessments of these interpretations, see my "Political Liberalization: The Ultimate Key to Economic Modernization in Mexico," in Riordan Roett, ed., *Political and Economic Liberalization in Mexico: At a Critical Juncture?* (Boulder: Lynne Rienner, 1993).

45. Luis Rubio, "Political Origins and Effects of Economic Reform in Mexico," in Riordan Roett, ed., *Political and Economic Liberalization in Mexico: At a Critical Juncture?* (Boulder: Lynne Rienner, 1993).

46. For background, see Enrique Alduncin Abitia, chapter on "Mexico: entre la tradición y la modernidad," in *Los Valores de los Mexicanos*, vol. 1, *México: entre la tradición y la modernidad* (Mexico: Fomento Cultural Banamex, 1986), 61–94.

47. In the 1988 elections, Cárdenas and the PAN candidate, Manuel J. Clouthier, combined, won four of Mexico's five largest cities: Mexico City, Guadalajara, Ciudad Juarez, and Ciudad Nezahualcóyotl. Together, they obtained 58.1 percent of the urban vote. See Colegio Nacional de Ciencia Politicas y Administración Publica, *Elecciones 1988, qué pasó?* (Mexico: Diana, 1988).

48. This has become more rather than less pronounced. As a result of the last reform, polling places increased 60 percent from 1988 to 1991, totaling 88,000 locations. Delal Baer, "The 1991 Mexican Mid-Term Elections, October, 1991" (Washington, D.C.: CSIS Latin American Election Studies Series, 1991), 23.

49. Javier Garrido, "The Crisis of *Presidencialismo*," in Wayne A. Cornelius et al., eds., *Mexico's Alternative Political Futures* (La Jolla: Center for U.S.-Mexican Studies, UCSD, 1989), 423.

50. Ted Bardacke, "Another Governor Strategically Displaced," *El Financiero Internacional*, October 19, 1992, 13.

51. For examples of these criticisms, and evidence of the abuse of funds, see Stephen D. Morris, "Political Reformism in Mexico: Salinas at the Brink," *Journal of Inter-American Studies and World Affairs* 34, no. 1 (spring 1992): 32–33.

52. For convincing evidence of this argument, see John J Bailey's statistical evidence and statement that, "State and local governments have become ever more dependent on the center for revenues, and the center has come to exercise greater control over investment spending." "Fiscal Recentralization in Mexico, 1979–91," paper presented at the Latin American Studies Association meeting, Los Angeles, September 1992, 14.

53. The first comprehensive, comparative analysis of opposition governments is offered in Peter Ward and Victoria Rodriguez, eds., *Opposition Government in Mexico: Past Experiences and Future Opportunities* (Albuquerque: University of New Mexico Press, 1993).

54. Bardacke, "Another Governor Strategically Displaced," 13.

55. Personal interview with Miguel Alemán, Jr., secretary of finances, CEN of PRI, August 1992.

56. Alberto Alvarez Gutiérrez, "Comó se sientan los mexicanos?" in Alberto Hernández

Medina and Luis Narro Rodriguez, eds., *Como somos los mexicanos* (Mexico: CREA, 1987), 86.

57. John Booth and Mitchell Seligson, "The Political Culture of Authoritarianism in Mexico," *Latin American Research Review* no. 1 (1984): 113.

58. World Values Survey, 1991.

59. "No newly politicized bloc of voters has entered Mexico's 'political space'. In 1988 and 1991, the principal effect of the irruption of Cardenismo was to reshuffle the voters among existing parties, not to mobilize the previously unmobilized." See Jorge I. Domínguez and James A. McCann, "Shaping Mexico's Electoral Arena: The Construction of Partisan Cleavages in the 1988 and 1991 National Elections," paper presented at the American Political Science Association meeting, Chicago, September 1992, and published in the *American Political Science Review* 89, no. 1 (1995): 1–15.

60. The president only encouraged speculations about his office making the decisions about electoral outcomes by calling and congratulating the PAN candidate on his election victory, Francisco Barrio, before the votes were actually counted.

61. Delal Baer concluded, "The United States reacted in 1985–1986 with studied indifference to electoral dramas that, had they occurred in almost any other nation in the world, would have drawn a sympathetic response." "Mexican Democracy Between Evolution and Devolution," *The Washington Quarterly* 11, no. 3 (summer 1988): 84.

62. Bush was quoted as saying, "We don't want to impose a replica of our own system on other countries even though the U.S. always supports free and fair elections." See the interesting comparisons, and the evolution of the U.S. position, in Judith Gentleman and Voytek Zubek, "International Integration and Democratic Development: The Cases of Poland and Mexico," *Journal of Inter-American Studies and World Affairs* 34, no. 1 (spring 1992): 84–85.

63. The Organization of American States adopted an American Convention on Human Rights. Unfortunately, the United States has not ratified this agreement. The provisions of this convention would, if enforced, according to Andrew Reading, abolish authoritarian rule. The National Action party has repeatedly filed petitions before the Inter-American Commission on Human Rights, which in a 1990 case determined that the Mexican government "had violated its citizens' rights to 'genuine' elections by failing to provide effective means of challenging electoral fraud. Then in 1991 it found that the electoral law of the northern state of Nuevo León violates Article 23 by not providing for balanced, independent electoral commissions. . . . the electoral law of Nuevo León is essentially identical to every other electoral law in the country, including the federal law enacted by President Carlos Salinas in 1990." Mexico did not accept the jurisdiction of the court. As Reading argues, if the United States signed the convention, that could all change. "Bolstering Democracy in the Americas," *World Policy Journal* (summer 1992): 406–07.

64. Many analysts are pessimistic about these possibilities, suggesting that the revival of pluralist political theories is premature. The best discussion of opposing points of view is Viviane Brachet-Márquez, "Explaining Sociopolitical Change in Latin America, the Case of Mexico," *Latin American Research Review* 27, no. 3 (1992): 111–12.

65. Delal Baer, who carefully analyzed the 1988 presidential elections, argued as one of three preconditions for electoral democracy in Mexico that an "electorally based political system requires a new set of understandings that guide the rules of the political game. Primarily, parties would agree to behave as true parties, defining their objectives electorally. Influence over policy would be commensurate with the ability to achieve electoral control of government posts. Essential is the establishment of mutual trust that permits all parties to accept wins and losses with

maturity and self restraint." "The Mexican Presidential Election, Post-electoral Analysis, Report No. 2, August 15, 1988," CSIS Latin American Election Study Series, 1988, 14.

2. "Deepening Democracy with Dominant Parties and Presidentialism," by Enrique A. Baloyra

1. R. Lynn Kelley, "Venezuelan Constitutional Forms and Realities," in John D. Martz and David J. Myers, eds., *Venezuela, the Democratic Experience*, rev. ed. (New York: Praeger, 1986), 32–53; Miriam Kornblith, "The Politics of Constitution-Making: Constitutions and Democracy in Venezuela," *Journal of Latin American Studies* 23, no. 1 (February 1991): 61–80; John D. Martz, "The Party System: Toward Institutionalization," in John D. Martz and David J. Myers, eds., *Venezuela, the Democratic Experience* (New York: Praeger, 1977), 93–112.

2. Daniel H. Levine, *Conflict and Political Change in Venezuela* (Princeton: Princeton University Press, 1973), 231–43; Martz, op. cit., 106–11; and Juan Carlos Rey, *El futuro de la democracia en Venezuela* (Caracas: IDEA, 1989), 213–19.

3. Described, among others, by Terry L. Karl, "Petroleum and Political Pacts: The Transition to Democracy in Venezuela," *Latin American Research Review* 20, no. 1 (1987): 63–94; and Humberto Njaim et al., *El sistema político venezolano* (Caracas: Editorial Arte, 1975). For a different interpretation, see Kevin Neuhouser, "Democratic Stability in Venezuela: Elite Consensus or Class Compromise?" *American Sociological Review* 67, no. 1 (February 1992): 117–35.

4. Juan Carlos Rey, "El sistema de partidos venezolano," *Politeia* 1 (1972): 224–28.

5. A point stressed by Juan Carlos Rey in *Continuidad y cambio en las elecciones venezolanas: 1958–1988* (Caracas: Instituto Internacional de Estudios Avanzados, 1989), 11–12. The method of "successive divisions," or D'Hondt system of proportional representation, utilized in Venezuela, unfairly rewards the major party in assigning additional seats from proportionality. For a recent critique, richly illustrated with examples, and a proposal for adopting a different model (the Saint Lague system) see Nerio Rauseo, *Los efectos políticos de un nuevo sistema electoral* (Caracas: Consejo Supremo Electoral, 1988), 37–73.

6. Juan Carlos Rey, "Polarización electoral, economía del voto y voto castigo en Venezuela, 1958–1988," *Cuestiones Políticas* 12 (1994): 19–25. Also José Enrique Molina Vega, *El sistema electoral venezolano y sus consecuencias políticas* (Valencia: Vadell Hermanos, 1991): 88–99.

7. More details in David J. Myers, "The Venezuelan Party System: Regime Maintenance Under Stress," in John D. Martz and David J. Myers, eds., *Venezuela, the Democratic Experience*, rev. ed. (New York: Praeger, 1986), 127–31.

8. See Manuel Caballero, "1973, ¿el fin del comienzo?," in Federico Alvarez et al., *La izquierda venezolana y las elecciones del 73* (Caracas: Síntesis Dos mil, 1974), 79–121.

9. Joaquín Marta-Sosa, "Elecciones y transformación social," paper delivered at the seminar, "Los Veinticinco Años de la Democracia en Venezuela," mimeo, Caracas, 24–26 January 1983.

10. "Presentational" and "participatory" techniques follow the usage proposed by John Martz in reference to campaign styles and practices, in John D. Martz and Enrique A. Baloyra, *Electoral Mobilization and Public Opinion: The Venezuelan Campaign of 1973* (Chapel Hill: University of North Carolina Press, 1976), xxxviii–xl.

11. Ibid., 71–75 and 151–60. Also see Teodoro Petkoff, *Del optimismo de la voluntad* (Caracas: Ediciones Centauro 1987), 49–94 and 251–54; and Demetrio Boersner, "El proceso electoral de 1973 y las perspectivas de la izquierda," in Federico Alvarez et al., *La izquierda venezolana*, 165.

12. See Steve Ellner, *Venezuela's Movimiento al Socialismo: From Guerrilla Defeat to Inno-*

vative Politics (Durham, N.C.: Duke University Press, 1988); Petkoff, op. cit., 61–76 and 93–94; and Andrés Stambouli, "La campaña electoral de 1978," *Politeia* 9 (1981): 53–132. Despite the obvious intuitive appeal of the economy-of-the-vote explanation, this is insufficient because it overlooks the dominant parties' careful attention to matters of political organization and strategy.

13. Ellner, op. cit., chapter 5. Also Pedro José Martínez, "La unidad de la izquierda en Venezuela, Su evolución hasta las elecciones nacionales de 1978 y 1979," *Politeia* 9 (1980): 351–53.

14. Ellner, op. cit., 123.

15. Molina Vega, op. cit., 148–52.

16. Reported by David J. Myers, "Perceptions of A Stressed Democracy," in Jennifer McCoy et al., eds., *Venezuelan Democracy Under Stress* (New Brunswick, N.J.: Transaction, 1995), table 25, p. 131.

17. Datanalysis, "La abstención electoral en 1989 (Informe analítico)," in Comisión Presidencial Para La Reforma del Estado (COPRE), *Reformas para el cambio político*, vol. 3, *Las transformaciones que la democracia reclama* (Caracas: Editorial Arte, 1993), especially 186–90.

18. Datanalysis, op. cit., 199–201.

19. For more on this election, see José E. Molina Vega and Carmen Pérez Baralt, "Elecciones estatales y municipales. Venezuela 6 de Diciembre de 1992," *Boletín Electoral Latinoamericano* 8 (July–December 1992).

20. There were 5,829,216 voters from the 9,994,689 registered.

21. DATOS poll of June 1993. For commentary and detail see Enrique Baloyra, "Elecciones generales, Venezuela, 5 de diciembre de 1993," *Boletín Electoral Latinoamericano* 10 (July–December 1993): 31–42.

22. This earned it 9 of 52 seats in the Senate and 40 of 201 seats in the Chamber of Deputies, a very respectable showing indeed.

23. See David Eugene Blank, *Politics in Venezuela* (Boston: Little, Brown, 1973), 174–81; John D. Martz, "The Minor Parties," in Howard R. Penniman, ed., *Venezuela at the Polls: The National Elections of 1978* (Washington, D.C.: American Enterprise Institute, 1980), 154–70; and Martz and Baloyra, op. cit., 160–63. For a direct reference, see Pedro Tinoco, *El estado eficaz* (Caracas: Italgráfica, 1973).

24. Martz and Baloyra, op. cit., 75–82.

25. This had a little more success and David J. Myers called them "recently attractive" in "Urban Voting, Structural Cleavages, and Party System Evolution, The Case of Venezuela," *Comparative Politics* (October 1975): 119–51.

26. See Robert O'Connor, "The Electorate," in Penniman, op. cit., 56–90; and Antonio Stempel-París, *Venezuela, Una democracia enferma* (Caracas: Editorial Ateneo, 1981).

27. John D. Martz, "The Malaise of Venezuelan Parties," in Donald Herman, ed., *Democracy in Latin America, Colombia and Venezuela* (New York: Praeger, 1988), 165–66.

28. For a discussion of these so-called "new caudillos," see Carina Perelli, "La personalización de la política," and Oscar Landi, "Outsiders, nuevos caudillos y media politics," in Carina Perelli, Sonia Picado, and Daniel Zovatto, eds., *Partidos y clase política en América Latina de los 90* (San José: Instituto Interamericano de Derechos Humanos, 1995), 163–204 and 205–17, respectively.

29. José Antonio Gil-Yepes, *El reto de las élites* (Madrid: Editorial Tecnos, 1978), 150–60 and 248–63.

30. For more details, see Michael Coppedge, "*Partidocracia* and Reform in Comparative Perspective," in McCoy et al., op. cit., 183–87.

31. Luis J. Oropeza, *Tutelary Pluralism: A Critical Approach to Venezuelan Democracy* (Cambridge: Harvard University Center for International Affairs, 1983), 27–31.

32. Oropeza, op. cit., 27–28.

33. Moisés Naim and Ramón Piñango, "El caso Venezuela: Una ilusión de armonía," in Moisés Naim and Ramón Piñango, eds., *El caso Venezuela: Una ilusión de armonía* (Caracas: IESA, 1984), 538–79; Aníbal Romero, *Decadencia y crisis de la democracia* (Caracas: Editorial Panapo, 1994), 59–68; and Brian F. Crisp, Daniel H. Levine, and Juan Carlos Rey, "The Legitimacy Problem," in McCoy et al., op. cit., especially 153–58.

34. Crisp, Levine, and Rey, op. cit., 154–58.

35. John D. Martz and David J. Myers, "Venezuelan Democracy: Performance and Prospects," in John D. Martz and David J. Myers, eds., *Venezuela: The Democratic Experience,* rev. ed. (New York: Praeger, 1986), 437–68; Myers, op. cit., 131–41; Naim and Piñango, op. cit., 548–50; Humberto Njaim, "El financiamiento de la maquinaria partidista en Venezuela," in Juan Carlos Rey et al., *El financiamiento de los partidos políticos y la democracia en Venezuela* (Caracas: Editorial Ateneo y Editorial Jurídica Venezolana, 1981), 25–76; Njaim et al., op. cit., 37–40; and Arístides Torres, "La campaña electoral de 1978," *Politeia* 9 (1981): 263–86.

36. Pedro Pablo Aguilar, "Rómulo Betancourt, Arquetipo político," in Pedro Pablo Aguilar et al., eds., *Situación y perspectivas de la democracia venezolana* (Caracas: Fundación Rómulo Betancourt, 1991), 49; Martz, "The Malaise," 166–67; Petkoff, op. cit., 146–52.

37. Terry Lynn Karl, "The Venezuelan Petro-State and the Crisis of "Its" Democracy," in McCoy et al., op. cit., 43–48; José Antonio Gil-Yepes, *Más y mejor democracia* (Caracas: Grupo Roraima, 1987), 11–13; also Naim and Piñango, op. cit., 562–63.

38. A proposition advanced by Juan Carlos Navarro in his penetrating essay, "In Search of the Lost Pact: Consensus Lost in the 1980s and 1990s," in McCoy et al., op. cit., 13–31.

39. Luis Gómez Calcaño and Margarita López Maya, *El tejido de Penélope* (Caracas: CENDES, 1990), 96–116. For COPRE's own evaluation of what transpired during 1986–1990 and what remained to be done, and for the text of many of its recommendations, see COPRE, *Reformas,* especially chapters 7 and 8.

40. For details, see Allan R. Brewer-Carías, *El Estado: Crisis y reforma* (Caracas: Academia de Ciencias Políticas y Sociales, 1982), 20–21. Also the diverse points of view expressed in Mary Sananes et al., *La Crisis: Responsabilidades y Salidas* (Caracas: Expediente Editorial, 1986).

41. Levine, *Conflict and Political Change,* 259; and Daniel H. Levine, "Venezuela: The Nature, Sources, and Prospects for Democracy," in Larry Diamond, Juan J. Linz, and Seymour Martin Lipset, eds., *Democracy in Developing Countries,* vol. 4, *Latin America* (Boulder: Lynne Reinner, 1989), 283–84.

42. Navarro, op. cit., 26.

43. Results reported by Myers in "Perceptions," op. cit., tables 13 and 21, pp. 120 and 125.

44. Enrique A. Baloyra, "Public Attitudes Toward the Democratic Regime," in John D. Martz and David J. Myers, eds., *Venezuela, The Democratic Experience* (New York: Praeger, 1977), 50–51.

45. Enrique A. Baloyra and John D. Martz, *Political Attitudes in Venezuela* (Austin: University of Texas Press, 1977), 46–58.

46. Baloyra, op. cit., 60.

47. Enrique A. Baloyra, "Criticism, Cynicism, and Political Evaluation: A Venezuelan Example," *American Political Science Review* 73, no. 4 (December 1979): 994–1000. Also see Arístides Torres, "Fe y desencanto democrático en Venezuela," *Nueva Sociedad* 77 (Mayo–Junio 1985): 52–64.

48. Enrique A. Baloyra, "Public Opinion and Support for the Regime," in John D. Martz and David J. Myers, eds., *Venezuela, the Democratic Experience*, rev. ed. (New York: Praeger, 1986), 57–58 and 62–68.

49. Judith Ewell, *Venezuela: A Century of Change* (London: C. Hurst and Company, 1984), 216; and Judith Ewell, "Venezuela: Interim Report on A Social Pact," *Current History* 85, 507 (January 1986): 25–26, 39–40.

50. Judith Ewell, "Debt and Politics in Venezuela," *Current History* 88, 536 (March 1989): 124 and 147–49; and Andrés Serbín, "Venezuela: Reversal or Renewal?" *Hemisphere* 4, no. 3 (summer 1992): 24.

51. Jennifer McCoy, "Labor and the State in a Party-Mediated Democracy: Institutional Change in Venezuela," *Latin American Research Review* 24, no. 2 (spring 1989): 35–67.

52. Charles Davis and John G. Speer, "The Psychological Bases of Regime Support Among Urban Workers in Venezuela and Mexico: Instrumental or Expressive?" *Comparative Political Studies* 24, no. 3 (October 1991): 319–43.

53. For an eyewitness account, see *El estallido de Febrero* (Caracas: Ediciones Centauro, 1989).

54. For a brief albeit lucid attempt at describing the motives and profile of the conspirators of 7 February, see Serbín, op. cit.

55. Teodoro Petkoff, "Treinta años de democracia venezolana a vuelo de pájaro," in Pedro Pablo Aguilar et al., eds., op. cit., 95. On the reforms and future commitments, see Navarro, op. cit., 16–19.

56. Marco Tulio Bruni-Celli, "La cultura política de la democracia," in Pedro Pablo Aguilar et al., eds., op. cit., 70–71.

57. Agustín Blanco-Muñoz, "La crisis de la crisis," and Domingo F. Maza-Zavala, "La crisis: Antecedentes, factores, responsabilidades, salidas," in Sananes et al., op. cit., 30–32 and 87, respectively.

58. Gil-Yepes, *El reto*, 53–54.

59. Arturo Sosa, "Dimensiones y perspectivas políticas de la crisis actual," in Sananes et al., op. cit., 295.

60. Moisés Moleiro, *Las máscaras de la democracia* (Caracas: Ediciones Centauro, 1988), 319–25.

61. Gómez Calcaño and López Maya, op. cit., 98–99.

62. Aguilar, op. cit., 59; Bruni-Celli, op. cit., 65–66; Petkoff, "Treinta años," op. cit., 95–96; and Ramón J. Velásquez, "El cuadro histórico de la actual crisis," in Sananes et al., op. cit., 116, 121.

63. Aguilar, op. cit., 59; Bruni-Celli, op. cit., 69.

64. Fernando Coronil and Julie Skurski, "Dismembering and Remembering the Nation: The Semantics of Political Violence in Venezuela," *Comparative Studies in Society and History* 33, no. 2 (April 1991): 288–337.

65. Arístides Torres, "Crisis económica y actitudes hacia el sistema político." Paper delivered

at the meeting of the World Association for Public Opinion Research, Caracas, 15–17 January 1990, p. 5, chart 1.

66. Myers, "Perceptions," table 22, p. 127.

67. Romero, op. cit., 82–90.

68. Enrique A. Baloyra, "Public Opinion About Military Coups and Democratic Consolidation in Venezuela," in Herman, *Democracy in Latin America*, 196, 210–14.

69. See Víctor Manuel Reinoso, "Corruption and Abuse of Power Caused the 4 February Coup," *El Nacional*, 25 May 1992, section D. Reported in *Foreign Broadcasts Information Service, Latin America*, FBIS-LAT-92-128, 2 July 1992, 49–51.

70. Baloyra, "Public Opinion and Support," 63.

71. Arístides Torres, "Opinión pública y evaluaciones de gobierno," *Suplemento Cultural, Ultimas Noticias*, September 11, 1988.

72. Baloyra, "Public Opinion and Support," 58.

73. Myers, "Perceptions," op. cit., table 24, p. 130.

74. Juan Rial, "Los partidos políticos en América del Sur en la primera mitad de los años noventa," in Perelli, Picado, and Zovatto, eds., *Partidos y clase política*, 38–40.

75. For more in-depth commentary and discussion, see José Enrique Molina-Vega and Carmen Pérez-Baralt, "Venezuela: ¿Un nuevo sistema de partidos? Las elecciones de 1993," *Cuestiones Políticas* 13 (1994): 63–89.

76. Perelli, op. cit., 172, 177.

77. Peter H. Merkl, "The Challengers and the Party System," in Kay Lawson and Peter H. Merkl, eds., *When Parties Fail* (Princeton: Princeton University Press, 1988), 561.

78. Some signs are positive. For example, in July 1992, the Venezuelan Congress finally approved a plan proposed by AD to amend Article 31 of the constitution and allow for the direct election of municipal and community boards.

3. "Partisan Decline and Presidential Popularity," by Julio F. Carrión

I would like to thank all the participants in the Pittsburgh conference, and the editors of this volume in particular, for their helpful comments. Criticisms from Carlos Franco, Fabian Echegaray, and an anonymous reviewer improved the final version.

1. For a detailed analysis of Peruvian politics in the 1960s see Julio Cotler, *Clases, Estado y Nación en el Perú* (Lima: Instituto de Estudios Peruanos, 1978).

2. General Juan Velasco Alvarado was replaced in a palace coup by General Francisco Moralez Bermudez in June 1975.

3. For an overview of the military government, see Carlos Franco, ed., *El Perú de Velasco* (Lima: CEDEP, 1984); Abraham F. Lowenthal, ed., *The Peruvian Experiment: Continuity and Change Under Military Rule* (Princeton: Princeton University Press, 1975); Cynthia McClintock and Abraham F. Lowenthal, eds., *The Peruvian Experiment Reconsidered* (Princeton: Princeton University Press, 1983); Alfred Stepan, *State and Society: Peru in Comparative Perspective* (Princeton: Princeton University Press, 1978).

4. Cynthia McClintock, "Peru: Precarious Regimes, Authoritarian and Democratic," in Larry Diamond, Juan J. Linz, and Seymour Martin Lipset, eds., *Democracy in Developing Countries*, vol. 4, *Latin America* (Boulder: Lynne Rienner, 1989), 335–86.

5. The Senderista phenomenon has been analyzed in Carlos I. Degregori, *El Surgimiento*

de Sendero Luminoso. Ayacucho 1969–1979 (Lima: Instituto de Estudios Peruanos, 1990); Gustavo Gorriti, *Sendero: Historia de la Guerra Milenaria en el Perú* (Lima: Editorial Apoyo, 1990); David Scott Palmer, ed., *Shining Path of Peru*, 2d. ed. (New York: St. Martin's Press, 1995); Deborah Poole and Gerardo Rénique, *Peru: Time of Fear* (London: Latin American Bureau, 1992).

6. See Catherine M. Conaghan and James M. Malloy, *Unsettling Statecraft: Democracy and Neoliberalism in the Central Andes* (Pittsburgh: University of Pittsburgh Press, 1994).

7. See Samuel Kernell, "Explaining Presidential Popularity," *American Political Science Review* 72 (1978): 506–72; Donald R. Kinder, "Presidents, Prosperity, and Public Opinion," *Public Opinion Quarterly* 45 (1981): 1–21; Michael Lewis-Beck, *Economics and Elections: The Major Western Democracies* (Ann Arbor: University of Michigan Press, 1990); Kristen Renwick Monroe, *Presidential Popularity and the Economy* (New York: Praeger, 1984); Helmut Norpoth, "Economics, Politics, and the Cycle of Presidential Popularity," in Heinz Eulau and Michael S. Lewis-Beck, eds., *Economic Conditions and Electoral Outcomes: The United States and Western Europe* (New York: Agathon Press, 1985), 167–86; Helmut Norpoth, Michael Lewis-Beck, and Jean-Dominique Lafay, eds., *Economics and Politics: The Calculus of Support* (Ann Arbor: University of Michigan Press, 1991). For a dissenting view, see James A. Stimson, "Public Support for American Presidents: A Cyclical Model," *Public Opinion Quarterly* 40 (1976): 1–21.

8. Jorge Buendía, "Economic Reform, Public Opinion and Presidential Approval in Mexico: The Salinas Years (1988–1993)" (M.A. dissertation, University of Chicago, 1994); Mitchell Seligson and Miguel Gómez, "Ordinary Elections in Extraordinary Times: The Political Economy of Voting in Costa Rica," in John Booth and Mitchell Seligson, eds., *Elections and Democracy in Central America* (Chapel Hill, N.C.: University of North Carolina Press, 1989), 158–84.

9. For an analysis of the 1990 elections see Gregory D. Schmidt, "Fujimori's 1990 Upset Victory in Peru: Electoral Rules, Contingencies, and Adaptive Strategies," *Comparative Politics* 29 (1996): 321–54.

10. See Catherine Conaghan, "Polls, Political Discourse, and the Public Sphere: The Spin on Peru's Fuji-golpe," in Peter H. Smith, ed., *Latin America in Comparative Perspective* (Boulder: Westview, 1995), 227–56.

11. I included the vote for Javier Pérez de Cuellar's UPP (Unión del Pueblo Peruano) as part of the partisan vote in the 1995 election.

12. For an analysis of the APRA origins, see Peter F. Klaren, *Modernization, Dislocation, and Aprismo: Origins of the Peruvian Aprista Party, 1870–1932* (Austin: University of Texas Press Institute of Latin American Studies, 1973); Steve Stein, *Populism in Peru* (Madison: University of Wisconsin Press, 1980). For more contemporary views on this party see Heraclio Bonilla and Paul Drake, eds., *El APRA: De la Ideología a la Praxis* (Lima: Editorial Nuevo Mundo, 1989); Carol Graham, *Peru's APRA: Parties, Politics, and the Elusive Quest for Democracy* (Boulder: Lynne Rienner, 1992); John Crabtree, *Peru Under García: An Opportunity Lost* (Pittsburgh: University of Pittsburgh Press, 1992).

13. This proportion is calculated without considering blank and void ballots. For the 1985 and 1990 presidential elections, and due to a law introduced by AP's congressional representation, the official percentages were computed including blank and void ballots. Thus, the official results are lower than those reported here. I have decided to use the first procedure to keep comparisons with pre-1985 results possible. In the 1995 presidential elections, the official results were calculated as they were in 1980.

14. An analysis of Belaunde's economic policies can be found in Conaghan and Malloy, *Unsettling Statecraft*.

15. For an analysis of the electoral strength of the Left in Peru see Henry Dietz, "Political Participation in the Barriadas: An Extension and Reexamination," *Comparative Political Studies* 18 (1985); Fernando Tuesta Soldevilla, *Peru 1985: El Derrotero de una Nueva Elección* (Lima: Centro de Investigaciones de la Universidad del Pacífico-Fundación Friedrich Ebert, 1986); idem, *Pobreza Urbana y Cambios Electorales en Lima* (Lima: Cuadernos DESCO, 1989).

16. Dietz, op. cit.

17. See Dietz, op. cit.; Fernando Tuesta Soldevilla, *Pobreza Urbana y Cambios Electorales en Lima*; Julio Cotler, "Los Partidos Políticos y la Democracia en el Perú," in Luis Pásara and Jorge Parodi, eds., *Democracia, Sociedad y Gobierno en el Perú* (Lima: CEDYS, 1988).

18. In a survey conducted in Lima a few days after the 1995 elections, 78 percent of those belonging to the socioeconomic status group A (the highest) declared to have voted for Fujimori. Among those belonging to the socioeconomic status group D (the poorest) that figure was 66 percent. Data taken from Apoyo, *Informe de Opinión*, Lima, April 1995, 12. Thanks to Catherine Conaghan for kindly sharing this information with me.

19. Maxwell Cameron, *Democracy and Authoritarianism in Peru: Political Coalitions and Social Change* (New York: St. Martin's Press, 1994).

20. Julio Cotler, "Political Parties and the Problems of Democratic Consolidation in Peru," in Scott Mainwaring and Timothy R. Scully, eds., *Building Democratic Institutions: Party Systems in Latin America* (Palo Alto: Stanford University Press, 1995), 323–53.

21. Romeo Grompone, "El Incierto Futuro de los Partidos Políticos," in Julio Cotler, ed., *Peru 1964–1994: Economía, Sociedad y Política* (Lima: Instituto de Estudios Peruanos, 1995), 181–200. See also Romeo Grompone, *El Velero en el Viento. Política y Sociedad en Lima* (Lima: Instituto de Estudios Peruanos, 1991).

22. For a sample of the voluminous literature on political socialization, see Fred I. Greenstein, *Children and Politics* (New Haven: Yale University Press, 1965); Kent M. Jennings and Richard Niemi, *Generations and Politics: A Panel Study of Young Adults and Their Parents* (Princeton: Princeton University Press, 1981). For more recent reviews see Yali Peng, "Intellectual Fads in Political Science: The Cases of Political Socialization and Community Power Studies," *PS: Political Science and Politics* 27 (1994): 100–109; Anders Westholm and Richard Niemi, "Political Institutions and Political Socialization: A Cross-National Study," *Comparative Politics* 25 (1992): 25–42.

23. A number of reasons can be offered to explain the short-lived nature of most Peruvian parties: military coups that interrupted the normal process of party development; personality-based politics that fosters party factionalization; ideological disputes that result in the formation of new parties.

24. Carlos Franco, *Imagenes de la Sociedad Peruana. La Otra Modernidad* (Lima: CEDEP, 1991), 97–100.

25. For an overview of Latin American populism, see Michael L. Conniff, ed., *Latin American Populism in Comparative Perspective* (Albuquerque: University of New Mexico Press, 1982); Torcuato Di Tella, "Populismo y Reforma en América Latina," *Desarrollo Económico* 4 (1965): 391–425; Robert Dix, "Populism: Authoritarian and Democratic," *Latin American Research Review* 20 (1985): 29–52. For a recent work on the transformations of populism in the context of ne-

oliberal economic policies, see Kenneth M. Roberts, "Neoliberalism and the Transformation of Populism in Latin America: The Peruvian Case," *World Politics* 48 (1995): 82–116.

26. There were 2,316,188 persons registered to vote in 1966, and 4,966,016 in similar condition in 1978. The difference between these two figures gives the proportion of new voters in 1978 (4,966,016 – 2,316,188 = 2,649,828, which is 53.36 percent of the number of registered voters in 1978). The number of registered voters in 1980 was 6,485,680; in 1985 was 8,290,846, and in 1990 was 9,923,062. I am the first to recognize the crude nature of this indicator, but its usefulness cannot be denied: it gives a rough measure of the proportion of voters that had not had the experience of casting a vote in a previous national contest.

27. Conaghan and Malloy, op. cit.; Julio Cotler, *Política y Sociedad en el Perú: Cambios y Continuidades* (Lima: Instituto de Estudios Peruanos, 1994), 173–200.

28. For instance, 17 percent declared to trust political parties in polls conducted in Lima in March 1989. Three years later, in March 1992, that figure was 13 percent. Data taken from various issues of Apoyo's *Informe de Opinión*, Lima.

29. See Efraín Gonzalez de Olarte and Lilian Samamé, *El Péndulo Peruano. Políticas Económicas, Gobernabilidad y Subdesarrollo 1963–1990* (Lima: Instituto de Estudios Peruanos-Consorcio de Investigación Económica, 1991); Manuel Pastor and Carol Wise, "Peruvian Economic Policy in the 1980s: From Orthodoxy to Heterodoxy and Back," *Latin American Research Review* 27 (1992): 83–118; Manuel Pastor, *Inflation, Stabilization, and Debt* (Boulder: Westview Press, 1992).

30. Economic Commission for Latin America and the Caribbean, *Preliminary Overview of the Economy of Latin America and the Caribbean* (Santiago: United Nations-ECLA, 1995), table A-1. Figures based on values at 1980 prices.

31. Belaunde and García had initial popularity rates of 75 and 96 percent, respectively. The average approval rates for their second year in office were 36 and 73 percent, respectively. After six months in office, the popularity rate was 25 percent for Belaunde, and 15 percent for García.

32. James A. Stimson, "Public Support for American Presidents: A Cyclical Model," op. cit.

33. *Caretas*, January 13, 1992, 28.

34. Apoyo, *Informe de Opinión*, February 1992.

35. For an analysis of Fujimori's shrewd use of polling data, see Catherine Conaghan, "Polls, Political Discourse, and the Public Sphere," op. cit.

36. Samuel Kernell, "Explaining Presidential Popularity."

37. Kernell, op. cit.; Richard A. Brody and Benjamin I. Page, "The Impact of Events on Presidential Popularity: The Johnson and Nixon Administrations," in Aaron Wildavsky, ed., *Perspectives on the Presidency* (Boston: Little, Brown, 1975), 136–48.

38. Of course, it also includes the effects of previous noneconomic variables.

39. Samuel Kernell, op. cit.

40. Damodar N. Gujarati, *Basic Econometrics*, 2d ed. (New York: McGraw Hill, 1988), 365.

41. Kristen R. Monroe informs us that "(1) Inflation and military expenditures are consistently significant influences on presidential popularity [in the United States]. (2) Unemployment, real personal income, and the stock market are not significant influences on popularity." See her "Economic Influences on Presidential Popularity," *Public Opinion Quarterly* 42 (1978): 360–69. In a similar vein, Kernell argues that inflation is a consistent predictor of presidential popularity, whereas unemployment is not (op. cit., 518). Similar findings have been reported by Norpoth, "Economics, Politics, and the Cycle of Presidential Popularity," and David G. Golden and James

M. Poterba, "The Price of Popularity: The Political Business Cycle Reexamined," *American Journal of Political Science* 24 (1980): 696–714.

42. Economic Commission for Latin America and the Caribbean, op. cit.

43. The polling firm Apoyo, S.A., has asked regularly the following question: "What do you think will be your family's economic situation within six months?" (starting in 1994, the question wording was changed from *within six months* to *within one year*). In September 1990, one month after Fujimori initiated his first administration, 39 percent declared that "it will be better." One year later, that figure dropped to 16 percent. In March 1995, one month before the end of Fujimori's first administration, 45 percent of those interviewed gave an optimistic answer, and only 12 percent believed that the economic situation of their families would be worse within a year. Data taken from various issues of Apoyo, *Informe de opinión*, Lima.

44. Economic Commission for Latin America and the Caribbean, op. cit.

45. To compete again, they would have to reregister, fulfilling a number of requisites, with the Electoral National Board.

46. For an analysis of the impact of authoritarian legacies on the prospects for democracy in Latin America, see Frances Hagopian, "After Regime Change: Authoritarian Legacies, Political Representation, and the Democratic Future of Latin America," *World Politics* 45 (1993): 464–500.

47. In June 1995, the Democratic Constituent Congress (CCD) approved an amnesty law for members of the police and armed forces convicted or indicted for violations of human rights in the fight against *Sendero Luminoso*. A poll conducted one month after the approval of the law indicated that 78 percent of those interviewed in Lima disagreed with it. See Apoyo, *Informe de Opinión*, July 1995.

48. For an analysis of Fujimori's disregard for public opinion see Catherine Conaghan, "Public Life in the Time of Alberto Fujimori," Working Paper No. 219, the Latin American Program, Woodrow Wilson International Center for Scholars, May 1996.

49. A former member of PPC, he was for some years mayor of Miraflores, an affluent district in Lima.

4. "Facing the Twenty-First Century," by Eduardo A. Gamarra

1. Thousands of unemployed mine workers and others affected by the economic crisis migrated to lowland valleys such as the Chapare in the department of Cochabamba where they joined thousands of others engaged in the cultivation of coca leaves.

2. For an in-depth treatment of this topic consult Eduardo A. Gamarra, *Entre la Droga y la Democracia* (La Paz: ILDIS, 1994).

3. Interview with Cossio, former minister of planning, La Paz, August 1995.

4. Under the terms of the MNR-UCS pact, Fernández's followers secured one ministry, two undersecretary posts, two embassies, the presidency of one regional development corporation, and the first vice-presidency of both the Chamber of Deputies and the Senate.

5. The MBL was promised one ministry, key congressional posts, and at least one embassy. Araníbar and the MBL extracted a high price, considering this party won only 5 percent. Subsequently, Araníbar was named minister of foreign affairs.

6. The debate over the Education Reform Law was the most intense. In 1995, the government faced an insurrection of sorts from teachers' unions that refused to allow the reform to go forward. As a result the government launched a state of siege, which it maintained in place for

ninety days. During this period, the leadership of the teacher's union was arrested and opposition was effectively demobilized.

7. The debate over the passage of the INRA bill was dramatic. As discussed below, thousands of peasants from around the country mobilized against the bill, the business sector rallied against it, and the government eventually gave in to demands from both sectors. The pattern of confrontation with each sector was recurrent. In each instance, the government announced an initiative, expected confrontation with the affected sectors, and attempted to co-opt the leadership of the opposition forces. Often the strategy worked. Other times, it failed dramatically and violent confrontations ensued.

8. The law was signed by President Gonzalo Sánchez de Lozada on April 20, 1994, and published in the Official Gazette of Bolivia as Law Number 1551 on April 21, 1994. The law came into effect as of the date of its publication.

9. To implement the reform, a reform of Article 60 of the constitution was necessary. As has been the case with every reform pushed by the Sánchez de Lozada government, the debate over Article 60 stirred great regional passions as some departments faced losing congressional representatives. In the end, the government secured a new Article 60 that paved the way for the 1997 national elections.

10. The only major exception to U.S. satisfaction after the June 30, 1994, ultimatum came in September 1995 when the DEA in collaboration with Peruvian police captured a Bolivian DC-6 plane loaded with four tons of cocaine. The plane departed from the La Paz airport under the watch of dozens of Bolivia's special counternarcotics police. After the capture of Amado Pacheco, the fallout was large. While nothing has been established, it appeared that the web of corruption reached high into quarters of the government.

11. Political parties were not the only ones facing egregious charges of corruption. Perhaps the most serious crisis involved the allegations of corruption against two members of the Supreme Court. The crisis in the Supreme Court began in mid-1993, when relatives of a member of the court solicited a bribe from Antonio Ibarra, a former official of the Nicaraguan government, who was facing extradition procedures. With U.S. assistance, the Bolivian police recorded the conversation and proceeded to indict the Supreme Court justices. In June 1994, in a Senate trial, the two justices were found guilty, sentenced to two years in prison, and barred from ever holding public office.

12. According to former ambassador Robert Gelbard, the MIR also financed its 1985 presidential campaign with drug money. Interview, May 4, 1996, Miami, Florida.

5. "Chilean Democracy Before and After Pinochet," by Sylvia Borzutzky

1. For a more detailed analysis see Silvia Borzutzky, "Social Security Policies and Chilean Politics" (Ph.D. dissertation, University of Pittsburgh, 1983).

2. Brian Loveman, *Struggle in the Countryside: Politics and the Rural Labor in Chile, 1919–1973* (Bloomington: Indiana University Press, 1977), 293–94, and *Chile, the Legacy of Hispanic Capitalism* (New York: Oxford University Press, 1979), 257.

3. Charles Anderson, *Politics and Economic Change in Latin America* (Princeton: D. Van Nostrand, 1967).

4. Julio Valenzuela, "The Chilean Labor Movement: The Institutionalization of Conflict,"

in Arturo Valenzuela and Julio Valenzuela, eds., *Chile: Politics and Society* (New Brunswick, N.J.: Transaction, 1974), 161.

5. Barbara Stallings, *Class Conflict and Economic Development in Chile, 1958–1973* (Palo Alto: Stanford University Press, 1978), 46.

6. Brian Loveman, *Chile*, 277–78; David Cusack, "The Politics of Chilean Private Enterprises Under Christian Democracy" (Ph.D. dissertation, University of Colorado, 1970).

7. For an analysis of the history of these laws and their political impact, see James O. Morris, *Elites, Intellectuals and Consensus: A Study of the Social Question and the Industrial Relations System in Chile* (Ithaca: Cornell University Press, 1966); Jorge Barria, *Breve Historia del Sindicalismo Chileno* (Santiago: INSORA, 1967); Alan Angell, *Politics and the Labour Movement in Chile* (London: Oxford University Press, 1973); and Silvia Borzutzky, op. cit., chaps. 1 and 2.

8. Crisóstomo Pizarro, "Rol de los sindiatos en Chile," *Estudios CIEPLAN* no. 22 (Marzo 1978): 40.

9. Nicholas Kaldor, "Problemas económicos de Chile," *Trimestre Económico* (Abril–Junio 1959): 179.

10. Isabel Heskia, "La distribución del ingreso en Chile," in CIEPLAN, ed., *Bienestar y Pobreza* (Santiago: Universidad Católica de Chile, 1974), 45.

11. Joseph Ramos, *Política de remuneraciones e inflaciones persistentes: El caso Chileno* (Santiago: Instituto de Economía, Universidad de Chile, 1970).

12. Kenneth Dyson, *The State Tradition in Western Europe* (New York: Oxford University Press, 1980), 119–21.

13. Tomás Moulián, "Desarrollo Político y Estado de Compromiso: Desajustes y Crisis estatal en Chile," *Colección Estudios CIEPLAN* no. 8 (Julio 1982): 105–60; Manuel Antonio Garretón, "Democratización y otro desarrolo: el caso chileno," *Revista Mexicana de Sociología* 42, no. 3 (September 1980): 1167–1213.

14. Jacques Maritain, *The Rights of Man and Natural Law* (New York: Charles Scribner and Sons, 1943), 17–42; Jaime Castillo Velasco, *Los caminos de la Revolución* (Santiago: Editorial del Pacífico, 1955), 370; Eduardo Frei, *Pensamiento de Eduardo Frei, Selección y Notas de Oscar Pinochet* (Santiago: Editorial Aconcagua, 1982).

15. Analyses of the economic program of the Frei administration are found in Barbara Stallings, *Class Conflict and Economic Development in Chile, 1958–1973* (Palo Alto: Stanford University Press, 1978); Ricardo French Davis, *Políticas Económicas en Chile, 1952–1970* (Santiago: Universidad Católica de Chile, 1973); Robert Kaufman, *The Politics of Land Reform in Chile, 1950–1970: Policy, Political Institution, and Social Change* (Cambridge: Harvard University Press, 1972); Theodore Moran, *Multinational Corporations and the Politics of Dependence* (Princeton: Princeton University Press, 1977); Brian Loveman, op. cit., 1975 and 1979.

16. Silvia Borzutzky, op. cit., chaps. 4 and 5.

17. Salvador Allende, Discurso Inaugural, Nov. 5, 1970, in Salvador Allende, *Historia de una Ilusión* (Santiago: La Señal, 1973), 11–23. For an analysis of the program and the Allende regime, see Sergio Bitar, *Transición, Socialismo y Democracia: La Experiencia Chilena* (Mexico City: Siglo XXI Editores, 1979); Regis Debrais, *Conversaciones con Allende* (Mexico City: Siglo XXI Editores, 1971): Federico Gil, *Chile at the Turning Point: Lessons of the Socialist Years 1970–1973* (Philadelphia: Institute for the Study of Human Issues, 1979); Ian Roxborough et al., *Chile: The State and the Revolution* (New York: Holmes and Meiers Publishers, 1977); Paul Sigmund, *The*

Overthrow of Allende and the Politics of Chile (Pittsburgh: University of Pittsburgh Press, 1979); Arturo Valenzuela, *The Breakdown of Democratic Regimes, Chile* (Baltimore: John Hopkins University Press, 1979).

18. Valenzuela, op. cit.

19. Augusto Pinochet Ugarte, Jose T. Merino Castro, Gustavo Leigh Guzman, and Cesar Mendoza Duran, "Declaration of Principles of the Chilean Government" (Santiago, 1974), 29.

20. On the history of the Chicago Boys in Chile, see J. G. Valdés, *La Escula de Chicago: Operación Chile* (Buenos Aires: Ediciones B., 1989); A. Fontaine, *Los economistas y el Presidente Pinochet* (Santiago: Editorial Zig-Zag, 1988).

21. Sergio de Castro, speech, Sesion Inaugural de la 2a Reunión Conjunta del Comite Interempresarial Chile—Japón, Sept. 8, 1980.

22. Manuel A. Garretón, "La Institucionalización política del regimen militar chileno," *Mensaje* 310 (Julio 1982): 329–33.

23. Interview, Santiago, August 1986.

24. Sergio de Castro, speech, "El Estado de las finanzas públicas," *El Mercurio*, September 8, 1980, 1-C, 10.

25. Sergio de Castro, speech, ibid., Sept. 8, 1980.

26. José Piñera, speech, Nov. 7, 1979.

27. Banco Central de Chile, *Indicadores Económicos y Sociales, 1960–1982* (Santiago, 1983), 24.

28. Silvia Borzutzky, "The Pinochet Regime: Crisis and Consolidation," in J. Malloy and M. Seligson, eds., *Authoritarians and Democrats: Regime Transition in Latin America* (Pittsburgh: University of Pittsburgh Press, 1986); A. Valenzuela and J. S. Valenzuela, *Party Oppositions Under the Chilean Authoritarian Regime* (Washington, D.C.: Wilson Center Working Papers, 1984); M. Barrera and J. S. Valenzuela, "The Development of Labor Movement Opposition to the Military Regime," in J. S. Valenzuela and A. Valenzuela, *Military Rule in Chile: Dictators and Oppositions* (Baltimore: Johns Hopkins University Press, 1986); M. A. Garreton, *Las complejidades de la transicion invisible: Movilizaciones populares y regimen militar en Chile* (Santiago: Flacso, Documento de Trabajo no. 334, Abril 1987).

29. S. Edward and A. Edwards, *Monetarism and Liberalization: The Chilean Experiment* (Cambridge: Ballinger Publishing Co., 1986), 80.

30. Hernan Buchi, "Programa macroeconómico de Chile 1985–1986 y su financiamiento," *Boletin Banco Central de Chile* (July–September 1985), 1689; R. French Davis, "El conflicto entre le deuda y el crecimiento en Chile: Tendencias y perspectivas," *Colección Estudios CIEPLAN 26*, June 1989; J. P. Arellano, "Crisis y recuperación económica en Chile en los años 80," *Colección estudios CIEPLAN 24*, June 1988.

31. Karen L. Remmer, *The Chilean Military Under Authoritarian Rule, 1973–1987* (Albuquerque, N.M.: Latin American Institute, University of New Mexico, Occasional Paper Series no. 1, March 1988), 34.

32. Apuntes CIEPLAN, no. 16, Balance Económico y Social del Regimen Militer, Dic 1988.

33. Analisis Económico, Informe bimestal, November-December 1991, 6.

34. Manuel A. Garretón, *Las Condiciones sociopolitícas de la inauguaración democràtica en Chile* (Notre Dame: Kellog Institute for International Studies, Working paper 142, June 1990).

35. Manuel A. Garretón, op. cit, 1990, 6.

36. Karen Remmer, op. cit., and *Military Rule in Latin America* (Boulder: Westview Press,

1991), 178.

37. Pamela Constable and Arturo Valenzuela, "Chile's Return to Democracy," *Foreign Affairs* 68, no. 5: 177.

38. Ibid., 176.

39. *Analisis*, 6 Julio 1992, 10–14.

40. *Analisis*, 9–22 Dec. 1991, interview of President Aylwin, 16–19.

41. Pilar Vergara, "Economía de Mercado, Estado de Bienestar y Consolidación Democrática en Chile," ms., 23.

42. Ibid.

43. *Analisis*, 17 Agosto, 1992, 27, 28.

44. For an analysis of these issues, see Brian Loveman, "Missión Cumplida? Civil Military Relations and the Chilean Political Transition" (prepared for the LASA meeting, April 1991).

45. *Analisis*, 17 Feb. 1992, 17 and 18.

46. Ibid.

6. "The Symbolic Value of Economists in the Democratization of Chilean Politics," by Verónica Montecinos

1. See J. Markoff, *Waves of Democracy* (Thousand Oaks, Calif.: Pine Forge Press, 1996); and J. Markoff and V. Montecinos, "The Ubiquitous Rise of Economists," *Journal of Public Policy* 13, no. 1 (1993): 37–68.

2. C. Conaghan, J. Malloy, and L. Abugattas, "Business and the 'Boys': The Politics of Neoliberalism in the Central Andes," *LARR* 25, no. 2: 3–30.

3. See V. Montecinos, "Economic Policy Elites and Democratization," *Studies in Comparative International Development* 28, no. 1 (1993): 25–53.

4. See V. Montecinos, "Economics and Power: Chilean Economists in Government: 1958–1985" (Ph.D. dissertation, University of Pittsburgh, 1988).

5. See Silva 1991 and Valdés 1995.

6. Mónica Madariaga in an interview with Arturo Valenzuela. See A. Valenzuela, "The Military in Power: The Consolidation of One-Man Rule," in P. W. Drake and I. Jaksic, eds., *The Struggle for Democracy in Chile 1982–1990* (Lincoln and London: University of Nebraska Press, 1991), 56.

7. Aylwin's finance minister, Alejandro Foxley, recognized that the policies promoted by his team benefitted from the experience accumulated by the Chicago Boys, but he vehemently rebuffed charges of continuity and claims of neoliberalist conversion. See *El Mercurio*, April 1–7, 1993. The quality of economic indicators added weight to the influence of government technocrats: Chile's growth rate in the 1990s appeared among the highest in the region, and inflation remained at record low levels. While the unemployment rate fell and real wages improved, private investment increased considerably.

8. When the candidacies for the 1993 presidential election were beginning to take shape, several professional economists were considered as possible candidates (Alejandro Foxley, Ricardo Lagos, Evelyn Matthei, Sebastián and José Piñera, Manfred Max-Neef). Some of these individuals are being mentioned again for the 1999 presidential race.

9. In 1994, Alejandro Foxley went from heading the Ministry of Finance to campaign for the presidency of the Christian Democratic party. He won with over 60 percent of the votes. This, however, is one of several cases of economists leading parties.

10. The organizational approach to the study of political parties has not received much attention in the literature on parties nor in organizational theory. Yet it offers important clues to understand recent changes in the composition of party elites and in the dynamics of party life. For an exception, see A. Panebianco, *Political Parties: Organization and Power* (Cambridge and New York: Cambridge University Press, 1988).

11. March and Olsen, for example, tell us that "A primary contribution of politics is in the development of meaning. . . . political institutions, rhetoric and the rituals of decision facilitate the maintenance and change of social values, and the interpretation of human existence." See J. March and J. Olsen, *Rediscovering Institutions: The Organizational Basis of Politics* (New York: Free Press, 1989), 94.

12. Ibid., p. 17, 48.

13. See A. Valenzuela and J. S. Valenzuela, "Party Opposition Under the Chilean Authoritarian Regime," in J. S. Valenzuela and A. Valenzuela, eds., *Military Rule in Chile: Dictatorship and Opposition* (Baltimore and London: Johns Hopkins University Press, 1986). See also T. Scully, "Reconstituting Party Politics in Chile" in S. Mainwaring and T. Scully, eds., *Building Democratic Institutions: Party Systems in Latin America* (Palo Alto: Stanford University Press, 1995).

14. Organization theorists point precisely to the state (for its power to enforce the rules that regulate what other organizations do) and to the professions (for their capacity to diagnose problems and prescribe solutions) as major sources of change in the institutional environment surrounding organizations in modern societies. The state and the professions provide the typifications, assumptions, rules, and normative definitions that guide the actions of organizational actors. See W. R. Scott, *Organizations: Rational, Natural and Open Systems* (Englewood Cliff, N.J.: Prentice Hall, 1992), 139.

15. See A. Valenzuela and J. S. Valenzuela, "Party Opposition Under the Chilean Authoritarian Regime," 1986; A. Valenzuela, "Partidos políticos y crisis presidencial en Chile: Proposición para un gobierno parlamentario," in J. Linz, A. Lijphart, A. Valenzuela, and O. Godoy, eds., *Hacia una democracia moderna: La opción parlamentaria* (Santiago: Ediciones Universidad Católica de Chile, 1990), 129–90; and S. Mainwaring, "Political Parties and Democratization in Brazil and the Southern Cone," *Comparative Politics* 21 (October 1988): 91–120.

16. On polarized pluralism, see Giovanni Sartori, *Parties and Party Systems* (Cambridge: Cambridge University Press, 1976). On the Chilean experience, see Arturo Valenzuela, *The Breakdown of Democratic Regimes: Chile* (Baltimore: Johns Hopkins University Press, 1979).

17. Pamela Constable and Arturo Valenzuela, *A Nation of Enemies: Chile Under Pinochet* (New York: W. W. Norton and Company, 1991), 54.

18. The junta had control over executive, legislative, and constitutional powers. Each commander enjoyed an indefinite term in office. The military courts were given jurisdiction over any crime linked to political subversion. On the "consolidation of one-man rule," see A. Valenzuela, "The Military in Power"; and Constable and Valenzuela, *A Nation of Enemies*.

19. On the internal divisions within the regime and the struggles among Pinochet's advisors, see A. Valenzuela, "The Military in Power."

20. See A. Fontaine Aldunate, *Los economistas y el presidente Pinochet* (Santiago: Empresa Editora Zig-Zag, 1988); P. Vergara, *Auge y caída del neoliberalismo en Chile* (Santiago: FLACSO, 1985); A. Foxley, *Experiments in Neoconservative Economics* (Berkeley: University of California Press, 1983); J. Ramos, *Neoconservative Economics in the Southern Cone of Latin America*

1973–1983 (Baltimore and London: Johns Hopkins University Press, 1986); S. Edwards and A. Cox, *Monetarism and Liberalization: The Chilean Experiment* (Cambridge: Ballinger, 1987).

21. On the story of the Chicago Boys, see J. G. Valdés, *Pinochet's Economists: The Chicago School in Chile* (Cambridge: Cambridge University Press, 1995).

22. For an analysis of the Chicago Boys' connections with financial conglomerates that, until the 1982 crisis, controlled the most dynamic sectors of the economy, see E. Silva, "The Political Economy of Chile's Regime Transition: From Radical to 'Pragmatic' Neo-liberal Policies," in P. W. Drake and I. Jaksic, eds., *The Struggle for Democracy in Chile 1982–1990* (Lincoln and London: University of Nebraska Press, 1991).

23. For economists in the opposition, it was difficult to understand their colleagues' passive attitude on issues concerning human rights. "Economists thought they had nothing to do with politics. Otherwise, I could not understand how [ministers] Cauas and de Castro coexisted with torture and exile." Former minister Pablo Baraona, a key member of the Chicago group, explained: "There was total ignorance among civilians in the government. Civilian ministers knew as much as you or me about what happened to Tucapel Jiménez [a labor leader murdered in 1982]. For me, it is mystery." (Interview, 1986.)

24. "Lawyers can only translate the ideas of economists into their language," I was told by a government economist in an interview in 1986.

25. Opposition economists were willing to recognize advances over previous practices of resource allocation in the public sector. They approved of project evaluation and a new national and regional inventory of projects but criticized the neglect of medium-term macroeconomic planning. Interview with Eduardo García d'Acuña, 1986.

26. "When the minister asked the entrepreneurs, 'Well, why do you think this subsidy will be favorable to Chile?,' there was a crisis. Never before had an entrepreneur been asked to justify a policy measure by saying it would be beneficial to the country. The military saw how the economists, supposedly from the right, were harsher on business than anyone else." Interview with former minister José Piñera, 1986.

27. A 1993 law approved the payment of benefits to 58,000 public employees who had been dismissed for political reasons in the period between 1973 and 1990, when almost any sign of political dissent was a cause of separation.

28. Constable and Valenzuela, *A Nation of Enemies*, 190.

29. March and Olsen, *Rediscovering Institutions*, 98.

30. Frederick von Hayek, the Societé Mont Pelerin, Milton Friedman, Gordon Tullock, and other international luminaries visited Chile in the 1970s and expressed their support to the experiment underway. The Chilean government, committed to the implementation of the most orthodox reforms in the region, received the approval of multilateral agencies in the form of abundant resources. (See P. Meller, "Revisión del proceso de ajuste chileno de la década de los 80," Colección Estudios CIEPLAN, 30, 1990, 5–54.)

31. Professors with unorthodox views were purged from the schools of economics.

32. March and Olsen, *Rediscovering Institutions*, 89, 51.

33. Until 1982, the Chicago Boys partly assured the implementation of their reforms by making it easy for entrepreneurs and private citizens to access the foreign credit bonanza of the 1970s and early 1980s. Expanded expenditures created a boom, accumulated an enormous foreign debt, and contributed to a major recessionary crisis in 1982–83. The economic team was then only temporarily replaced by a group of businessmen and military officers. From 1985 until the presiden-

tial election, neoliberal technocrats regained dominance. With more pragmatic policies and a less exclusionary style, they managed to recover output and employment, increase public revenues, recapitalize insolvent banks and firms, reduce the foreign debt, and promote nontraditional exports.

34. Some organizations face stronger technical demands and are rewarded on the basis of the quality and quantity of their outputs. Others (churches, schools) face mostly institutionalized requirements. Among the latter, the structural capacities of the organization (the qualifications of their personnel, their academic degrees, their access to crucial and powerful networks) and the processes followed (the plans, the models, the data gathered, the contacts made) become the preferred indicators to grant legitimacy. See W. R. Scott and J. W. Meyer, "The Organization of Societal Sectors," in J. W. Meyer and W. R. Scott, eds., *Organizational Environments: Ritual and Rationality* (Beverly Hills: Sage, 1983); W. R. Scott, "Unpacking Institutional Arguments," in W. W. Powell and P. J. DiMaggio, eds., *The New Institutionalism in Organizational Analysis* (Chicago: University of Chicago Press, 1991).

35. Political parties, like other organizations with ambiguous goals (power, votes?) and unclear technologies (resource mobilization?), are likely to change their organizational structures by copying each other and adopting forms that are institutionalized in their environment. The rational design of political entrepreneurs may not have been the most important source of the changes introduced by political parties. The political engineers, more than sources of rationality, were themselves serving as symbols of compliance.

36. Parties on the right had welcomed the coup and voluntarily relinquished their right to exist in exchange for military protection against their own electoral decline of the 1960s and 1970s.

37. Interview with UDI economist, former minister Luis Larraín (August 1992). Before becoming a prominent neoliberal, Jaime Guzmán, a party founder and one of Pinochet's ideologues, had been a law professor and charismatic leader of the "gremialista" movement in the Catholic University. Lawyers from that university are heavily represented in the party.

38. UDI also made contacts with the international "new right" and tried to incorporate some of the tactics that during the 1980s had given strength to conservatism in the United States and other countries.

39. The economist Sebastián Piñera joined the Political Commission of RN only three months after becoming a member of the party. As a senator, he tried to run for president in an unsuccessful internal campaign against a fellow party economist, deputy Evelyn Matthei. Both had to withdraw their candidacies after being involved in a case of political espionage in early 1993. Deputy Matthei resigned as party member and ran for reelection as an independent.

40. The Instituto Libertad, a think tank created in 1990, gives technical advice to party leaders and legislators of Renovación Nacional. On occasion, members of the Instituto Libertad and the Instituto Libertad y Desarrollo (UDI) collaborate. Many of them were former colleagues in the Pinochet administration.

41. Interview with Carlos Correa, former state manager under Pinochet (July 1992).

42. Interview with Felipe Larraín, July 1992. At the time, Sebastián Piñera's presidential bid still seemed viable and Larraín was collaborating in the campaign program.

43. Economists in RN reportedly exasperate politicians. They are seen as arrogant when adopting the role of technical advisors ("we are slowly educating politicians," a party economist told me). In executive roles, economists' political style is perceived as alien: "Sebastián acts like

an efficient entrepreneur; lyrics and speeches bore him, and he gives little time to lobbying."

44. Interview with Roberto Ossandón (August 1992).

45. Mechanisms of internal discipline and strong organizational structures had been developed during several years of clandestine operations in the late 1940s and 1950s. In the 1970s and 1980s, the party decided to maintain a unified direction, although there was a point in which the majority in the Central Committee and all of the members of the Political Commission were in exile (see "Informe al Pleno del Partido Comunista," in Frei et al., *Democracia Cristiana y Partido Comunista* (Santiago: Editorial Aconcagua, 1986).

46. Interview, July 1988.

47. Quote from I. Walker, *Socialismo y democracia: Chile y Europa en perspectiva comparada* (Santiago: Cieplan-Hachette, 1990), 193. Analyses of the "renovation" of Chilean Socialists include P. Politzer, *Altamirano* (Santiago: Ediciones Melquíades, 1990); R. Nuñez, *Socialismo: Diez años de renovación* (Santiago: Las Ediciones del Ornitorrinco, 1991); and J. Arrate, "El exilio: Origen y proyección," in J. Gazmuri, ed., *Chile en el umbral de los noventa* (Santiago: Editorial Planeta, 1988), 113–35.

48. An economist at the technical department of the Christian Democratic party put it this way: "In the PS Almeyda, there are some economists of the old School of Economics, but they are not respected. It is not enough to be an economist. It is also important to be at the top and not among the lumpen in the profession."

49. One of Almeyda's followers explained: "The renovated Socialists have taken the European socialism as a model, but that is not the kind of socialism appropriate for a poor country. The politics of negotiation, international contacts, meetings and academic articles is more comfortable, but it does not create consciousness at the base. They cannot mobilize the rank-and-file." Interview with Rodolfo Galvez (July 1988).

50. See P. Silva, "Technocrats and Politics in Chile: From the Chicago Boys to the CIEPLAN Monks," *Journal of Latin American Studies* 23, no. 2 (May 1991): 385–410.

51. T. Scully, *Los partidos de centro y la evolución política chilena*. (Santiago: Cieplan-Notre Dame, 1992), 254–59.

52. In 1980, when the economy was booming and Pinochet obtained the plebiscitarian approval of a new constitution, various attempts to structure party cooperation failed. The formation of a broad multiparty coalition was not achieved until 1988. The Concertación de Partidos por el NO, that organized the triumph against Pinochet in the 1988 plebiscite, was later transformed into the Concertación de Partidos por la Democracia, the center-left alliance that brought Aylwin to the presidency in 1989 and Eduardo Frei in 1993.

53. Some referred to "Latin America's obvious need for more illustrated politicians." Others emphasized the lessons to be learned from the tragic political consequences of "careless economic management." For many, reflecting on the "modernization" of political parties became "an obsession." One of these analysts asked, "How can we make parties less ideological and more programmatic? How can we provide them with the scientific-technical capacity to come up with less ideological formulations? How can we make the political class more permeable to the concrete demands of a society that must go simultaneously through modernization and democratization?" See M. A. Garretón, participation in round table discussion, in N. Lechner, *Partidos y democracia* (Santiago: FLACSO, 1985), 215.

54. Interview with Alejandro Foxley (December 1987). Consider also the rise of economist Ricardo Lagos as the most prominent political figure on the left: "Originally, Lagos came from

nowhere. He was neither an Altamiranista nor an Almeydista. He was a "Swiss" who began to gather *técnicos* and did not make ideological judgments." Interview with Luis Maira (July 1988).

55. "Politicians have [an inferiority] complex: economists know things that the politicians do not know. And what economists do not know, they are thought of as capable of learning." Interview with Alejandro Foxley (December 1987). Another party economist said, "politicians have trouble sitting down for hours to evaluate the pros and cons of a decision. . . . When the ideological level of the debate subsides, the politician loses relative weight."

56. I interviewed Clodomiro Almeyda in July 1988, while he was imprisoned in Santiago.

57. On the involvement of social scientists in the politics of redemocratization, see J. Puryear, *Thinking Politics: Intellectuals and Democracy in Chile, 1973–1988* (Baltimore: Johns Hopkins University Press, 1994).

58. Significant groups within these parties were skeptical of or plainly hostile to exercises in "political engineering."

59. On recently formulated criticisms of the professional socialization of economists, see D. Colander and R. Brenner, *Educating Economists* (Ann Arbor: University of Michigan Press, 1992).

60. "The *técnicos* have allowed a faster renovation of the party, but we have not succeeded in getting them to say what we want. There is a double discourse: one of convergence, the private discourse of economists. The other is the public discourse of the parties. Parties hate to recognize that they converge!" Interview with Jorge Marshall R., minister of economy under Aylwin (July 1988).

61. Scott, "Unpacking Institutional Arguments," 237.

62. Interview with Augusto Aninat of the Technical Department of the Christian Democratic party (July 1988). The perception of a "conspiracy of the *técnicos*" led the parties to react. The Economic Commission of the Socialist party, for example, was restructured in the early 1990s to link a "miniclub" of select party economists more directly to the party's political leadership. Interview with Oscar Landerretche, a Socialist economist at the Ministry of Economy (July 1992).

63. Interview with Ignacio Balbontín (July 1988).

64. Interview with Sergio Molina, minister of planning under Aylwin and minister of education under Frei Ruiz-Tagle (January 1988).

65. Interview with economist Carlos Hurtado, minister of public works under Aylwin (July 1988).

66. Senator Valdés was a key negotiator during the transition, as president of the Christian Democratic party and director of CED (interview, July 1992).

67. Panebianco asserts that professionalization "is the distinguishing feature of the organizational change political parties are currently undergoing." See A. Panebianco, *Political Parties: Organization and Power* (Cambridge: Cambridge University Press, 1988), 230.

68. Scott, "Unpacking Institutional Arguments," 348–58.

69. J. W. Meyer and B. Rowan, "Institutionalized Organizations: Formal Structure as Myth and Ceremony," *AJS* 83 (1977): 340–63; P. J. DiMaggio and W. W. Powell, "The Iron Cage Revisited: Institutional Isomorphism and Collective Rationality in Organizational Fields," *ASR* 48 (1983): 147–60.

70. Panebianco, *Political Parties*, 230.

7. "Direct Appeals, Political Machines, and Reform," by Kurt von Mettenheim

1. This trajectory was largely unexpected by social scientists who either emphasized the hope that new independent organizations from civil society would democratize Brazil or argued that parliamentary institutions were required to avert the instability supposedly caused by presidentialism.

2. These mechanisms are direct popular appeals during campaigns for executive office and alliances with patronage machines through the spoils system thereafter.

3. Assis Brasil, *Democracia Representativa* (Rio de Janeiro: Editora Nacional, 1932).

4. On party-electoral politics from 1945–1964, see Maria C. C. Souza, *Estado e Partidos Politicos no Brasil, 1930–1964* (São Paulo: Paz e Terra, 1976).

5. Juan Linz, "The Transition from an Authoritarian Regime to Democracy in Spain: Some Thoughts for Brazilians." Memo, Yale University, 1983.

6. On the prolonged transition from military to civilian rule in Brazil, see Thomas Skidmore, *The Politics of Military Rule in Brazil, 1964–1985* (New York: Oxford University Press, 1988).

7. On the broader problem of economic policy and democracy, see Joan Nelson, ed., *Intricate Links: Democratic Politics and Market Reform in Latin America and Eastern Europe* (New Brunswick, N.J.: Transaction, 1994).

8. Patronage is a classic theme in Brazilian political studies. See Richard Graham, *Patronage and Politics in Nineteenth Century Brazil* (Palo Alto: Stanford University Press, 1990).

9. Their central works on this subject are: Oliveira Vianna, *Instituições Políticas Brasileiras* (Rio de Janeiro: Editora Nacional, 1954); and Paula Beiguelman, *Formação Política do Brasil* (São Paulo: Pioneiro, 1973).

10. The current description of Old Republic politics as *politica dos governadores* (governor's politics) focuses on the emergence of specific electoral and party practices that linked local and regional political machines with national politics. On the concept of *politica dos governadores*, see Paula Beiguelman, "A Primeira Republica no Periodo de 1891 a 1909," appendix to *Pequenos Estudos de Ciência Política* (São Paulo: Pioneiro, 1967); and Maria C. C. Souza, "O Processo Político-Partidario na Primeira Republica," in Carlos G. Motta, ed., *Brasil em Perspectiva* (São Paulo: Difel, 1969).

11. On the influence of American federalism in the 1891 Brazilian constitution, see Souza, "O Processo Político-Partidario na Primeira Republica," 150.

12. Party development in the nineteenth-century United States occurred largely through senators who served as the primary link between local patronage machines and the federal government. Although Brazilian governors lost the prerogative to seat congressional delegations in 1930 and never regained it, their influence in electoral and party politics on the state and federal levels remains critical until today.

13. On the spoils system from 1945 to 1964, see Barry Ames, "The Congressional Connection: The Structure of Politics and the Distribution of Public Expenditures in Brazil's Competitive Period," *Comparative Politics* (January 1987): 147–71.

14. The concept of late party development means that modern, mass parties emerged after state agencies and bureaucracies were already established.

15. In contrast to this rapid sequence of alliances during transition from military rule in Brazil, the concept of realignment suggests that electoral change in the United States trickles

down from presidential elections through state and local politics over decades. See James Sundquist, *Dynamics of the Party System*, 2d ed. (Washington, D.C.: Brookings, 1983), 1.

16. Interview, Fernando Henrique Cardoso, November 4, 1986.

17. The 1989 presidential election was held outside the Brazilian historical norm of holding executive elections with proportional representation contests for legislatures. Since 1932, the Brazilian electoral code has used this mechanism first proposed by Assis Brasil in his 1897 book *Democracia Representativa*.

18. Over 85 percent of registered voters viewed four televised debates, while two hours of party campaign programs were broadcast every day on prime-time television and radio for two months prior to November 15, and for two weeks preceding the December 15 runoff election.

19. While Collor's popularity fell steadily after July, endorsement by media personality Silvio Santos reinforced Collor's image after Santos's own last-minute bid for the presidency was rejected by the Supreme Electoral Court (STE).

20. While social pacts were critical for imposing economic adjustment in Mexico and Argentina, Brazil lacks the corporatist organizations or political parties capable of enforcing pacts. Collor's appeals for a national understanding with labor and business also failed because of poor political timing; the government sought to organize a pact as inflation increased and the recession deepened.

21. On the impeachment process, see Kurt Weyland, "The Rise and Fall of President Collor and Its Impact on Brazilian Democracy," *Journal of Interamerican Studies and World Affairs* 35, no. 1 (1993): 1–37.

22. Estimates from the Fundação Instituto de Pesquisas Economicas da Universidade de São Paulo and DIEESE (Departamento Intersindical de Estatistica e Estudos Socioeconomicos) reported in *Folha de S. Paulo*, March 26, 1995, section 2, p. 5.

23. On inertial inflation in Brazil, see Luiz C. Bresser Pereira and Yoshiaki Nakamo, *The Theory of Inertial Inflation: The Foundation of Economic Reform in Brazil and Argentina* (Boulder: Lynne Rienner, 1987).

24. According to Brazilian electoral legislation, executive contests require a second round unless a candidate wins over 50 percent plus one of valid votes (not including blank or null ballots), or unless the votes received by a candidate exceed the sum of votes for all other candidates.

25. On electoral stability and change in Europe, see S. Bartolini and P. Mair, *Identity, Competition and Electoral Availability* (Cambridge: Cambridge University Press, 1990).

26. On the Worker's Party, see Margaret Keck, *The Workers' Party and Democratization in Brazil* (New Haven: Yale University Press, 1992).

27. Francisco Weffort, longtime advisor of Luiz Inacio da Silva and member of the Worker Party central committee (and who accepted the Ministry of Culture in Cardoso's cabinet) argued that the 1994 election may be remembered as a political watershed in Brazilian history, perhaps equal to the 1930 revolution. See his editorial, *Folha de S. Paulo*, October 4, 1994.

28. See coverage in the *Folha de S. Paulo*, March 26, 1995.

29. On Social Security in Brazil, see James Malloy, *The Politics of Social Security in Brazil* (Pittsburgh: University of Pittsburgh Press, 1979).

30. The description of civil society resurrection under authoritarianism and during transitions to democracy can be found in Guillermo O'Donnell and Phillipe Schmitter, "Transitions From Authoritarian Rule: Tentative Conclusions," in G. O'Donnell, P. Schmitter, and L. White-

head, eds., *Transitions From Authoritarian Rule: Prospects for Democracy* (Baltimore: Johns Hopkins University Press, 1986). On the superiority of parliamentarism, see: Arturo Valenzuela and Juan Linz, *The Failure of Presidential Democracy: The Case of Latin America* (Baltimore: Johns Hopkins University Press, 1994). Also see Kurt von Mettenheim, ed., *Presidential Institutions and Democratic Politics: Comparing Regional and National Contexts* (Baltimore: Johns Hopkins University Press, 1997).

31. For Weber, the precocious organization of mass parties in the United States occurred because of the popular appeals of presidential elections and the prerogative of presidents to nominate party professionals directly to administrative posts (facilitating alliances with the patronage systems of senators). See "Politics as a Vocation" in H. H. Gerth and C. Wright Mills, eds., *From Max Weber* (New York: Oxford University Press, 1946); and "Parliament and Government in a Reconstructed Germany," in *Economy and Society* (Berkeley: University of California Press), 2:1381–1462.

32. Note Weber's analysis of the organization of parties during the German transition from empire to democracy: "In the beginning there were new kinds of party apparatuses emerging. First, there were amateur apparatuses. They are especially often represented by students of various universities, who tell a man to whom they ascribe leadership qualities: we want to do the necessary work for you; carry it out. Secondly, there are the apparatuses of businessmen. But, both apparatuses were fast-emerging bubbles which swiftly vanished again." "Politics as a Vocation," 113.

8. "Between Restructuring and Impasse," by Aldo C. Vacs

1. For a general analysis of Argentina's political history since 1930 see, for instance, David Rock, *Argentina 1516–1982: From Spanish Civilization to the Falklands War* (Berkeley: University of California Press, 1985), 214–376. For an examination of Uruguay's political evolution in the same period see Martin Weinstein, *Uruguay: Democracy at the Crossroads* (Boulder and London: Westview Press, 1988), 23–112.

2. On the decline of the post-1930 Argentine political economy and the attempts to establish new foundations for economic growth, social modernization, and political stability see, for instance, Guido DiTella and Rudiger Dornbusch, eds., *The Political Economy of Argentina, 1946–1983* (Pittsburgh: University of Pittsburgh Press, 1989); Mónica Peralta-Ramos, *The Political Economy of Argentina: Power and Class since 1930* (Boulder: Westview Press, 1992); Guillermo O'Donnell, *1966–1973, El Estado burocrático autoritario: Triunfos, derrotas y crisis* (Buenos Aires: Editorial de Belgrano, 1982); and William C. Smith, *Authoritarianism and the Crisis of the Argentine Political Economy* (Palo Alto: Stanford University Press, 1989).

3. Juan Carlos Portantiero, "La crisis de un régimen: Una mirada retrospectiva," in José Nun and Juan Carlos Portantiero, eds., *Ensayos sobre la transición democrática en la Argentina* (Buenos Aires: Puntosur, 1987), 57–80.

4. See Adolfo Canitrot, *La disciplina como objetivo de la política económica: Un ensayo sobre el programa económico del gobierno argentino desde 1976* (Buenos Aires: Estudios Cedes, vol. 2, no. 6, 1979).

5. On the inability of the authoritarian regime to accomplish its political economic goals and the circumstances that led to this failure see Jorge Schvarzer, *Expansión económica del estado subsidiario, 1976–1981* (Buenos Aires: CISEA, 1981), and *Martínez de Hoz: La lógica política*

de la política económica (Buenos Aires: CISEA, 1983); Juan V. Sourroville and Jorge Lucangell, *Política económica y procesos de desarrollo: La experiencia argentina entre 1976 y 1981* (Santiago, Chile: CEPAL, 1983); and Aldo C. Vacs, *The Politics of Foreign Debt: Argentina, Brazil and the International Debt Crisis* (Ph.D. dissertation, University of Pittsburgh, 1986), 265–366.

6. On the changes in Argentina's socioeconomic structure fostered or accelerated by the authoritarian regime's policies see, for instance, D. Aspiazu, E. Basualdo, and M. Khavisse, *El nuevo poder económico en la Argentina de los años ochenta* (Buenos Aires: Legasa, 1986); Carlos Filgueira, "El estado y las clases: Tendencias en Argentina, Brasil y Uruguay," *Pensamiento Iberoamericano* no. 6 (July–December 1984): 35–61; José Nun, "Cambios en la estructura social de la Argentina," in J. C. Portantiero and J. Nun, eds., *Ensayos sobre la transición*, 117–37; Héctor Palomino, *Cambios ocupacionales y sociales en Argentina, 1947–1985* (Buenos Aires: CISEA, 1987); and Juan M. Villareal, "Changes in Argentine Society: The Heritage of the Dictatorship," in Mónica Peralta-Ramos and Carlos H. Waisman, eds., *From Military Rule to Democracy in Argentina* (Boulder: Westview Press, 1987).

7. On the rise and decline of the post-1930 Uruguayan model of development see, for instance, CINVE (Centro de Investigaciones Económicas), *La crisis uruguaya y el problema nacional* (Montevideo: CINVE/Ediciones de la Banda Oriental, 1984); Luis A. Faroppa, *El desarrollo económico del Uruguay. Tentativa de explicación* (Montevideo: CECEA, 1965); M. H. J. Finch, *A Political Economy of Uruguay since 1870* (New York: St. Martin's Press, 1981); and Luis Macadar, *Uruguay 1974–1980: Un nuevo ensayo de reajuste económico?* (Montevideo: CINVE/Ediciones de la Banda Oriental, 1982).

8. For an excellent analysis of these attempts see Luis Macadar, *Uruguay 1974–1980*, 19–49.

9. On the features of the 1967 Constitution see Gerónimo de Sierra, *El Uruguay post-dictadura. Estado-política-actores* (Montevideo: Facultad de Ciencias Sociales—Departamento de Sociología, 1992), 107–21.

10. See, for instance, Martin Weinstein, *Uruguay*, 45, 56; and Alfred Stepan, *Rethinking Military Politics: Brazil and the Southern Cone* (Princeton: Princeton University Press, 1988), 14. For a critique of this characterization of the Uruguayan regime as totalitarian, see Paul C. Sondrol, "1984 Revisited? A Re-examination of Uruguay's Military Dictatorship," *Bulletin of Latin American Research* 11, no. 2 (1992): 187–203.

11. On the model of economic development sponsored by the Uruguayan dictatorship, see Luis Macadar, *Uruguay 1974–1980*; Jorge Notaro, *La política económica en el Uruguay, 1968–1984* (Montevideo: CIEDUR/Ediciones de la Banda Oriental, 1984); and Martin Weinstein, *Uruguay*, 55–67.

12. On the ultimate political goals of the authoritarian rulers see, for instance, Charles G. Gillespie and Luis E. González, "Uruguay: The Survival of Old and Autonomous Institutions," in Larry Diamond, Juan Linz, and Seymour Martin Lipset, eds., *Democracy in Developing Countries*, volume 4, *Latin America* (Boulder: Lynne Rienner, 1989), 207–45; and Paul Sondrol, "1984 Revisited?".

13. On the factors leading to the breakdown of the regime and the transition to democracy see Gillespie and González, "Uruguay: The Survival of Old"; Charles Gillespie, "Uruguay's Transition from Collegial Military-Technocratic Rule," in G. O'Donnell, P. Schmitter, and L. Whitehead, eds., *Transitions From Authoritarian Rule: Latin America* (Baltimore and London: Johns Hopkins University Press, 1986), 173–95; and Weinstein, *Uruguay*, 74–92.

14. For an analysis of the plebiscite and the gradual political opening that followed see Luis

E. González, "Uruguay, 1980–1981: An Unexpected Opening," *Latin American Research Review* 18, no. 3 (1983): 63–76.

15. The Uruguayan system of *lemas* allows permanent parties (those that elected representatives in the two last contests) to participate in elections presenting under their title (*lema*) different lists (*sub-lemas*) of factional candidates for the presidential, vice presidential, and gubernatorial (*intendencia*) offices. The candidate of the *sub-lema* who obtains the most votes within the party *lema* that has gathered the highest total vote is elected. In this "double simultaneous vote" system the voter selects, at the same time, the party and candidate of his or her preference but, unlike what happens in a primary followed by a general election, it is uncertain not only which party will win but also which of the party candidates will prevail. This system has facilitated the multiplication of factions (at least in the traditional parties) and the election of individual candidates who have obtained fewer votes than candidates from other losing *lemas*. However, it also allows the parties to widen their popular appeal by offering a wide array of ideological and personal choices to the electorate, without destroying their formal unity.

16. For an in-depth analysis of the Uruguayan political system and the characteristics and significance of the 1984 elections see Luis E. González, *Political Structures and Democracy in Uruguay* (Notre Dame: University of Notre Dame Press, 1991), esp. 53–135.

17. Gerónimo de Sierra, *El Uruguay post-dictadura*, 66–67. On the changes in Uruguay's socioeconomic structure see also Filgueira, "El estado y las clases."

18. For an analysis of the initial economic program of the Radical administration see Vacs, *Politics*, 367–93.

19. On the evolution of the Radical administration economic policies in a liberal direction see Aldo Vacs, "Argentina," in James M. Malloy and Eduardo Gamarra, eds., *Latin America and Caribbean Contemporary Record*, volume 7, 1987–1988 (New York and London: Holmes and Meier, 1990), B3–B9; José Luis Machinea, *Stabilization Under Alfonsín's Government: A Frustrated Attempt* (Buenos Aires: Documento CEDES 42, 1990).

20. For an insightful analysis of the last period of the Alfonsín administration see William C. Smith, "Hyperinflation, Macroeconomic Instability, and Neoliberal Restructuring in Democratic Argentina," in Edward C. Epstein, ed., *The New Argentine Democracy: The Search for a Successful Formula* (Westport and London: Praeger, 1992), 35–41.

21. For instance, the currency change contained in the Austral plan as well as a number of foreign debt agreements were enacted through executive decrees ignoring explicit constitutional provisions that required congressional participation and legislation to pass these measures.

22. For the nature and development of Bunge and Born, including references to the confrontations between the company and the early Peronist administrations, see Raul Green and Catherine Laurent, *El poder de Bunge and Born* (Buenos Aires: Legasa, 1989).

23. See República Argentina, Ministerio de Economía, *Discurso del Ministro de Economía*, 07/9/89, and *Principales medidas económicas del 07/9/89* (Buenos Aires: Ministerio de Economía, Press release no. 2/89, July 9, 1989).

24. On these bills and the means used to ensure their approval by Congress see *Clarín*, 18 August 1989 and 2 September 1989; and Jorge Garfunkel, *59 semanas y media que conmovieron a la Argentina* (Buenos Aires: EMECE, 1990), 239–49.

25. The evolution throughout August–October 1989 of the confrontation between Ubaldini and the *Mesa de Enlace* is reported in *El bimestre político y económico* 46 (October 1989): 37, 41–42, 48, and 53–54; and ibid. 47 (December 1989): 19, 22, 27, 33, 41–42, and 43–44.

26. *Clarín*, 13 August 1989 (for the reduction of agricultural export taxes); *Clarín*, 2 September 1989 (for the reduction of manufactured export taxes).

27. *Clarín*, 19 December 1989.

28. *Clarín*, 2 January 1990.

29. *Clarín*, 5 March 1990.

30. On the increase in poverty prior to 1989 see, for instance, Instituto Nacional de Estadísticas y Censos (INDEC), *La pobreza en el conurbano bonaerense* (Buenos Aires: Estudios INDEC no. 13, 1989); and INDEC, *La pobreza urbana en la Argentina* (Buenos Aires: INDEC, 1990). On the regressive trends in the distribution of income under Menem see, for instance, Alberto Minujin, ed., *Cuesta abajo: Los nuevos pobres* (Buenos Aires: UNICEF/Losada, 1992); Alberto Minujin, ed., *Desigualdad y exclusión* (Buenos Aires: UNICEF/Losada, 1993); and Alberto Minujin and Gabriel Kessler, *La nueva pobreza en la Argentina* (Buenos Aires: Planeta Argentina, 1995).

31. For an analysis of the Argentine privatization program and its implementation see Luigi Manzetti, "The Political Economy of Privatization Through Divestiture in Lesser Developed Economies: The Case of Argentina" (Miami: North-South Center, 1992). A strong criticism of the privatization process as corrupt and inefficient is found in Horacio Verbitsky, *Robo para la corona* (Buenos Aires: Planeta, 1991). For Menem's presentation and defense of his program (written in collaboration with his minister of public works and services) see Carlos Menem and Roberto Dromi, *Reforma del Estado y transformación nacional* (Buenos Aires: Ed. Ciencias de la Administración, 1990).

32. See, for instance, Domingo Cavallo, *Volver a crecer* (Buenos Aires: Sudamericana-Planeta, 1982); and D. Cavallo, R. Domenech, and Y. Mundlak, *La Argentina que pudo ser. Los costos de la represión económica* (Buenos Aires: Fundacion Mediterránea/Manantial, 1989).

33. On Cavallo's "Convertibility Plan" see *Clarín*, 21, 22 March 1991. Analyses from different perspectives of the economic plan and the results of its application can be found in Pablo Gerchunoff and Juan Carlos Torre, *Argentina: La política de liberalización económica bajo un gobierno de base popular* (Buenos Aires: Instituto Torcuato Di Tella, 1996); Naúm Minsburg and Héctor W. Valle, eds., *Argentina hoy: Crisis del modelo* (Buenos Aires: Ediciones Letra Buena, 1995); and World Bank, *Argentina: From Insolvency to Growth: A World Bank Country Study* (Washington, D.C.: World Bank, 1993).

34. *Clarín—edición internacional*, 29 October–4 November 1991.

35. *Clarín—edición internacional*, 20–26 August 1990.

36. *Clarín—edición internacional*, 15–21 October 1990.

37. See *Foreign Broadcast Information Service (FBIS)—Latin America*, 15 July 1992, 29; and 5 March 1993, 25–26.

38. On the fall of Cafiero and the reassertion of presidential control over the Peronist party see *Clarín—edición internacional*, 6–12 August 1990.

39. *La Nación*, 7 April 1990.

40. On the ideological revival of economic neoliberalism and political conservatism in Argentina see Edward L. Gibson, *Class and Conservative Parties: Argentina in Comparative Perspective* (Baltimore: Johns Hopkins University Press, 1996).

41. On the political crisis in Jujuy, Chubut, and Tucumán see *Clarín—edición internacional*, 29 October–4 November 1990. On the rise of conservative provincial parties and the evolution of the party system see Gerardo Adrogué, "El nuevo sistema partidario argentino," in Car-

los H. Acuña, ed., *La nueva matriz política argentina* (Buenos Aires: Nueva Visión, 1995), 27–70.

42. On the military question and the issue of human rights see Carlos Acuña and Catalina Smulovitz, *Ni olvido ni perdón? Derechos humanos y tensiones cívico-militares en la transición argentina* (Buenos Aires: Documento de Trabajo CEDES No. 69, 1991); Carlos Acuña and Catalina Smulovitz, "Militares en la transición argentina: del gobierno a la subordinación constitucional," in Carlos H. Acuña, ed., *La nueva matriz*, 153–202; and Rosendo Fraga, *Menem y la cuestión militar* (Buenos Aires: Centro de Estudios Unión para la Nueva Mayoría, 1991).

43. On the decline of judicial independence under Menem see Catalina Smulovitz, "Constitución y poder judicial en la nueva democracia argentina," in Carlos H. Acuña, ed., *La nueva matriz política*, 71–114; and Horacio Verbitsky, *Hacer la Corte* (Buenos Aires: Planeta, 1993).

44. See *FBIS—Latin America*, 22 July 1992, 18.

45. Statements by Bernardo Neustadt to *Somos* (22 June 92) reproduced in *FBIS—Latin America*, 7 August 1992, 15.

46. Menem's statements in *La Prensa* (4 November 1992, 11) reproduced in *FBIS—Latin America*, 3 December 1992, 20.

47. For the English translation of the complete text of the new constitution, see *Constitution of the Argentine Nation—1994* in *FBIS—Latin America*, 14 October 1994.

48. For the results of the presidential elections see *Clarín*, 15, 16, 17 May 1995.

49. On the features of Uruguay's restored liberal democracy, political culture, and relations between state and civil society see, among others, de Sierra, *El Uruguay*; Alfredo Errandonea, *El sistema político uruguayo* (Montevideo: Ediciones La República, 1995); and González, *Political Structures*.

50. On Uruguay's economic situation by the end of the authoritarian regime and at the time of Sanguinetti's inauguration see Notaro, *La política económica*; Ricardo Petrissans Aguilar, *Políticas de estabilización y reforma estructural a la luz de su contexto político-social. El caso uruguayo* (Buenos Aires: CIEDLA, 1993); and Inter-American Development Bank (IADB), *Economic and Social Progress in Latin America. 1986 Report* (Washington, D.C.: IADB, 1986), 368–74.

51. On the debate on modernization and the rejection by important Uruguayan political and socioeconomic actors of the neoliberal model promoted by the Sanguinetti administration, see de Sierra, *El Uruguay*, 173–76.

52. On the contents and implications of this limited notion of governability in the Uruguayan case see Francisco Panizza, "Mirando hacia el futuro," in Tabaré Vera, ed., *Uruguay hacia el 2000. Desafíos y opciones* (Caracas: Nueva Sociedad/UNITAR/PROFAL-FESUR, 1991), 127–61.

53. On Uruguay's bilateral economic agreements with Argentina and Brazil and its integration into MERCOSUR, see Nicolás Betancur, "La integración regional como generadora de cambios en el sistema político uruguayo," in Gerardo Caetano, ed., *El Uruguay hacia el siglo XXI* (Montevideo: Trilce, 1994), 75–87; Néstor Huici and Eduardo Jacobs, *Primeros pasos de la integración Argentina-Brasil-Uruguay* (Buenos Aires: CISEA, 1989); Miguel Kaplan, "Integración: un camino posible," in Vera, ed., *Uruguay hacia el 2000*, 33–60; and G. Margarinos, *Uruguay en el Mercosur* (Montevideo: FCU, 1991).

54. On the reconstruction of the Uruguayan labor movement and its activities during the last period of the dictatorship and the democratic period see de Sierra, *El Uruguay*, 213–32; Juan Rial, "El movimiento sindical uruguayo ante la redemocratizacion," in PREALC, *Políticas*

económicas y actores sociales (Santiago: PREALC, 1988); and Weinstein, *Uruguay,* 67–68 and 102–04.

55. Sanguinetti's statements (June 1986) quoted in Weinstein, *Uruguay,* 104.

56. On the military policies and human rights issues during the Sanguinetti period see Weinstein, *Uruguay,* 104–12; and Paul W. Zagorski, *Democracy vs. National Security: Civil-Military Relations in Latin America* (Boulder and London: Lynne Rienner, 1992).

57. Analyses and interpretations of the 1989 election results can be found in de Sierra, *El Uruguay,* 233–43; González, *Political Structures,* 155–61; and Pablo Mieres, *Desobediencia y lealtad. El voto en el Uruguay de fin de siglo* (Colonia, Uruguay: Editorial Fin de Siglo, 1994), 57–162.

58. President Luis A. Lacalle Herrera was the grandson of Luis Alberto de Herrera, a right-wing *Blanco* leader who supported Terra's 1933 coup, participated in the division of state patronage spoils, agreed with the *Colorados* in the infamous *"Pacto del Chinchulín,"* and remained a perennial candidate for the presidency until his death in 1959. Since the 1970s, Lacalle headed an influential Blanco faction called the *Consejo Nacional Herrerista* that vowed to follow the old leader's conservative line.

59. *FBIS—Latin America,* 2 October 1991, 40–41.

60. *FBIS—Latin America,* 6 January 1992, 56–57.

61. *FBIS—Latin America,* 31 January 1992, 43.

62. *FBIS—Latin America,* 15 May 1992, 26.

63. *FBIS—Latin America,* 8 April 1992, 26.

64. *FBIS—Latin America,* 26 May 1992, 53.

65. *FBIS—Latin America,* 17 September 1992, 42.

66. *FBIS—Latin America,* 27 May 1992, 43.

67. *FBIS—Latin America,* 16 July 1992, 29.

68. On the characteristics and behavior of the Uruguayan entrepreneurial associations see Gerardo Caetano, "Partidos, estado y cámaras empresariales en el Uruguay contemporáneo (1900–1991)," and Jorge L. Lanzaro, "Las cámaras empresariales en el sistema político uruguayo: acciones informales e inscripciones corporativas," in CIESU-Fesur-CP, *Organizaciones empresariales y políticas públicas* (Montevideo: Ediciones Trilce, Colección Logos, 1992), 15–83.

69. Lacalle's address to the nation (30 January 1992) quoted in *FBIS—Latin America,* 31 January 1992, 43.

70. *FBIS—Latin America,* 15 December 1992, 29.

71. On the 1994 elections see Gerónimo de Sierra, *Elecciones uruguayas: Cambios en el sistema de partidos y bloqueos emergentes* (Montevideo: CIEDUR, Serie Seminarios y Talleres No. 83, 1994); and Errandonea, *El sistema político uruguayo.*

72. Among the most influential studies of liberal democracy that define its formal operative aspects and analyze its empirical manifestations see Robert A. Dahl, *Polyarchy: Participation and Opposition* (New Haven and London: Yale University Press, 1971); and G. Bingham Powell, Jr., *Contemporary Democracies: Participation, Stability, and Violence* (Cambridge: Harvard University Press, 1982). On the procedural aspects of democracy see Robert A. Dahl, "Procedural Democracy," in Peter Laslett and James Fishkin, eds., *Philosophy, Politics and Society: Fifth Series* (New Haven: Yale University Press, 1979), 97–133. The current wave of democratization in Latin America appears to have generated what Dahl calls "procedural democracy in a narrow sense" rather than the more inclusive "full procedural democracy."

73. On these trends see Peter Dicken, *Global Shift: The Internationalization of Economic Activity*, 2d ed. (New York and London: Guilford Press, 1992); Howard M. Wachtel, *The Money Mandarins: The Making of a Supranational Economic Order* (London: Pluto Press, 1990); and Maria da Conceição Tavares and José Luís Fiori, *(Des)ajuste global e modernização conservadora* (Rio de Janeiro: Paz e Terra, 1993). Relevant analyses of the transnational processes from the interdependence perspective can be found in Robert Keohane and Joseph Nye, *Power and Interdependence: World Politics in Transition* (Boston and Toronto: Little, Brown, 1977); and Robert O. Keohane, *After Hegemony: Cooperation and Discord in the World Political Economy* (Princeton: Princeton University Press, 1984).

74. On the "Washington Consensus" see John Williamson, ed., *Latin American Adjustment: How Much Has Happened?* (Washington, D.C.: Institute for International Economics, 1990), esp. 7–38.

75. On the different foundations on which it is possible to build legitimate orders, see Max Weber, *Economy and Society* (Berkeley-Los Angeles-London: University of California Press, 1978), 1:31–36.

76. For a popular exposition of the thesis of the connection between liberal economics and political democracy see Milton Friedman, *Capitalism and Freedom* (Chicago and London: University of Chicago Press, 1982). A more philosophical presentation of similar ideas is found in F. A. Hayek, *The Constitution of Liberty* (Chicago: University of Chicago Press, 1960). A critical analysis of these links from a historical perspective is found in John A. Hall, *Liberalism: Politics, Ideology and the Market* (Chapel Hill: University of North Carolina Press, 1987).

"Conclusion," by Kurt von Mettenheim and James Malloy

1. Joseph Schumpeter, *Capitalism, Socialism, and Democracy* (New York: Harper, 1942).

2. On participatory democratic theory, see Benjamin Barber, *Strong Democracy* (Berkeley: University of California Press, 1984).

3. Perhaps the classic statement remains Fernando Henrique Cardoso and Enzo Falleto, *Dependent Development in Latin America* (Berkeley: University of California Press, 1979).

4. It should be noted that theories of political development also challenged this core formula of liberal scholarship. See Robert Packenham, *Liberalism and the Third World: Political Development Ideas in Foreign Aid and Social Science* (Princeton: Princeton University Press, 1973).

5. Cardoso and Falleto's concept of dependent development criticized both liberal and marxist assumptions of the time. See their preface to the English edition, *Dependent Development in Latin America*.

6. The literature on transitions from authoritarian rule is voluminous. For overviews, see the following collections: James Malloy and Mitchell Seligson, *Authoritarians and Democrats* (Pittsburgh: University of Pittsburgh Press, 1987); Guillermo O'Donnell, Phillipe Schmitter, and Laurence Whitehead, eds., *Transitions from Authoritarian Rule: Southern Europe and Latin America* (Baltimore: Johns Hopkins University Press, 1986); and Larry Diamond, Juan Linz, and Seymour Martin Lipset, eds., *Democracy in Developing Countries* (Boulder: Lynne Rienner, 1988).

7. For a classic statement on political parties and political development, see Samuel Huntington, *Political Order in Changing Societies* (New Haven: Yale University Press, 1968), chap. 5.

8. For work that shifts away from European assumptions, see Douglas Chalmers, "Parties

and Society in Latin America," in Steffen W. Schmidt et al., eds., *Friends, Followers and Factions* (Berkeley: University of California Press, 1977), 401–19.

9. On corporatism in the region, see James Malloy, ed., *Authoritarianism and Corporatism in Latin America* (Pittsburgh: University of Pittsburgh Press, 1977).

10. On the importance of the communication function of competitive elections, see Giovanni Sartori, *Democratic Theory Revisited* (Chatham, N.J.: Chatham House, 1987), 110.

11. See Arturo Valenzuela and Juan Linz, eds., *The Failure of Presidential Democracy: The Case of Latin America* (Baltimore: Johns Hopkins University Press, 1994), and Kurt von Mettenheim, ed., *Presidential Institutions and Democratic Politics: Comparing Regional and National Contexts* (Baltimore: Johns Hopkins University Press, 1997).

12. For a review of issues in Brazil, see Kurt von Mettenheim, *The Brazilian Voter: Mass Politics in Democratic Transition* (Pittsburgh: University of Pittsburgh Press, 1995).

13. Pocock's work recuperates central aspects of Machiavelli's original writings compatible with the liberal and democratic tradition. See Pocock, *The Machiavellian Moment: Florentine Political Thought and the Atlantic Republican Tradition* (Princeton: Princeton University Press, 1975).

The late **Enrique A. Baloyra** pioneered studies of public opinion, electoral campaigns, and party politics in Latin America. His distinguished career as professor in the Political Science Department and director of the Graduate School of International Studies, University of Miami, left generations of grateful students and colleagues. A very select list of his publications includes: "Criticism, Cynicism, and Political Evaluation: A Venezuelan Example"; *Political Attitudes in Venezuela* (with John Martz); and *Electoral Moblization and Public Opinion: The Venezuelan Campaign of 1973* (with John Martz).

Sylvia Borzutzky has taught Latin American politics at the University of Pittsburgh and Carnegie Mellon University and published on social security policy in Chile and the dyamics of military government and regime change in Chile.

Roderic Camp is professor in the Tulane University Department of Political Science. His publications include *Politics in Mexico; Polling for Democracy: Public Opinion and Political Liberalization in Mexico; Modernization and Political Recruitment: The Case of Mexico; Generals in the Palacio: The Military in Modern Mexico;* and *Entrepreneurs and the State in Twentieth Century Mexico*.

Julio F. Carrion is assistant professor in the University of Delaware Department of Political Science and International Relations. His dissertation on Peruvian politics defended at the University of Pittsburgh is currently under revision for publication.

Eduardo A. Gamarra is associate professor in the Department of Political Science, Florida International University. Recent publications include: *Dictators, Democrats, and Drugs: A Brief History of U.S.–Bolivia Counternarcotics Policy; Democracy, Markets, and Structural Reform in Latin America: Argentina, Bolivia,*

Brazil, Chile, and Mexico (co-editor); *Latin American Political Economy in the Age of Neoliberal Reform: Theoretical and Comparative Perspectives for the 1990s* (co-editor); and *Revolution and Reaction: Bolivia 1964–1985*. Professor Gamarra is editor of both *Hemisphere* magazine and the annual *Latin American and Caribbean Contemporary Record*, and has testified before the United States Congress on Andean counternarcotics policy.

James Malloy is professor in the University of Pittsburgh Department of Political Science. His many publications include *Unsettling Statecraft: Democracy and Neo-Liberalism in the Central Andes* (with Catherine M. Conaghan); *The Politics of Social Security in Brazil; Bolivia: The Uncompleted Revolution;* editor of *Authoritarianism and Corporatism in Latin America; Authoritarians and Democrats: Regime Transition in Latin America* (with Mitchell Seligson) and former editor of the *Latin American and Caribbean Contemporary Record*.

Veronica Montecinos is assistant professor in the Department of Sociology, The Pennsylvania State University, McKeesport Campus. Her Ph.D. dissertation on Chilean economists, defended at the University of Pittsburgh Department of Sociology, has been followed by a series of publications on the relation between economists, political organization, and questions of regime change in Latin America.

Aldo C. Vacs is associate professor of political science at Skidmore College. He has published widely on the political economy of debt in Argentina and Brazil, Soviet-Argentine relations, and questions of regime change in the Southern Cone of Latin America.

Kurt von Mettenheim is author of *The Brazilian Voter: Mass Politics in Democratic Transition, 1974–1986,* and editor of *Presidential Institutions and Democratic Politics: Comparing Regional and National Contexts.* He has taught at Columbia University, the University of Pittsburgh, the Universidade de São Paulo, and is currently writing a study of the Brazilian presidency in comparative perspective.

INDEX